Corporate Governance and Sustainability

Corporations and governments are now confronted with managing the [illegible]ns of a society newly alerted to the social and environmental risks associated with economic development. There is dawning recognition at many levels of society that achieving a sustainable world is dependent upon the democratic management and equitable distribution of these risks for now and for the future.

Corporate Governance and Sustainability argues that better systems of governance at a number of different levels hold the key to transforming economic development so that it is in line with sustainability principles, including those of social and environmental justice. New systems of governance appear crucial to transforming corporate behaviour in accordance with sustainability principles.

Sustainability poses new and major challenges for the theory and practice of corporate governance. This book attempts to identify and address these challenges. It recognizes the complex and contested nature of both sustainability and governance, and that these key concepts have been redefined considerably over time. This is the first systematic examination of how these two areas need to be interrelated in the future.

Suzanne Benn is Senior Lecturer in the School of Management at the University of Technology, Sydney. She is a biochemist and social scientist with a strong research background in corporate sustainability and stakeholder collaboration.

Dexter Dunphy is Distinguished Professor in the School of Management at the University of Technology, Sydney. His main research and consulting interests are in the management of organizational change, human resource management and corporate sustainability.

The *Routledge Contemporary Corporate Governance* series aims to provide an authoritative, thought-provoking and well-balanced series of textbooks in the rapidly emerging field of corporate governance. The corporate governance literature traditionally has been scattered in the finance, economics, accounting, law and management literature. However the international controversy now associated with corporate governance has focused considerable attention on this subject and raised its profile immeasurably. Government, financial institutions, corporations and academics have become deeply involved in tackling the dilemmas of corporate governance due to widespread public concerns.

The *Routledge Contemporary Corporate Governance* series will make a significant impact in this emerging field: defining and illuminating problems; going beyond the official emphasis on regulation and procedures to understand the behaviour of executives, boards, and corporations; analysing the wider impact and relationships involved in corporate governance. Issues that will be covered in this series include:

Exploring the impact of the globalization of corporate governance
Assessing the ongoing contest between shareholder/stakeholder values
Examining how corporate governance values determine corporate objectives
Analysing how financial interests have overwhelmed corporate governance
Investigating the discourse of corporate governance
Considering the imperative of sustainability in corporate governance
Addressing the contemporary crises in corporate governance and how they might be resolved.

Titles available:
Corporate Governance and Sustainability: Challenges for Theory and Practice
Edited by Suzanne Benn and Dexter Dunphy

Titles forthcoming:

Governance and the Market for Corporate Control
John L. Teall

The Governance of Strategic Alliances
Antoine Hermens

Project Governance: Integrating Corporate, Program and Project Governance
Edited by Lynn Crawford, Christophe Bredillet and J. Rodney Turner

Corporate Governance and Sustainability

Challenges for Theory and Practice

Edited by Suzanne Benn
and Dexter Dunphy

LONDON AND NEW YORK

First published 2007
by Routledge
2 Park Square, Milton Park, Abingdon, Oxon 0X14 4RN

Simultaneously published in the USA and Canada
by Routledge
270 Madison Ave, New York, NY 10016

Routledge is an imprint of the Taylor & Francis Group, an informa business

Typeset in Perpetua and Bell Gothic by
Keystroke, 28 High Street, Tettenhall, Wolverhampton
Printed and bound in Great Britain by
Antony Rowe Ltd, Chippenham, Wiltshire

British Library Cataloguing in Publication Data
A catalogue record for this book is available from the British Library

Library of Congress Cataloging in Publication Data
Corporate governance and sustainability : challenges for theory and practice / edited by Suzanne Benn and Dexter Dunphy.
p. cm.
"Simultaneously published in the USA and Canada."
Includes bibliographical references and index.
ISBN 0-415-38062-6 (hard cover) — ISBN 0-415-38063-4 (soft cover)
1. Corporate governance. 2. Social responsibility of business.
3. Organizational change. 4. Sustainable development. I. Benn, Suzanne.
II. Dunphy, Dexter C. (Dexter Colboyd), 1934-
HD2741.C77494 2006
338.9′27—dc22
2006010670

ISBN10: 0–415–38062–6 (hbk)
ISBN10: 0–415–38063–4 (pbk)

ISBN13: 978–0–415–38062–1 (hbk)
ISBN13: 978–0–415–38063–8 (pbk)

Contents

Illustrations

FIGURES

TABLES

Notes on Contributors

EDITORS

Suzanne Benn is Senior Lecturer in the School of Management at the University of Technology, Sydney. She is a biochemist and social scientist with research interests in corporate sustainability, business education for sustainability and stakeholder collaboration. Her research is published in a number of books and international journals. She is the co-author of *Organisational Change for Corporate Sustainability*, published by Routledge in 2003 and currently under revision for the second edition.

Dexter Dunphy is Distinguished Professor, University of Technology, Sydney. Dexter's main research and consulting interests are in corporate sustainability, the management of organizational change and human resource management. He also has a special interest in comparative management, particularly in East Asia. His research is published in over 80 articles and 22 books.

CONTRIBUTING AUTHORS

Jem Bendell has been involved in, advised on, analysed and written about corporate and NGO responses to the challenges of globalization for over ten years. Jem is a Visiting Fellow at the University of Nottingham and an Adjunct Professor with Auckland University of Technology. His research on partnerships for sustainable development and other aspects of sustainability is published in two books on cross-sector relations, a column in the *Journal of Corporate Citizenship*, and over 30 other publications. He is a consultant to a variety of UN organizations on related issues.

Krista Bondy is a PhD student with the International Centre for Corporate Social Responsibility, Nottingham University Business School. Her PhD looks at how corporations implement CSR codes within a cross-cultural environment. Recent research appears in *Business and Society Review*.

Thomas Clarke is Professor of Management and Director of the Centre for Corporate Governance at UTS Sydney. He is editor of *Theories of Corporate Governance: The*

Philosophical Foundations of Corporate Governance (Routledge 2004); *Corporate Governance: Critical Perspectives* (Routledge 2005); and author of *International Corporate Governance: A Comparative Approach* (Routledge 2006).

Rachel Davies has worked in the Financial Services Industry for over four years and is currently an Equity Research Associate at a Canadian Investment Dealer. Rachel received a BSc H (biochemistry) from Queen's University in Kingston, Ontario and an MBA specializing in finance and business and sustainability from the Schulich School of Business.

Andrew Griffiths is a Senior Lecturer at the University of Queensland Business School. He has published in leading international management journals including *Academy of Management Review* and *Journal of Management Studies*. He is also a recipient of the UQ Research Excellence Foundation Award. He directs and undertakes research on the corporate sustainability programme in the business school.

Nardia Haigh is a PhD student at the University of Queensland Business School. Her research interests include sustainability strategy, organizational response and adaptation to climate change, and the impact of institutional systems on these issues.

Soochen Low is a design consultant with a strong interest in sustainability. She also lectures part-time at the School of Management at the University of Technology, Sydney. She is a postgraduate student at UTS and researches corporate sustainability and education for sustainability in the School of Management at UTS.

Andrew Martin is a practising barrister at the criminal bar in New South Wales and a doctoral student at the Australian Centre for Environmental Law, Sydney University Law School. His area of research is adaptive management and governance in water management. He is highly involved in community-based environmental activities and is Chair of Hunter Region Landcare Network.

Dirk Matten is Professor of Business Ethics and Director of the Centre for Research into Sustainability at Royal Holloway, University of London. He is interested in international aspects of ethics and corporate social responsibility. Recent work appeared in *Academy of Management Review*, *Journal of Management Studies*, *Organization Studies*, *Human Relations* and *Business Ethics Quarterly*.

Tudor J. Maxwell is a consultant, and a part-time business school lecturer of analytical techniques and research methods. Tudor is a portfolio partner at the IFPM-Centre for Corporate Governance at the University of St Gallen, Switzerland, where he completed a doctorate in corporate governance and sustainability. He is currently based in Johannesburg, South Africa.

Jeremy Moon is Professor and Director of the International Centre for Corporate Social Responsibility, Nottingham University Business School. Research interests include CSR and government, comparative CSR, and corporations and citizenship.

Recent research appears in *Journal of Business Ethics*, *Business Ethics Quarterly*, *Business and Society*, *Business and Society Review* and the *Journal of Management Studies*.

Professor Benjamin J. Richardson is an environmental lawyer trying to make the world a better place. To this end, he has taught and published widely on various environmental law topics at Osgoode Hall Law School, and previously at the Universities of Auckland and Manchester.

Sally Russell is a doctoral student at the University of Queensland Business School and her research is in the area of organizational behaviour and organizations and the natural environment. Her PhD examines the role of individuals in driving organizational response to environmental issues.

Aarti Sharma teaches Strategic Management at the College of Business Administration in the University of South Florida, USA. She is pursuing her PhD study on multi-stakeholder dialogic collaborations for sustainability from the Auckland University of Technology, New Zealand. Aarti has worked in projects across a range of social and environmental sustainability issues that spanned from local to bilateral (Indo-US government) levels, and involved India, the USA, and New Zealand. She has served the US Departments of Health and Human Services and State, and The Energy and Resources Institute in New Delhi, India, before pursuing her academic career in New Zealand and the USA.

David Wheeler is Director and Erivan K. Haub Professor in Business and Sustainability at the Schulich School of Business, York University, Toronto. He is also the Founding Director of the York Institute for Research and Innovation in Sustainability – a strategic initiative of York University embracing all ten faculties. Previous to his current appointments, David Wheeler worked in international development and international business. He has advised a wide range of businesses, national governments and civil society organizations.

Louise Wilson is Senior Manager, Leadership and Culture at Insurance Australia Group (IAG). Louise has worked in Malaysia, Italy, the UK and Australia across change management, organizational design, leadership development and culture change. Louise's role at IAG is to work with group executives and business units to embed a high performance culture that is united and committed to IAG's purpose, values and long-term growth.

Series editor's preface

This pioneering work edited by Suzanne Benn and Dexter Dunphy is the first to attempt to bridge the dangerous divide between corporate governance and sustainability. For too long corporate governance was defined both in law and practice in terms of the narrow pursuit of shareholder value, allowing the dismissal of the wider social and environmental impact of corporate activity as *externalities* which company boards of directors need not be concerned with. A stunted set of commercial values has allowed corporations to despoil communities and natural environments all in the name of the generation of *wealth*. This irresponsible approach to free enterprise has reached its limits in a world threatened with irreparable ecological damage. The *license to operate* of corporations now inescapably involves the imperative of social and environmental sustainability.

The original and challenging focus of this work is upon how corporate governance can help to deliver sustainability. This involves a new understanding of the nature of governance, with a profound rethinking of the values, relationships and objectives of corporate activity. As the authors indicate, however challenging and complex this reconceptualization of the purpose the corporation may be, it is now necessary. Achieving a sense of the inter-connectedness of business with the community and environment, and appreciating the responsibility of business to ensure that it does not impair social and ecological stability, is an important step forward. Working towards a business philosophy of mutuality and inter-dependence is the next stage. The contributors to the book offer extensive analysis and evidence in support of corporations adopting a strategic focus on achieving sustainability, and renewing the legitimacy of economic endeavour.

Thomas Clarke
Series Editor

Acknowledgements

The assembling and editing of this book would not have been possible without the assistance of our extraordinarily capable editorial assistant, Gabriela Pulczynski. Her patience, intelligence and graciousness have enabled our contributing authors to work together in reaching the many deadlines associated with the production of an edited volume and we really cannot thank her enough.

We have also benefited from the support of many of our colleagues in the School of Management, University of Technology, Sydney. In particular, we are grateful to the ongoing encouragement and support we have received from Professor Thomas Clarke, the series editor.

Last but not least, we thank our contributing authors for their excellent work and collaboration.

Suzanne Benn
Dexter Dunphy

Introduction

This book seeks to bring together research from the disciplinary areas of sociology, law, political science, organization studies and natural resource management in order to address the increasingly urgent challenge of governance for sustainability. It draws on the work of researchers and practitioners from Canada, Australia, South Africa and the United Kingdom in order to contribute to the debate on this complex subject. The book takes as its starting point the fact that corporations and governments are now confronted with managing the expectations of a society newly alerted to the social and environmental risks and negative impacts associated with economic development. In this collection we explore the implications for the theory and practice of corporate governance.

In assembling the various contributions to this book, our aim is to develop the argument that systems of governance need to be redesigned at a number of different levels if they are to assist in transforming economic development to bring it in line with sustainability principles. This is particularly the case if they are to promote social and environmental justice. Our specific area of interest is the governance and sustainability of the corporation. We have selected this area for two reasons. First, because the corporation is the core unit of economic development, and second, because new systems of governance appear crucial to transforming corporate behaviour in accordance with sustainability principles.

In tackling our task, we recognize the complex and contested nature of both sustainability and governance, and that these key concepts have been considerably redefined over time. We and our other contributors aim to examine the shifts in both corporate governance and corporate sustainability theory and the relationship between the two bodies of theory and practice. Most importantly, we hope to foster critical debate on the subject of governance for sustainability in the context of the contemporary corporation. We do this around three key themes. A section of the book is devoted to each theme.

PART I: GOVERNANCE AND SUSTAINABILITY CHALLENGES

The chapters in this section introduce two key challenges that sustainability poses for corporate governance. First, sustainability is an open and contestable concept with many layers of meaning. Second, it raises issues of major organizational change.

Sustainability is a values-based concept and consequently readily politicized. It also raises special problems of multiple scales – problems of different magnitudes concerning many different policy objectives, over different levels of government, geographical areas and affecting different generations. This requires decision-makers to balance many different priorities – a key factor in corporate governance. For instance, global concerns must be balanced against the local concerns, economic objectives against social and environmental objectives, natural capital against the other forms of capital and long-term targets against short-term targets.

In the opening chapter, Benn and Dunphy take up the issue of competing priorities in identifying the issues that sustainability poses for current theories and practice of governance. They argue that balancing these priorities highlights the need for adaptive and flexible systems of governance rather than controls imposed through top-down, hierarchical authority. Governance systems that can address sustainability criteria must have the capacity to respond to differences in power and access to resources between and within stakeholder groups and to enable inclusive decision-making. These authors propose that themes drawn from ecopolitical theory could usefully inform the development of such models of governance.

The second chapter in Part I, by Russell, Haigh and Griffiths, is based on empirical data which explores variations in how corporate sustainability is understood in differing social contexts. The authors argue that different governance regimes have a marked impact on understandings of sustainability. They show, for instance, how corporate sustainability is understood in very different ways across industry sectors and between public and private organizations.

PART II: LIMITATIONS OF EXISTING MODELS OF CORPORATE GOVERNANCE

The chapters in this section of the book provide empirical support for the thesis that traditional models of governance, preoccupied with the task of ensuring control of delegated power, have limited capability to address the normative, standard-setting challenges of organizational sustainability. Overall, the section highlights the fact that, in creating momentum toward sustainability, the top-down governance of the powerful bureaucracies and corporations of the industrial era is counterproductive. Several contributors to this section argue that the dominance of economic liberalism in traditional models of corporate governance has resulted in an emphasis on market fundamentalism, economically 'rational' behaviour and the primacy of shareholder interest. This perspective on governance gives no accord to the management of public goods, such as ecosystem needs or to the importance of social capital and reputation in adding long-term value and sustainability to the firm.

The chapter by Wheeler and Davies, for instance, reports on a study which compares shifts in the position of Canadian companies' 'benchmark' corporate governance ranking to shifts in market capitalization. Their results point up the limitations of an over-reliance on rules and structures in predicting the future performance of a firm and add weight to an alternative perspective that 'self-reinforcing networks of stakeholders with loyalty to the firm' are very important in generating improved long-term market value. The chapter provides indirect empirical evidence of the business case for sustainability and corporate social responsibility and for the stakeholder approach to governance.

Increasingly, achieving sustainability involves inter-organizational relations and partnerships between governments, corporations, NGOs and community members. These relationships are formed for several reasons including furthering organizational learning, ensuring accountability, maintaining credibility and reducing resistance to change. Sustainability therefore exemplifies the new 'problem field' for managers and corporate leaders: an emergent network-based organizational world where corporations must maintain consistency of purpose and identity yet be flexible enough to interact and compete in conditions of constant change and flux.

In addressing some of these issues, the chapter by Benn, Dunphy and Griffiths argues that corporate sustainability can only be achieved if firms are supported by a governance system that encourages going beyond compliance to a more strategic form of sustainability. This is itself dependent upon high levels of innovation and inter-relatedness with a range of organizations such as government, NGOs and other corporations. Case material presented in the chapter highlights the limitations of dominant pluralist systems of democracy and decision-making in supporting such organizational behaviour. The authors raise the alternative of deliberative decision-making as a means of ensuring interaction and fostering corporate awareness of sustainability criteria.

The contribution by Martin, Benn and Dunphy explores the limitations of legal, bureaucratic and market-based governance models in terms of incorporating change. To create a suitable working model, the chapter draws on a study of collaborative arrangements between corporations and other forms of organizations involved with sustainable land practices in Australia. The authors suggest a model of sustainable governance based on the social networks and shared values that they argue will enable the development of the new knowledge required for sustainability.

The final chapter in Part II, by Richardson, reflects on the role of the financial markets in environmental governance. He reviews the rise of ethical investment funds – rapid but still miniscule compared to overall funds. Richardson explores legal, institutional, information and market barriers to more environmental financing. He questions the adequacy of current policy instruments and raises the issue of reflexive regulation as an alternative. The chapter raises a number of important issues for further research such as the adequacy of assessment criteria for ethical investment and the comparison between activist shareholder deliberation and passive investment as drivers of change.

PART III: REDESIGNING GOVERNANCE FOR SUSTAINABILITY

Part III continues our exploration into new models and practices of governance that are compatible with sustainability criteria. An overall theme linking the contributions in this section is a concern with the power relations underpinning governance for sustainability. Several contributors, for instance, argue for the importance of coordination, commitment and participation over control as mechanisms of governance. This in turn requires redesigning the structures, processes and relationships which control access to decision-making and information and the distribution of resources. There is a strong practical base to this section of the book, as we look to some of the ways companies are carrying out such redesign with the aim of progressing towards sustainability.

Tudor Maxwell's chapter is a case study of the world's third largest mining company, Anglo American PLC. Maxwell finds the board of this firm supporting sustainability through a number of measures. Overall he finds the firm taking a more holistic approach to governance, based on more positive arrangements with stakeholders that reduce both operating costs for the company as well as environmental impacts. This finding supports his argument that a multitheoretic approach to corporate governance is necessary if corporations such as Anglo are to reduce their environmental externalities.

Increasingly standards are not set by governments but by non-profit organizations and industry associations. This section of the book also looks at the increasing use of codes for assessing and classifying corporate behaviour. In a highly reflexive and critical age, concerned with the effects of corporate activity on the sustainability of the ecosystem and society, it is not just who contributes to decision-making which must be legitimized, but the output of decision-making. Accountability is an issue of legitimacy.

The chapter by Bondy, Matten and Moon examines the role that codes of conduct can play in examining a corporation's behaviour at the interface with society. This chapter also takes up risk management as a facet of corporate social responsibility and emphasizes codes as a tool to facilitate self-regulation. The authors admit that codes by themselves cannot make that happen without commitment of key decision-makers in the organization and the concurrent use of tools such as reports and policies. But they make the strong point that clear standards and assessment criteria in effect act as a means of adjusting the power differentials between different stakeholders of the firm.

As Bondy *et al.* acknowledge, interpretations of corporate governance need to move from a rules-based perspective to a broader understanding of the structures, processes and relationships which control and coordinate organizations. The chapter by Benn, Wilson and Low is a case study of a leading Australian insurance firm which has made sustainability a key feature of its business strategy. The insurance sector has been sensitized to sustainability issues through the effects of climate change on global weather patterns. IAG is only one of a number of insurance firms worldwide increasingly committed to sustainability. In this study, the authors, one of whom is a senior manager at IAG, explore the structures, strategies and processes that IAG has put in place with the aim of developing a shared purpose of sustainability within the firm and across its stakeholder networks.

In their chapter, Bendell and Sharma point to the increasing importance of corporations in every aspect of society and contrast this with the increasingly limited power of democratically elected governments. This leads to their argument in support of stakeholder democracy. In calling for a more democratic focus of governance, and linking to points made by Benn and Dunphy in their first chapter of the book, Bendell and Sharma stress the importance of differences in power in the relationship between different stakeholders.

The last chapter in this book, by Clarke, touches on a number of key points made throughout the book. The author explores the revitalization of CSR as a real demonstration that corporate stakeholders are prepared to act to end the stalemated opposition between agency and stakeholder governance. He argues that a dynamic stakeholder model is now emerging that is driving enlightened shareholder value and bringing together the complex picture of how corporations can be redesigned to achieve sustainability. This will involve an intersection between governance and reporting systems at the levels of the corporation, the nation and global society and will build on work already begun through the Global Reporting Initiative.

Overall, if we look over the contributions made in this book, we see that for corporations to move beyond compliance to address sustainability criteria their leaders and managers will need to engage with a broader interpretation of governance than the rules and structures they have been accustomed to. The push towards corporate sustainability is seeing the emergence of different types of leaders and different types of decision-making models. Sustainable corporations are likely to be less mechanistic and hierarchical, more holistic in their management planning and to have more network-based multidirectional information flows and feedback mechanisms fostering reflexive management.

The interdisciplinary approach taken in this book has generated new questions and understandings on the subject of governance for sustainability. We hope that these combined contributions will stimulate your thinking and lead you too to contribute to this crucially important debate.

Part I

Introduction

Governance and sustainability challenges

Chapter 1

New forms of governance

Changing relationships between corporates, government and community

Suzanne Benn and Dexter Dunphy

INTRODUCTION

This chapter provides a framework for analysing corporation–government–community interactions. This framework is developed within the context of the forms of governance required to coordinate these interactions and achieve social and environmental sustainability.

Corporations and governments are now confronted with managing the expectations of a society newly alerted to the social and environmental risks associated with economic development. There is dawning recognition at many levels of society that achieving a sustainable world is dependent upon anticipating and reducing risks where possible and on the equitable distribution and democratic management of the remaining risks. However, action of this kind is reliant upon relevant interest groups being prepared to move beyond narrow self-interest and on the capacity for enlightened policy-making by government and corporate leaders. Fundamentally, these are requirements of governance, for they relate to the structures and processes which determine the sharing of responsibilities and the appropriate allocation of power in society (Bressers and Rossenbaum 2003; Clarke 2004). Governance of this kind entails not only transparency and accountability but also active collaboration between a range of social actors (Clarke 2004). As Bertels and Vredenburg (2004) argue, governance at the level of the multiple stakeholder or interorganizational domain must consider the complex interdependencies between the actors.

In the face of these demands for governance, the traditional closed decision-making of the powerful bureaucracies and corporations of the industrial era is no longer either appropriate or acceptable. This raises two key questions. How equipped is the standard body of democratic theory to deal with issues of governance that relate to sustainability? To the extent that democratic theory is inadequate, can the leading concepts of management theory provide guidance for more appropriate models of governance and norms of management practice that will foster the transition to a sustainable society?

DRIVERS OF CHANGE

Global pressures from above and below

Climate change, toxic waste legacies and human rights abuses are examples of the issues of global survival which are mobilizing actors at two levels on the world stage. From above, governments, corporations and NGOs are negotiating agreements designed to enable a more equitable distribution of social and environmental risk within and between the generations. Examples of the so-called 'globalization from above' include the global Stockholm Treaty for Persistent Organic Pollutants, the UN Global Compact and the Global Reporting Initiative (Falk, quoted in Beck 1999: 38).

At the same time, organized by transnational NGOs, assisted by activist individuals and spread on the internet, the 'globalization from below' movement has emerged, reflecting a re-emphasis on sustainability values, often linked to post-materialist concerns. Both 'globalization from above' and 'below' are forcing organizations to open up their decision-making structures and processes for perusal and participation. For example, the worldwide movement for corporate reporting on sustainability and CSR issues is increasing the transparency of corporate decision-making.

The discourse of risk and uncertainty

Complexity, chaos, uncertainty and change are now almost standard terms in the lexicon of most organizations. On the one hand, risk, as the language of rational discourse, has become the 'generic unit of governance', useful in justifying a governmental focus on efficiency and cost–benefit based decision-making (Fisher 2003). On the other hand, we see the emergence of a World Risk Society dominated by themes of uncontrollable financial, ecological and terrorist risk; according to Beck a new public is surfacing that is united by fear (Beck and Beck-Gernsheim 2002: 46). In these conditions, it is not surprising that there is a widespread loss of faith in traditional systems of authority (Kochan 2003). Feigning 'control over the uncontrollable' (Beck and Beck-Gernsheim 2002: 41) by governments and corporations is a recipe for mistrust.

Corporations in particular are suffering a crisis in credibility, demonstrated by repeated surveys and polls in recent years. For example:

- According to the 2002 global survey conducted by Environics, 48 per cent of people have little or no trust in public companies (Business in the Community, *Research Review* 2004; Grayson and Hodges 2004).
- The 2003 Mori Trust Monitor carried out on behalf of the British Medical Association found that 60 per cent of British adults do not expect corporate leaders to tell the truth (Grayson and Hodges 2004).

Increasing shareholder activism and the upsurge in the socially responsible investment industry demonstrate growing public preparedness to question corporate power. An apparent factor is heightened recognition of the powerful role that corporates have played in setting priorities in the capitalist world (Stanfield and Carroll 2004). The recent dramatic collapses of corporations such as Enron confirm belief that corporations cannot maintain their relative independence unless a new system of governance is installed to ensure transparency, morality and ethics (Clarke 2004). The passing of the Sarbanes–Oxley Act in the US is an illustration of one government's reaction to this perceived need.

However, such legislation needs to be accompanied by structures and processes designed to enable governance of the shared responsibilities for the management of social and environmental risk. The interconnected phenomena of increased information flows, heightened conditions of risk and uncertainty and growing mistrust of established institutions point to the importance of public inclusion and external assessment. Corporations and organizations of all types are now aware that they must obtain a 'licence to operate' from a sceptical and aware public (Elkington 1998). In an ecological age and a discursive society, increasingly challenged by conditions of uncertainty and risk, organizations regard legitimacy and symbolic capital as key resources and sources of power (Beck 1992; Tsoukas 1999). In Livesey's (2001:78) words: 'the function of corporations has become, willy-nilly, political, and the production of green ideologies may be as important to competitive survival as the production of goods and services'.

THEMES IN POLITICAL THEORY

Traditional systems of democracy

Risk brings with it the need for coordination and control: matters for the governance of nations and of all types of organizations. The question is how to redesign current systems of governance to ensure that power is exercised in a way which is inclusive and where the parties can be held publicly accountable.

How well equipped is democratic political theory to deal with these new challenges for governance? In the capitalist world, two constellations of ideologies are typically contrasted as opposing systems of democracy: the 'New Right' and social democracy. The former is associated with a belief in individual freedom and property rights, free enterprise and market fundamentalism; the latter with a more proactive role for the state whose contract is to intervene in order to protect collective interests. Each ideology has apparent compatibilities and incompatibilities with a system which could support the democratic management of risk and the development of a sustainable society.

Reflecting the public choice reasoning that individuals in organizations will always act in their own self-interest, 'New Right' principles support the devolution of state authority to decentralized decision-making arenas (Pierson 1993; Bellamy 1999). This may seem to privilege civil society and foster more community-based involvement in decision-making. However, the New Right principles of minimalist government, individualization and market fundamentalism do not in fact support the protection and management of public goods (Eckersley 1992; Giddens 1998; Stewart and Jones 2003).

In the other camp, supporters of social democracy argue that specific policy incentives implemented by an interventionist state are crucial if corporate governance is to take account of the precautionary principle and encourage production of ecologically and socially responsible goods and services (Mol and Sonnenfeld 2000). However, critics of social democracy highlight the reliance of its governance systems upon bureaucratic rationality. In this view, the dependence of the interventionist social democratic state on administrative and planning systems restricts the sense of community and collaboration necessary for effective participatory risk management (Goodin 1992; Farrell and Morris 2003).

Given these limitations on both sides, an increasing number of political theorists now argue that neither system is suitable for dealing with complex decision-making, particularly where it involves social and environmental risk. Basically, both points of view rest on shared understandings of liberal pluralism: both aim 'to reach a fair and efficient compromise' between differing individual points of view (Miller 1993: 74). Limitations to the principle of fair and reasonable assessment of individual preferences are well recognized. They include the difficulties in ensuring individual preferences are aggregated fairly and preventing voters from strategically manipulating their vote (Miller 1993: 80). These limitations are compounded when powerful actors such as corporations have considerable economic resources and strategic interests at stake in the allocation and management of risk. The ideal of consensus reached between the interest groups leads to an emphasis on short-term social stability, which again can be exploited by powerful elites or authority figures and counter the long-term perspective required for genuine environmental governance that produces genuinely sustainable outcomes.

The key principle of the pluralist tradition is the competition between interest or pressure groups which are seen as composed of coalitions of like-minded citizens. The assumption is that all citizens have similar capacity (such as time and information) to form interest groups. Hence many minorities which do not are effectively excluded. Pluralist theory also does not give consideration to the potentially diverse make up of any particular interest group – homogeneity within the group is assumed whereas there can be very diverse interests within a group.

These issues become further problematic when alternatives presented to voters involve highly technical and interdisciplinary areas of knowledge associated with high degrees of uncertainty. The dependence of many environmental decisions on knowledge of this kind further compromises the capacity of a pluralist system to ensure all interest groups are equally equipped with the resources needed to fully understand and then defend their interest position (Eckersley 2004).

These limitations underpinning the traditional systems of democracy have prompted the development of a number of more radical governance theories.

EMERGENT POLITICAL THEORIES

Reflexive modernization

Reflexive modernization theorists argue that in post-industrial society the processes of globalization are parallelled by processes of individualization (Beck 1992, 1995, 1997, 1999; Beck *et al.* 1994; Beck and Beck-Gernsheim 2002). The factors underpinning this dynamic include the global information revolution, the heightened perception of risk resulting from industrialization, the shrinking of the welfare state and the dislocation of individual members of society from their traditional context of class, union, family or hierarchical firm (Beck 1997: 98). The effect is the emergence of an increasingly self-critical, reflexive society – termed the 'risk society' (Beck 1992). Since the transition from industrial to post-industrial society involves new and often incalculable forms of risk – financial, social and environmental – we need new institutions, new practices, new relationships, structures and processes in order to provide adequate governance (Backstrand 2003; Beck *et al.* 1994).

According to Beck, the individualization of politics resulting from the retreat of traditional institutions will lead to more inclusive decision-making in a new 'sub-political', extra-parliamentary arena (Beck 1992). In this arena, it is argued that temporary and multiple stakeholder networks operating as decentralized, self-determining, flexible arenas for decision-making will also enable new and more democratic ways of decision-making around areas of risk (Beck 1992; Beck *et al.* 1994). A key factor in this challenge to established political systems is growing recognition that traditional systems of authority, be they political, administrative, legal or scientific have facilitated and legitimated modernization processes associated with an institutionalized underestimation of risk. Reflexive modernization theorists argue that these new political structures will not only be more inclusive but will allow the entry of new forms of knowledge. As Tsoukas (1999: 509) points out, the ongoing 'reflexive monitoring of action' will have major implications for both individuals and organizations.

Arguably, however, as the theory stands, application of the 'sub-political' model relies upon high levels of communication and reaching of consensus between competing interests. Unless the theory is redefined and the method of decision-making more specifically addressed, the reflexive modernization model shares the limitations of liberal pluralism (Schlosberg 1999).

Deliberative democracy

Luskin and Fishkin (2004: 1) define the processes of deliberative democracy as follows:

> Deliberating citizens seek relevant information, reflect on the issues, and exchange views with others. The most valuable kind of deliberation is balanced, taking account of information both convenient and inconvenient to given arguments and alternatives, although much naturally occurring deliberation is of course highly imbalanced.

Based on their research, these writers argue that the process of deliberation makes citizens better informed and better able to contribute to the critical assessment of policy issues. In short, it increases their political efficacy.

Deliberative democracy aims to overcome problems associated with traditional systems of democracy by moving from a focus on votes to a focus on processes of public deliberation. In a system which emphasizes the processes of reflection and deliberation, citizens are selected (randomly or on the basis of representational criteria), then consider relevant information from a number of different perspectives, are given opportunity for critical conversation on the issues and then reconsider their original opinion (Carson 2001). Rather than consensus, the aim is to achieve impartiality and full knowledge of critical issues, concepts akin to Habermas' ideal of full communication (Habermas 1984). The theory presumes some degree of communality and a belief in human ability to be swayed by logical argumentation, an assumption of human nature which is clearly different from the liberal view (Miller 1993).

The limitations of deliberative democracy relate to the post-modernist critique of Habermas and to the potential for the deliberative forum to be influenced by political manipulation and differences in power. However, its techniques are strongly advocated by many public policy and civic science theorists. For instance, deliberative democracy methods which aim to foster public debate through ensuring fuller information can be used to bring together lay, expert and indigenous knowledge and thus establish a more communicative model of science. Such a model is more relevant to decision-making for governance in conditions of uncertainty and risk. As Backstrand (2003) points out, traditional science is not well equipped to deal effectively with the uncertainty characterizing many environmental decisions.

Radical pluralism

Radical pluralism has emerged in reaction to the well-known problems with classical pluralism, discussed previously. As a critique of classical pluralism, radical pluralism draws from the postmodern concerns for identity, challenging the assumption of conventional pluralism that the interest group has an 'essential' identity. According to radical pluralist theory, interest group identity is constructed in relation to others – a process necessarily involving exclusion (Wenman 2003). As a consequence, diverse viewpoints within interest groups are often suppressed.

Radical pluralism has been taken up by theorists concerned with environmental justice who part company with Beck's (1992) interpretation of the democratically experienced nature of risk in the 'risk society'. For example, the main concern of the environmental justice movement is that the risks associated with industrial development have been borne by those communities and individuals least able to deal with the consequences of these risks. As well, those groups or individuals within interest groups who are less resourced, either in economic or expert terms, can be marginalized through the process of pluralist interest group construction.

Schlosberg (1999) argues that contemporary environmental movements are characteristically pluralistic. They encompass many different understandings of, and experiences with, risk but these differences are not recognized by conventional pluralism. According to Schlosberg (1999: 184), if process and content are taken together by applying the principles of deliberative democracy, both inclusive decision-making and equitable distribution of risk can be achieved. In this case, the deliberative process will allow 'for an institution of discursive practices among a plurality of positions, knowledges and understandings' (1999: 90). Radical pluralism thus brings together Habermas' concepts of ideal forms of communication with more postmodernist understandings of diversity and identity.

Non-hierarchical networks within and between the less-resourced elements of society are a way of organizing against the exploitative 'divide and conquer' strategies often used by corporations and government organizations. The network does not imply unity and admits differences. As Schlosberg says (1999: 118):

> It is crucial to note that networks do not necessarily form around one single unifying commonality. Instead, networks form and hold themselves together around numerous issues where there are similarities or solidarities across groups. The resulting mosaic itself – the movement – becomes the major commonality. Within a network there remains both multiplicity and commonality.

Many of the arguments made by proponents of deliberative democracy and radical pluralism are also put by social movement theorists who stress the benefits of face-to-face interaction in the public space as a means of dealing with complexity (see for example: Melucci and Avritzer 2000).

New institutionalism

Governance of ecological problems at one scale prompts issues of control and co-ordination at other social, temporal and environmental scales (see for example: Dryzek 1997; Bressers and Rosenbaum 2003; Eckersley 2004). Environmental issues do not fit neatly within established governmental or geographic boundaries and their effects are not immediate. The transport and disposal of toxic waste, for example, may raise governance problems at local, regional, national and international levels. Inter-governmental and intersectoral issues may also be involved as well as effects extending well beyond the short term of the traditional political cycle. Environmental and social risks do not necessarily fit into neat regional and temporal boundaries.

New institutional theory has been used to grapple with the issue of resistant institutional practices. In the seminal work in political science by March and Olsen, institutions are seen as often resistant to change because social actors within them act according to institutional norms and policies rather than according to an understanding of the rational consequences of decisions (March and Olsen 1984; Peters 1999).

As Brujin points out: 'institutions develop robust resistance toward changes in their functional and normative environments, as well as toward reform attempts' (Brujin 2003: 283). Researchers using these concepts have focused on what institutional factors and types of adaptive pressures result in the most resistance to change. For instance, what causes resistance to bringing social actors together from across many different governance levels, or to the introduction of considerations of intergenerational equity into decision-making frameworks? How can such resistance be circumvented? Key conclusions to date are that shared policy styles and horizontal interactions between social sectors can lower institutional resistance to change (Brujin 2003; Lulofs *et al.* 2003).

Ecological modernization

Some of the challenges raised by the new institutionalists have been addressed in ecological modernization theory. Ecological modernization rests on the optimistic principle that neither the economies nor the polities of advanced capitalist systems are necessarily in conflict with environmental concerns (York *et al.* 2003). The argument is based on the assumptions that a concerned public will try to ensure institutional change and that further modernization involving innovation and knowledge development can reduce environmental impacts and lessen the likelihood of complex issues of risk management (Mol and Sonnenfeld 2000). In this view, current economic systems can be modified in line with sustainability if principles such as the precautionary principle are built into governmental policy-making in such areas as planning, product warranty, corporate regulation and procurement.

Ecological modernization is a systems-based approach which looks to the interconnections between policy formation, the economy and the natural environment. Partnerships, cooperation and the building of social capital between stakeholders such corporations and governments are crucial to the ecological modernization platform (Dryzek 1997; Lulofs *et al.* 2003). So-called 'weak' ecological modernization (Christoff 1996), the dominant understanding of this theory, has however come under considerable criticism for not addressing perceived inherent contradictions between techno-economic development and sustainability and for an excessive focus on techno-scientific solutions.

From the perspective of this chapter, the 'weak' version of the theory does not address the issue of inclusiveness raised previously in our analysis of the limitations of liberal pluralism. Disparities in power between and within the cooperating organizations and sectors of society are not adequately addressed.

Ecological democracy

Writers attempting to develop a vision of an ecological democracy have focused strongly on how to articulate the public interest through the development of civil society and on governance problems arising from issues that affect a range of social, temporal and ecological scales.

For instance, Eckersley (2004) argues that, given the short-term perspective of policy-makers in current democratic systems of liberal pluralism, environmental considerations are inevitably downgraded in the current competition for power. If a democracy is to incorporate ecological concerns it must specifically ensure that collaborative deliberation and problem solving, not competition, underpin governance structures and processes (Eckersley 2004). Legislation would be specifically designed for the democratic management of risk by enabling the enforcement of the precautionary principle and minimizing externalization of risks through measures such as polluter-pays. Eckersley (2004) argues that a green public space would be the crucial aspect of a green state: a civil society whose citizens possess the critical awareness necessary to contribute as equal stakeholders in the determination of appropriate governance measures.

Dryzek's (2000) interpretation of ecological democracy is also built on the concept that more genuine, inclusive forms of communication would ensure more ecologically rational decision-making. He focuses on an achievable, rather than on an idealized, system of ecological democracy. According to Dryzek, the most appropriate political strategy would be to develop awareness that better governance of the natural environment would benefit society as a whole.

From even such a brief summary we can see themes emerging in political theory that address governance issues of inclusion and equity not recognized in more traditional pluralist forms of decision-making.

MANAGEMENT THEORY

We can conclude that emergent versions of political theory are more relevant to our question of governance for the equitable management of risk than traditional concepts of democracy. This section of the paper examines the relevance of leading themes in management theory in this context.

LEADING THEMES IN MANAGEMENT THEORY

Resource-based and strategic management theory

The history of management theory shows that cultural changes associated with globalization and information flows have forced management theorists to gradually reconceptualize organizations as open structures. Leading this trend, contingency theory emerged in the 1960s as a situational, 'no one best way' approach which contrasts with the rigid 'one best way' and inward-looking principles of scientific management and Taylorism (see for example: Pfeffer 1982). Since then, strategic management theory, resource-based theory, and stakeholder theory have increasingly dominated management theory. Most of the following discussion will focus on stakeholder theory as it is this theory which most informs management practice concerning social and environmental issues.

Porter's ideas on strategic management, first developed in the late 1970s, continue to have enormous influence on management theory and practice. His 'five forces model', and the numerous other models of strategic management spawned since, largely focus on the company's external competitive environment (Porter 1980). The relationship between this body of theory and ecological or democratic concerns is limited and very much one way. While the strategic management literature largely ignores these concerns (Bubna-Litic and Benn 2003), ecological modernization theory incorporates the principles of strategic management into its framework for integrating economic and environmental decision-making.

The internal focus of resource-based theory, also highly influential on contemporary management practice, stands in contrast to the external focus of traditional strategic management. It highlights the need for a fit between the external business environment and internal organizational capabilities such as human resources. For instance, employee knowledge can become a key source of competitive advantage (Drucker quoted in Kochan 2003). From the internal organizational perspective, resource-based theory can encompass democratic systems of governance. Engaging employees through representation and share ownership is seen as a means of preventing CEO excesses and expanding awareness of financial, human resource and reputational risk factors (Kochan 2003). Positive community relationships and NGO partnerships are another way of developing a strategically important resource because such relationships give the corporation the 'licence to operate and grow' (Elkington 1998). Through the lens of this theory, bridging relationships to external organizations and community bodies builds reputational and social capital – both tradeable resources (Petrick *et al.* 1999; Adler and Kwon 2002).

The highly instrumental resource-based approach, however, has limited compatibility with a governance system grounded in ethical principles or one which gives an inherent value to the environment. Basically both resource-based and strategic management theories assume that organizations, even non-profit organizations, are necessarily 'narcissistic and self-serving' (Starkey and Crane 2003: 229). Both rest on the established parameters of development, growth, personal potential and technocratic innovation (Crane 2000).

Stakeholder theory

Broader versions of resource-based theory have been merged with traditional corporate social responsibility theories and reconceptualized as stakeholder theory (see for example: Warhurst 2001; Zadek 2001; Waddock *et al.* 2002). The broadest definition of stakeholder is 'any group or individual who can effect or is affected by the achievement of the organization's objectives' (Freeman 1984: 46). In this vein, a successful organization is one which at least satisfies but preferably adds value for all stakeholders, not just shareholders. Some writers have made serious attempts to conceptualize an ideal or an 'ecocentric' organization which could also feature the natural environment as a key stakeholder (Starik and Rands 1995; Dunphy *et al.* 2003). In general, these theorists argue for corporations to integrate a strong version of sustainability into their business operations with clear consequences for their structures and operations. According to Shrivastava (1995: 130):

> Organisations in the ecocentric paradigm are appropriately scaled, provide meaningful work, have decentralised participative decision-making, have low earning differentials among employees, and have non-hierarchical structures. They establish harmonious relationships between their natural and social environments. They seek to systematically review natural resources and to minimise waste and pollution.

To be ecocentric also requires cultural change at the organizational level. Gladwin *et al.* (1995: 899) argue the values required for the 'sustaincentric' organization are: 'stewardship, equity, humility, permanence, precaution and sufficiency'. According to these broad versions of stakeholder theory, governance for social and environmental risk also involves organizations internalizing all their social and environmental costs.

Limitations of stakeholder theory

Despite the claims for the importance of stakeholder engagement in creating sustainable organizations, stakeholder theory has a limited capacity to address the equitable management of risk. The theory does not really address how to operationalize a system of governance which will integrate the concerns of humans and non-humans as stakeholders. For instance, the 'ecocentric' theorists draw on industrial ecology (Ehrenfeld 2000) and natural capitalism models (Hawken *et al.* 1999) in order to explain how corporations can operationalize economic and environmental goals simultaneously. Yet both industrial ecology and natural capitalism rest upon technocentric principles. Neither is concerned with the principles of participatory or inclusive decision-making and both neglect the fact that people make technical solutions either work or fail.

Another limitation relates to the ideological battlefield surrounding the interpretation of stakeholder. The accepted perspective is a narrow version of stakeholder theory based in concepts of agency theory and individualism, while a broader version is based on stewardship theory and the obligations of the collective (Sundaramurthy and Lewis 2003). But governance, stakeholder and sustainability are loose terms which, when used in conjunction, can make for ready appropriation by ideological or vested interests. Hence we have the broad version of stakeholder theory espoused in the rhetoric of 'green evangelism' and the 'win-win' case for sustainability. (See for example: Warhurst 2001; Grayson and Hodges 2004.) This interpretation tends to gloss over any conflict between economic development and strong sustainability values (Newton and Harte 1997). One reason why the approach lacks a critical perspective on the power relations within and between stakeholder groups (Banerjee 2003) is that the discourse has been taken up by numbers of consultants, many working in the community or public relations field (Beder 2001). For these practitioners, differences in interests are to be smoothed-out through consensus-based dialogue but the 'consensus' is often dictated by the most powerful actors.

On the other hand, we have the view, underpinned by market fundamentalism, that good governance is about getting the best management of shareholder assets. According to Clarke (2004), this point of view is based on the individualist assumption that if systems of control are not implemented, managers will follow the characteristic human pattern of self-serving behaviour. In this narrow, shareholder-based view, broad stakeholder theory is limited by issues of multiple accountability and weakening agency (Sternberg 2000; Bergkamp 2002). If organizations are accountable to all stakeholders, so the narrow stakeholder theorists argue, then genuine accountability is lost. As Bergkamp (2002: 147) puts the narrow stakeholder case:

> Measuring performance against a profit maximisation objective is relatively easy but measuring performance against the objective of balanced stakeholder benefits is fraught with difficulty.

Recently, however, the picture has become more complex. The finance model has been drawn in with concepts from resource-based theory to support the broad stakeholder argument. Blair (2004: 184) points out that the wealth-generating capacity of the firm is no longer so much 'the capital investments and entrepreneurial efforts of the investor'. In the contemporary firm, sources of competitive advantage are more likely to reflect the skills of employees and intangibles such a brand, reputation, strategic management of litigation issues and ability to communicate with customers and local communities.

This instrumental perspective on the broad stakeholder view reveals a problem common to both combatants. Neither address the ethical guidelines which could underpin a more inclusive and ecologically equitable management of risk (Grace and Cohen 1998). As Orts and Strudler point out, some moral issues, such as the obligation to consider the impact of environmental risks on social groups and the environment, are 'more important than stakeholder theory can accommodate' (Orts and Strudler 2002: 228). This raises the suggestion that instead of the endless search for stakeholder priority we should be looking to set these issues in law in the form of concrete criteria for providing a 'license to operate' (Elkington 1998; Banerjee 2005). Others argue that these measures will only be meaningful if they emerge from the 'moral transformation' of corporate leaders – an issue which is not informed by the stakeholder concept (Crane 2000: 673). Effective change may well depend both on rules and leadership.

In summary, we would agree with numerous other critics that narrow stakeholder theory rests on a base of market fundamentalism and individualism and hence has no means of addressing our concerns with governance. Neither does broad stakeholder theory, which promised some solutions, offer an operational framework for implementing an integrated perspective on governance for a sustainable society. It remains conceptually limited by the unwarranted pluralist assumption that all stakeholders can compete with equal resources in the decision-making arena. Governance systems across multiple and diverse stakeholders have been little analysed in terms of disparities of power between and within interest groups and how to manage them. As we have argued, power differences and ethical principles in the management of risk are often downplayed in an eager approach to get business on board the 'sustainability makes good business sense' bandwagon and issues of power are smoothed out in support for a consensus-based dialogue.

We conclude therefore that the leading forms of management theory have real problems in incorporating democratic concerns for the distribution of environmental or social risk.

EMERGENT THEMES IN MANAGEMENT THEORY

How therefore can we realistically address the issue of relations of power between and within diverse stakeholder groups. Marginalizing political concerns by maintaining the narrow or shareholder perspective, for instance, or by implementing standardized operational systems, reflects a management determination to limit conflict, disorder and indeterminacy (Coopey and Burgoyne 2000). Yet reducing disorder through reducing diversity can have major implications for the creative problem solving required if solutions are to be found for challenging and seemingly intractable issues of social and environmental risk and sustainability (Vaughan 1999; Backstrand 2003). Traditional management theory fails to recognize that differences within and between stakeholder groups are better used to reach more creative solutions to social and environmental issues.

In this section of the chapter we point to some emergent themes which highlight the importance of diversity in both interorganizational and intraorganizational relations. We also consider the leadership qualities required to determine value from these diverse relationships. We argue that these themes, while not nearly as well developed, show some correspondence with the more critical political theories we have discussed. This correspondence justifies our recommendation that these themes be incorporated into new models of interorganizational governance for social and environmental risk.

Cultural framing and organizational change

Management theory has traditionally focused on cohesion and consensus. However, a relatively recent interest in organizational culture is beginning to draw attention to the construction of stakeholder identity. This theme corresponds to the radical pluralist rejection of essentialist pluralist understandings of the stakeholder. The work of Howard-Grenville *et al*. (2003: 70) shows, for instance, when they are setting their organizational agenda that managers and change agents choose from an array of cultural frames in negotiating with other stakeholders on social or environmental initiatives. These cultural frames may change or be changed as a result of relationships if, for example, an organization perceives itself under attack. This work highlights the importance of cultural determination of stakeholder identity and indicates its shifting and fluid nature.

This research also shows the importance of the cultural change agent in working with organizations to address social or environmental issues not previously seen as business priorities. The corporation, for instance, may be required by new legislation to share decision-making about risk with the wider community. It is important in this context for the change agent to recognize that the organization is not monolithic in its interpretation of social and environmental initiatives, but may in fact include a number of different factions, functions or units whose cultural frames shape very different perspectives on social and environmental issues. Howard-Grenville *et al.* (2003: 81) argue that selection of culturally appropriate language and other ways of communicating the issue at hand can 'stretch' frames already existent in the organization to 'accommodate new issues and new approaches'. As they point out (2003: 70):

> While successful implementation of social initiatives involves moving the organisation beyond its current practices, it also must tap into accepted ways of representing problems and enacting solutions.

Narrative theory

Recent developments in narrative theory shed some light on the complex picture of organizational orientations towards social and environmental issues such as the internalization of risk. Livesey's (2001) analysis suggests that eco or socially responsible discourse may have many layers of meanings and intentions. In embracing the discourse of community consultation or environmental reform, an organization may be merely engaging in 'symbolic politics'; on the other hand, the new language may reflect a more genuine determination to reform practices. Importantly, Livesey's work shows that many unintentional and unpredictable results may result from an organization engaging with the discourse of sustainability as a form of 'storytelling'. As well as shaping relationships with other stakeholders, the discourse may have the unintentional effect of an organization developing a greener or more responsible culture. Used intentionally, then, green or socially responsible narratives can foster cultural change. Starkey and Crane (2003), for instance, claim that if used critically and in conjunction with defamiliarizing narratives for change, then 'green narratives' can enable the co-evolution of differing sub-group perspectives towards a shared and more ecocentric perspective within an organization.

Stakeholder interaction

Matten and Crane (2005) argue that the lessening influence of nation-states as a result of globalization can increase the role played by corporations in the administration of citizenship, and conclude that political theory needs to examine multiple stakeholder interaction more seriously.

As well, some management theorists now recognize that diversity in inter-organizational relations encourages the development of reflexive practices and facilitates knowledge creation. Developing bridging social capital through developing diverse external ties is dependent on transparent and reciprocal communication processes between organizations. These organizations may be community groups, government or corporate organizations. The process of dialogue across corporate boundaries (Roberts 2003) stimulates innovation and facilitates organizational learning (Adler and Kwon 2002; Benn *et al.* 2004a). Hardy *et al.*'s 2003 research has shown that organizational interactions or relationships which are 'embedded' (that is characterized by interactions with third parties, representation and multidirectional information flows) and show deep involvement (that is, have interactions between many levels of the collaborators) facilitate the generation of new practices, technologies or rules and the building of sustainable and distinctive capacities.

Our own research has shown that interorganizational relationships are more likely to be embedded if the multiple stakeholder arrangement includes community-based networks and that the inclusion of these networks facilitates the development of new practices useful in the management of environmental risks (Benn *et al.* 2004a). One key reason behind this finding appears to be that the inclusion of the community-based networks enables the bringing together of different forms of knowledge, such as lay and expert knowledge (Benn *et al.* 2004a). In a sense, the network enables the development of a shared perspective based on valuing different types of knowledge of environmental and social issues.

Leadership

In addition, research dealing with gender and diversity on leadership is adding to our understanding of the value of different types of leadership styles. 'Feminine' leadership in particular encourages a diversity of values, experiences and opinions and appears to have advantages in developing a communicative culture both within and between organizations (Benn *et al.* 2004b). In a major study of Australian senior managers, Ross-Smith *et al.* (2003) have shown that a developing critical mass of female managers results in changes in organizational practice such as more team-based work, less competitive behaviour, changes in styles of communication and a more flexible culture. Leaders who value and can deal with diversity develop more communicative and flexible relationships between stakeholders which facilitates effective risk management.

Finally, as Berry (2000: 11) points out, reflexive management requires leaders who are prepared to engage with both inter- and extra-organizational tasks, and in so doing 'combine private advantage with public acknowledgement of the obligation to engage in critical reflexiveness of values and beliefs, intentions and consequences'. To some extent these relationships are dependent on the formation of institutions such as self-regulatory reflexive legal frameworks and incentives (Orts and Strudler 2002) designed to induce management to internalize their environmental risks and costs (Tirole quoted in Webb 2004).

Organic governance

In summary, governance for the equitable and inclusive management of risk is posing new challenges for management theory. As Nobel Prize winner Professor Joseph Stiglitz (2004: 3) has put it: 'good management is a public good. There is no perfect solution'. The shift is away from a single-minded emphasis on efficiency which dominated the governance interpretations of the 1990s. The contemporary organization is seen by some theorists as a complex adaptive system; it is more complex, more interconnected, less involved in linear cause–effect strategies and planning and more concerned with learning, adaptiveness and reflexivity as organizational qualities than the traditional form (Clarke 2004). 'Organic' or self-organizing systems of governance are argued to be more appropriate for the control and coordination of such forms. The organic or cluster model proposed by Potapchuk *et al.* (1999: 221), for instance, is conceptualized as being fluid with multiple nodes, involving clusters of multiple stakeholders linked by informal and formal connections and employing deliberative processes in decision-making.

Synthesizing political and management theory

In Table 1.1, we show that there are areas of correspondence between the emergent themes in political and management theory. Structurally, these emergent concepts from management and political theory can be synthesized into governance systems which can coordinate multiple and diverse stakeholders and achieve full and open debate. Governance for reflexive management aims to achieve change by involving people in doing it. The management of interorganizational relations provides a useful conceptual approach to this challenge.

We argue that the areas of correspondence mapped out in Table 1.1 can form the basis of a more productive model of governance which emphasizes organizational leadership geared to diversity, communication, flexibility, reflexivity and inclusion. We argue that this model fosters the trusting relationships necessary for managing issues of environmental and social risk for the long term while taking into account real difference in the interests of stakeholders (Kochan 2003). We admit to some inconsistencies or paradoxes.

Redesigning the practice of governance

In this section we provide some suggestions for the practical implementation of a governance model which has the characteristics listed in the left-hand column of Table 1.1. Our previous analysis of the shortcomings of traditional systems of democracy

Table 1.1 *Areas of correspondence between emergent bodies of theory*

Key issue	*Emergent political theory*	*Key contribution*	*Emergent management theory*	*Areas of correspondence*
Cluster governance	Reflexive modernization	A decentralized 'sub-political' arena enables reflexive and inclusive decision-making	Stakeholder interaction	Community-based networks involving multiple stakeholders link different types of knowledge and facilitate knowledge development and diffusion
Decision-making based on high communication frequency	Deliberative democracy	Open and critical debate can increase awareness and the political efficacy of all participants	Narrative theory	Defamiliarizing narratives and storytelling can develop a shared 'ecocentric' understanding across organizations
Leadership for diversity and flexibility	Radical pluralism	Non-hierarchical networks can support a multiplicity of meanings yet allow ongoing collaboration	Leadership styles	'Feminine' collaborative leadership styles support diverse understandings of values, knowledge, experience and opinions
Adaptiveness through cultural change	New institutionalism	Horizontal interactions reduce institutional resistance to change	Cultural framing	Cultural framing and analysis of stakeholder identity improves strategies for organizational change

continued

Table 1.1 *continued*

Key issue	*Emergent political theory*	*Key contribution*	*Emergent management theory*	*Areas of correspondence*
Partnership formation	Ecological modernization	Institutional innovation and knowledge development is enabled by government/ corporate partnerships	Bridging social capital	Open and reciprocal communication systems build trust and enable knowledge sharing between organizations
Reflexivity	Ecological democracy	Legislation needs to be precautionary and reflexive	Reflexive management	Reflexivity can be fostered through engaging in extra organizational tasks

and theories of management has led us to conclude that more than just coordination and accountability are required for the effective governance of sustainability. A key requisite is the creation of decentralized arenas of decision-making including community-based networks where new and creative solutions can be fostered. In these new units of governance, it is necessary to rethink decision-making, leadership, the role of the change agent in cultural change, the nature of partnership models and how reflexivity can be effectively encouraged. We deal with each of these areas in turn.

The cluster approach to governance

Both reflexive modernization and stakeholder interaction theories argue that decentralization encourages inclusiveness. We argue that, in addition, embeddedness is a vital component. Embeddedness results from high levels of interaction and deep involvement in stakeholder relations and this facilitates the shared development of new practices, skills and techniques for dealing with risk issues. Where the cluster approach to governance has these characteristics, it avoids the top-down and inflexible approach, which is incompatible with a reflexive, adaptive system (Potapchuk *et al.* 1999). The cluster-based model focuses on the development of networks or coalitions of those who are potentially at risk or critical to successfully ensuring that sustainable practices are instituted. A cluster can include organizations of all types as well as individual members of the community. In order to identify the boundaries of a cluster, it is necessary to define the nature of the risk, the scope of the risk, the relevant stakeholders (i.e. those potentially affected by the risk) and the extent of the risk to various stakeholders. This would not usually occur prior to the cluster coming into existence but would evolve as the relevant parties explore the nature of the risk – actual membership of a cluster can evolve over time with the increasing definition and clarification of the issues.

There is a major challenge in the development of such networked clusters, where, say, the organizations are firms or not-for-profit organizations involved in ongoing and structured relationships (Jones *et al.* 1997). Coordination between autonomous organizations is difficult enough. But where there are issues of wide social and environmental risk to consider, the members of the 'network' may not be only discrete organizations. They may include, for instance, individual activist and diverse interest groups within a broader community which faces potential risk due to, for example, the building of a new chemical plant.

These difficulties suggest the need for negotiating, at an early stage of cluster development, the deliberative strategies that will be adopted. Issues here include: deciding on whether to use direct or indirect representation of stakeholders, the appointment of a coordinator or coordinating group, choosing appropriate forms of communication within the networks, developing a timeline for the process and anticipated stages, gaining agreement to decision-making methods including how the final decision will be reached, providing for arbitration in case of failure to reach agreement (the citizen's jury is one method used by advocates of deliberative democracy) and designing support to overcome relative disadvantages of some stakeholders.

The diversity of ethical norms in such a cluster will require agreement on decision-making procedures. Potapchuk *et al.* (1999) suggest that there needs to be one coordinating entity to lead a cluster of organizations or individuals linked by both formal and informal governance structures. Ideally prior agreement will take place on the coordinating entity and the rules for decision-making.

Rethinking decision-making

Both deliberative democracy and narrative theory emphasize that high levels of communication ensure more shared understandings of changes required to address risk situations. In conditions of uncertainty and historical lack of trust between participants in decision-making concerning risk, the characteristics outlined in Table 1.1 are often lacking in the organizations participating at the 'sub-political', cluster-based level and communication is reduced or avoided. Assessing the range of participant responses is an essential element of the adaptive management required to address the lack of trust. Luginaah *et al.* (2004) suggest several tools to map public responses related to risk, hazard, trust, accountability and fairness in conditions of scientific uncertainty and lack of trust in decision-makers. They argue these qualitative tools enable the development of adaptive management techniques which, by respecting stakeholder differences of perception and resources, can build trust.

Table 1.2 Key themes and decision support tools for risk management

Key theme	Decision support tools
Managing information	Informational: provides information on the risk issue.
	Diagnostic: aims to uncover which groups or individuals may be exposed and the nature of exposure to the risk.
Managing uncertainty	Impact: responds to questions about the kinds of impact on stakeholders and how these impacts can be mitigated.
	Iterative: helps stakeholders respond to new circumstances as the risk issue is constantly changing.
Managing the environment	Process (scanning): allows for the assessment of the socio-political context, identification of stakeholders and the classification of these groups to map out the influence structure.
	Contextual (scoping):provides issue managers with updates on existing protocols and strategies from elsewhere.

We would add that there are additional methodologies which can be readily adapted from the organization development and change management fields, for example, future search methodology and participatory design processes (Holman and Devane 1999).

Rethinking leadership

We have noted that both radical pluralism and 'feminine' understandings of leadership focus on recognition of diversity. As we have discussed, one problem with the techniques set out in Table 1.2 is with the interpretation of stakeholder identity, which is subject to the failings of pluralism. Carson (2001) argues that the consultation process is more likely to go beyond the superficial and recognize diversity if it is interactive and community-focused. These characteristics do not simply evolve – they are brought into being by competent and skilled leaders. Hughes and Hosfeld have recently identified some distinctive characteristics of outstanding leaders of sustainable organizations (Hughes and Hosfeld 2005). They found that these leaders were characterized by:

- having passion and vision;
- systems thinking with a long time horizon;
- innovation and a willingness to learn;
- encouraging a participatory organizational culture;
- willingness to teach others, including competitors and clients – creating a 'knowledge commons' (2005: 16–18).

These leadership characteristics are entirely compatible with the participatory democracy approaches we have outlined.

There must be participation by all stakeholders in the problem definition process if the governance of interorganizational or multiple stakeholder arrangements is to engender trust and go beyond the corporate drive to accumulate symbolic capital (Tsoukas 1999). Participants need to acknowledge their mutual dependence and interconnectedness with each other in order to develop bridging social capital (Demirag 2004). As we have discussed, this contrasts with the construction of stakeholder identity through heightening the sense of 'otherness' – a process which leads to the smoothing-out of difference, lessens participation and in the end results in a less creative solution to a shared problem.

Rethinking the role of the change agent in cultural change

It is crucial to recognize that activists bring about change from within as well as from outside organizations. Change agents working to develop effective inquiry need to challenge their own assumptions first in order to develop the quality of self-leadership that Dunphy *et al.* (2003) argue is the key to success as a change agent.

Skilled change agents have a range of technical and interpersonal micro-skills. Figure 1.1 gives a summary outline of the range of relevant micro-skills needed to make

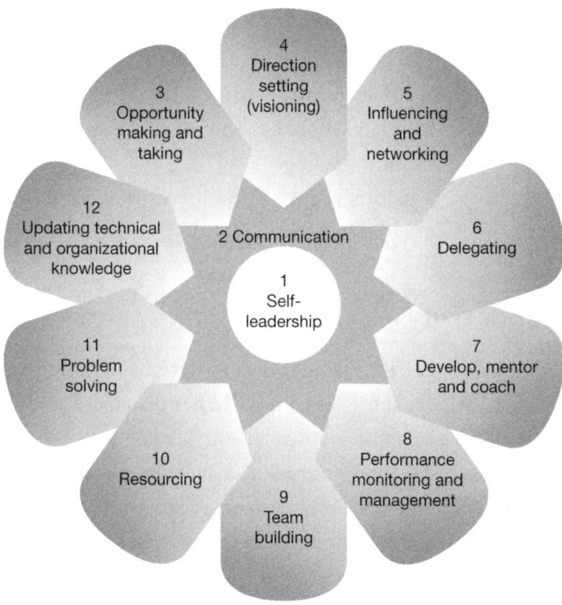

Figure 1.1 *Micro-skills of effective change agents (taken from Dunphy* et al. *2003: 276)*

the macro change strategies work effectively (Dunphy *et al.* 2003; Benn *et al.* 2004b). The core skills that support all other skills are self-leadership and communication. The other skills are those of handling interpersonal relations in a way that builds human capability plus more task-related project management skills. It is rare for a single change agent to have the full range of skills needed for a complex organizational change programme and this is particularly true for change towards sustainability. This suggests the need for a team approach to the implementation of democratic governance systems. Note that both in the internal operation of such teams and in their working out the implementation of change with other interest groups inside and outside the organization, the skills of conflict resolution are vital in resolving tensions without smoothing out the differences we have argued are essential for creativity.

Rethinking partnership models

Based on research conducted by Rondinelli and London (2003) we conclude that building the bridging social capital upon which the successful coordination of clusters, networks or coalitions depend requires the organizations involved to develop the following qualities:

- Assignment of participation in the cluster, network or coalition to managers who can serve as champions for the decision-making process. These managers must represent a cross-section of administrative and operational units within the organization.
- Measurement tools which can assess the organizational progress towards any requirements for change that are made through the decision-making process.
- Strong commitment by organizational executives that they will follow through on the outcomes of the decision-making.
- Leaders who see participation in the cluster, network or coalition as part of the long-term vision of the organization.

Encouraging reflexivity

Patently we need to move past the conventional structures of 'command and control' governance if we are to achieve these outcomes. Rather than fixed rules, reflexive regulation encourages self-reflection of industry through some process of self-regulation (Gunningham and Sinclair 2002). Government may be involved and sometimes other actors such as NGOs (Matten 2004). The reflexive capacity may derive, for instance, from the requirement to establish a safety management system, including reporting and monitoring.

Matten (2004) argues that strong governmental involvement is essential to ensure that reflexive regulation does not merely represent corporate attempts to gain in legitimacy without making environmental or social change. We argue that these procedures are best developed if deliberative democracy principles are employed to ensure that the diversity of the interest groups is recognized and built on in order to extend the reflexive capacity of the risk community and deliver creative outcomes (Dedeurwaerdere 2002). The reflexive capacities of adjustment and learning can then deliver the creative outcomes required for the democratic governance of risk. While we agree some government involvement is necessary, we are wary of the tendency for a coalition to form between the similar bureaucratic cultures of government, expert science and corporation. Such a coalition can exclude non-bureaucratic community groups.

A key aspect of governance based on the sharing of responsibility is the capacity of individual citizens and organizations to develop a broad, informed perspective on the issue for decision-making. Civic education is crucial to the development of new ways of managing risk that build trust and enable creative solutions to intractable social and environmental problems.

CONCLUSION

We end on a recommendation for a re-consideration of ideas for governance that might enable the democratic management of risk. The goal should be to create an inclusive system based on recognition of diversity; the tools for achieving this are decentralized networks, including community-based networks rather than selected individuals acting on behalf of communities. Resulting shifts in practice would entail a replacement of short-termism by long-termism and of organizational competition by interdependence and mutuality. Yet we have argued that this ideal cannot be achieved without creativity – knowledge creation and innovative practices fostered by a governance system which enables debate and challenges the established order.

REFERENCES

Adler, P. and Kwon, S. (2002) 'Social capital: prospects for a new concept', *Academy of Management Review*, 27(1): 17–40.

Backstrand, K. (2003) 'Civic science for sustainability: reframing the role of experts, policy-makers and citizens in environmental governance', *Global Environmental Politics*, 3(4): 24–41.

Banerjee, S.B. (2003) 'Who sustains whose development? Sustainable development and the reinvention of nature', *Organization Studies*, 24(1): 143–80.

Beck, U. (1992) *The Risk Society*, trans. M. Ritter, London: Sage.

Beck, U. (1995) *Ecological Politics in the Age of Risk*, Cambridge: Polity Press.

Beck, U. (1997) *The Reinvention of Politics*, Cambridge: Polity Press.

Beck, U. (1999) *World Risk Society*, Cambridge: Polity Press.

Beck, U. and Beck-Gernsheim, E. (2002) *Individualization*, London: Sage Publications.

Beck, U., Giddens, A. and Lash, S. (1994) *Reflexive Modernisation: Politics, Tradition and Aesthetics in the Modern Social Order*, Stanford: Stanford University Press.

Beder, S. (2001) *Global Spin*, 2nd edn, Newham: Scribe Publications.

Bellamy, R. (1999) 'Liberalism' in R. Eatwell and A. Wright (eds) *Contemporary Political Ideologies*, London: Pinter, pp. 23–50.

Benn, S., Dunphy, D. and Martin, A. 2004a. 'Networks for knowledge creation: interorganizational collaborations for sustainability', paper presented at 18th Australia and New Zealand Academy of Management Conference in Dunedin, December 2004.

Benn, S., Dunphy, D., Griffiths, A. and Ross-Smith, A. 2004b, 'Building the sustainable organisation: synergies, tensions and implications for change and leadership', paper presented at 18th Australia and New Zealand Academy of Management Conference in Dunedin, December 2004.

Bergkamp, L. (2002) 'Corporate governance and social responsibility: a new sustainability paradigm', *European Environmental Law Review*, May: 136–52.

Berry, A. (2000) 'Leadership in a new millennium: the challenge of the 'risk society', *Leadership and Organisation Development Journal*, 21(1/2): 5–13.

Bertels, S. and Vredenburg, H. (2004) 'Broadening the notion of governance from the organisation to the domain: a study of municipal water systems in Canada', *Journal of Corporate Citizenship*, 15: 33–47.

Blair, M. (2004) 'Ownership and control: rethinking corporate governance for the twenty-first century', in T. Clarke (ed.) *Theories of Corporate Governance*, London: Routledge, pp. 174–88.

Brujin de, T. (2003) 'The impact of policy style on policy choice across scales: the EU experience' in H. Bressers and W. Rosenbaum (eds) *Achieving Sustainable Development*, Westport: Praeger, pp. 281–306.

Bressers, H. and Rossenbaum, W. (2003) 'Social scales, sustainability and governance: an introduction' in H. Bressers and W. Rosenbaum (eds) *Achieving Sustainable Development*, Westport: Praeger, pp. 2–24.

Bubna-Litic, D. and Benn, S. (2003) 'The MBA at the crossroads: design issues for the future', *Journal of Australia and New Zealand Academy of Management*, 9(3): 25–36.

Business in the Community (2004) *Research Review*, Issue 1 March 2004. Online. Available at: http://www.bitc.org.uk/resources/research/ (accessed on 29 December 2004).

Carson, L. (2001) 'Innovative consultation processes and the changing role of activism', *Third Sector Review*, 7(1): 7–22.

Christoff, P. (1996) 'Ecological modernisation, ecological modernities', *Environmental Politics*, 5(3): 476–500.

Clarke, T. (2004) 'Introduction: theories of governance – reconceptualising corporate governance theory after the Enron experience' in T. Clarke (ed.) *Theories of Corporate Governance*, London: Routledge, pp. 1–31.

Coopey, J. and Burgoyne, J. (2000) 'Politics and organisational learning', *Journal of Management Studies*, 37(6): 869–85.

Crane, A. (2000) 'Corporate greening as amoralization', *Organization Studies*, 21(4): 673–97.

Dedeurwaerdere, T. (2002) 'Ethics and learning: from state regulation towards reflexive self-regulation of the information society', paper presented at the World Computer Congress in Montreal, August 2002.

Demirag, I. (2004) 'Introduction: towards better governance and accountability: exploring the relationships between public, private and the community', *Journal of Corporate Citizenship* (Theme Issue), 15: 19–25.

Dryzek, J. (1997) *Politics of the Earth: Environmental Discourses*, Oxford: Oxford University Press.

Dryzek, J. (2000). *Deliberative Democracy and Beyond*, Oxford: Oxford University Press.

Dunphy, D., Griffiths, A., and Benn, S. (2003) *Organizational Change for Corporate Sustainability*, London: Routledge.

Eckersley, R. (1992) *Environmentalism and Political Theory*, Albany: State University of New York Press.

Eckersley, R. (2004) *The Green State – Rethinking Democracy and Sovereignty*, Cambridge, MA: MIT Press.

Ehrenfeld, J. (2000) 'Industrial ecology', *American Behavioral Scientist*, 44(2): 229–45.

Elkington, J. (1998) *Cannibals with Forks*, Oxford: Capstone Press.

Farrell, C.M. and Morris, J. (2003) 'The "neo-bureaucratic" state', *Organization*, 10(1): 129–56.

Fisher, E. (2003) 'The rise of the risk commonwealth and the challenge of administrative law', *Public Law*, Autumn: 455–78.

Freeman, R. (1984) *Strategic Planning: A Stakeholder Approach*, London: Pitman Publishing.

Giddens, A. (1998) *The Third Way*, Cambridge: Polity Press.

Gladwin, T., Kennelly, J. and Krause, T. (1995) 'Shifting paradigms for sustainable development: implications for management theory and research', *Academy of Management Review*, 20(4): 874–908.

Goodin, R. (1992) *Green Political Theory*, Cambridge: Polity Press.

Grace, D. and Cohen, S. (1998) *Business Ethics*, 2nd edn, Melbourne: Oxford University Press.

Gunningham N. and Sinclair, D. (2002) *Leaders and Laggards: Next Generation Environmental Regulation*, London: Greenleaf Publications.

Grayson, D. and Hodges, A. (2004) *Corporate Social Opportunity: Seven Steps to Make Corporate Social Responsibility Work for Business*, London: Greenleaf Publications.

Habermas, J. (1984) *Theory of Communicative Action* (vol. 2), Boston: Beacon Press.

Hardy, C., Phillips, N. and Lawrence, T. (2003) 'Resources, knowledge and influence: the organizational effects of interorganizational collaboration', *Journal of Management Studies*, 40: 321–47.

Hawken, P., Lovins, A. and Lovins, H.L. (1999) *Natural Capitalism: Creating the Next Industrial Revolution*, New York: Little, Brown, and Company.

Holman, P. and Devane, T. (1999) *The Change Handbook: Group Methods for Shaping the Future*, San Fransisco: Berret-Kochler.

Howard-Grenville, J.A., Hoffman, A.J., Wirtenberg, J. (2003) 'The importance of cultural framing to the success of social initiatives in business', *Academy of Management Executive*, 17(2): 70–88.

Hughes, P. and Hosfeld, K. (2005) 'The leadership of sustainability: A study of characteristics and experiences of leaders bringing the "triple-bottom-line" to business', Centre for Ethical Leadership, Spring. Online. Available at: http://www.ethical leadership.org/Publications/Sustainability%20Report.pdf (accessed on 19 December 2005).

Jones, C., Hesterly, W. and Borgatti, S. (1997) 'A general theory of network governance: exchange conditions and social mechanisms', *Academy of Management Review*, 22: 911–45.

Kochan, T. (2003) 'Restoring trust in American corporations: addressing the root cause', *Journal of Management and Governance*, 7: 223–31.

Livesey, S. (2001) 'Eco-identity as discursive struggle: Royal Dutch/Shell, Brent Spar, and Nigeria', *Journal of Business Communication*, 38(1): 58–92.

Luginaah, I., Eyles, J. and Elliott, S. (2004) 'Informing the development of decision support tools for risk management: the case of electrical and magnetic fields', *Journal of Environmental Planning and Management*, 47(4): 601–21.

Lulofs, K., Bultmann, A., Eames, M., Schucht, S. and Watzols, F. (2003) 'Implementing environmental regulations across governance scales in the EU', in H. Bressers and W. Rosenbaum (eds) *Achieving Sustainable Development*, Westport: Praeger, pp. 307–26.

Luskin, R. and Fishkin, J. (2004) 'Deliberation and better citizens', Centre for Deliberative Democracy, Stanford University. Online. Available at: http://cdd.stanford.edu/research/index.html (accessed 1 October 2004).

March, J.G. and Olsen, J.P. (1984) 'The new institutionalism: organizational factors in political life', *American Political Science Review*, 78: 734–49.

Matten, D. (2004) 'The impact of the risk society thesis on environmental politics and management in a globalizing economy – principles, proficiency, perspectives', *Journal of Risk Research*, 7(4): 377–99.

Matten, D. and Crane, A. (2005) 'Corporate citizenship: towards an extended theoretical conceptualization', *Academy of Management Review*, 30(1): 166–80.

Melucci, A. and Avritzer, L. (2000) 'Complexity, cultural pluralism and democracy: collective action in the public space', *Social Science Information*, 39(4): 507–27.

Miller, D. (1993) 'Deliberative democracy and social choice' in D. Held (ed.) *Prospects for Democracy*, Cambridge: Polity Press, pp. 74–92.

Mol, A. and Sonnenfeld, D. (eds) (2000) *Ecological Modernisation Around the World: Perspectives and Critical Debates*, London: Frank Cass.

Newton, T. and Harte, G. (1997) 'Green business: technicist kitsch?', *Journal of Management Studies*, 34: 75–98.

Orts, E. and Strudler, A. (2002) 'The ethical and environmental limits of stakeholder theory', *Business Ethics Quarterly*, 12(2): 215–33.

Peters, B.G. (1999) *Institutional Theory in Political Science*, London: Pinter.

Petrick, J.A., Scherer, R.F., Brodzinski, J.D., Quinn, J.F. and Ainina, M. (1999) 'Global leadership skills and reputational capital: intangible resources for sustainable competitive advantage' *Academy of Management Executive*, 13(1): 58–69.

Pfeffer, J. (1982) *Organizations and Organization Theory*, Boston: Pitman Publishing.

Pierson, C. (1993) 'Democracy, markets and capital: are there necessary economic limits to democracy?' in D. Held (ed.) *Prospects for Democracy*, Cambridge: Polity Press, pp. 179–99.

Porter, M. (1980) *Competitive Strategy*, New York: The Free Press.

Potapchuk, W., Crocker, J. and Schechter, W. (1999) 'The transformative power of governance', *National Civic Review*, 88(3): 217–48.

Roberts, J. (2003) 'The manufacture of corporate social responsibility', *Organization*, 10(2): 249–66.

Rondinelli, D. and London, T. (2003) 'How corporations and environmental groups collaborate: assessing cross-sector alliances and collaborations', *Academy of Management Executive*, 17(1): 61–76.

Ross-Smith, A., Chesterman, C. and Peters, M. (2003) 'Getting there and staying there: identifying the characteristics of organisational cultures that keep women in academic leadership roles', *McGill Journal of Education* (Special Edition on Gender Issues in Commonwealth Higher Education), 38 (3): 421–36.

Schlosberg, D. (1999) *Environmental Justice and the New Pluralism*, Oxford: Oxford University Press.

Shrivastava, P. (1995) 'Ecocentric management in a risk society', *Academy of Management Review*, 20(1): 118–38.

Stanfield, J. and Carroll, M. (2004) 'Governance and the legitimacy of corporate power: a path for convergence of heterodox economics?', *Journal of Economic Issues*, 38(2): 363–71.

Starik, M. and Rands. G. (1995) 'Weaving an integrated web: multilevel and multisystem perspectives in ecological sustainability organisations', *Academy of Management Review*, 20(4): 908–35.

Starkey, K. and Crane, A. (2003) 'Toward green narrative: management and the evolutionary epic', *Academy of Management Review*, 28(2): 220–38.

Sternberg, E. (2000) 'How the strategic framework for UK company law reform undermines corporate governance', *Hume Papers on Public Policy*, 8: 54–73.

Stewart, J. and Jones, G. (2003) *Renegotiating the Environment*, Sydney: The Federation Press.

Stiglitz, J. (2004) 'Governance for a sustainable world', paper 01/04 presented at Centre for Corporate Responsibility and the Sustainability Forum in Zurich, January 2004.

Sundaramurthy, C. and Lewis, M. (2003) 'Control and collaboration: paradoxes of governance', *Academy of Management Review*, 28(3): 397–416.

Tsoukas, H. (1999) 'David and Goliath in the risk society: making sense of the conflict between Shell and Greenpeace in the North Sea', *Organization*, 6: 499–528.

Vaughan, D. (1999) 'The rôle of the organization in the production of techno-scientific knowledge', *Social Studies of Science*, 31: 913–43.

Waddock, S., Bodwell, C. and Graves, S. (2002) 'Responsibility: The new business imperative', *Academy of Management Executive*, 16(2): 132–49.

Warhurst, A. (2001) 'Corporate citizenship as corporate social investment', *Journal of Corporate Citizenship*, 1: 57–73.

Webb, E. (2004) 'An examination of socially responsible firms' board structure', *Journal of Management and Governance*, 8(3): 255–77. Online. Available at: http://www.kluweronline.com/issn/1385-3457/contents (accessed on 19 December 2005).

Wenman, M. (2003) 'What is politics? The approach of radical pluralism', *Politics*, 23(1): 57–65.

York, R., Rosa, E. and Dietz, T. (2003) 'Footprints on the earth: the environmental consequences of modernity', *American Sociological Review*, 68(2): 279–300.

Zadek, S. (2001) *The Civil Corporation*, London: Earthscan Publications.

Chapter 2

Understanding corporate sustainability

Recognizing the impact of corporate governance systems

Sally Russell, Nardia Haigh and Andrew Griffiths

INTRODUCTION

The concept of corporate sustainability is one that is gaining increasing importance as progressively more research suggests the need for organizations to address sustainability issues in order to resolve environmental and social problems they have helped create (Starik and Marcus 2000; Bebbington 2001; Dunphy *et al.* 2003). A perusal of bibliographic data over the last ten years reveals a dramatic increase in reference to corporate sustainability. Furthermore, a perusal of annual reports published by the Global Reporting Initiative (GRI 2002) provides evidence of the millions of dollars spent annually by companies around the world in the pursuit of corporate sustainability. However, there is growing evidence of complications in the pursuit of corporate sustainability, as people find it difficult to make sense of and operationalize the term (Munda *et al.* 1994; Bosshard 2000). This challenge of developing corporate sustainability as an operational concept is amplified by a dearth of empirical research that examines the meaning of the concept directly. Scholars agree that the extant research on corporate sustainability is fundamentally theoretical, extremely limited and that it is therefore an area promising for future research (Sharma 2002).

Several researchers have examined corporate sustainability theoretically (see for example: Gladwin, Kennelly and Krause 1995; Jennings and Zandbergen 1995; Starik and Rands 1995), yet to date there is little empirical research that examines how corporate sustainability is understood and enacted within organizations. While some research has examined managers' perceptions of corporate environmentalism (Banerjee 2001) and the moral position of managers in relation to the natural environment (Fineman 1997), none has examined the notion of corporate sustainability specifically. This chapter makes a unique contribution to these issues by exploring how corporate sustainability is understood.

We also make a second contribution by examining the understandings of managers in both private industry and public institutions. We suggest that individual understandings of corporate sustainability differ according to the dominant governance structures of the organization of which they are a member (Scott 2001). Furthermore, we suggest that as firms adopt more collaborative relationships with regulatory agencies and public organizations through public–private partnerships (Darnall 2002) such differences in understanding will likely have important implications for public–private partnerships and also for flexible regulatory arrangements between government and industry. In this context we now examine current literature and debate around the concept of corporate sustainability.

What is corporate sustainability?

Corporate sustainability largely stems from the broader concept of sustainability. This concept, as it is conceived of today, has a history beginning in the 1950s, when it was used to discuss the relationships between population growth, resource consumption, and environmental impacts (Kidd 1992). Sustainability is a concept that has been defined and described in many different ways (Bosshard 2000; Phillis and Andriantiatsaholiniaina 2001), and authors often address the difficulty people have in making sense of it (Bosshard 2000). For example, in a study assessing the meaning of sustainability, Bosshard (2000: 29) described it as '. . .one of the most challenging and, at the same time, most fuzzy contemporary paradigms'. Similarly, Kidd suggests that:

> The roots of the term 'sustainability' are so deeply embedded in fundamentally different concepts, each of which has valid claims to validity, that a search for a single definition seems futile. The existence of multiple meaning is tolerable if each analyst describes clearly what he [sic] means by sustainability.
>
> (Kidd 1992: 1)

In 1987, the World Commission on Environment and Development (WCED) related sustainability to corporations and the economy by coining and defining the term 'sustainable development': 'Sustainable development is development that meets the needs of the present without compromising the ability of future generations to meet their own needs' (WCED 1987: 43). The term has become widely accepted in management and industry as an approach to achieving sustainability (Munda *et al.* 1994), particularly since it was endorsed at the 1992 Earth Summit (Dunphy *et al.* 2003).

The concept of corporate sustainability is a term for which the meaning is debated by authors and used to mean many things. For example Diesendorf (2000) warns against using the term, and suggests it is most commonly interpreted to mean a long-lived corporation and not one that is necessarily contributing to ecological or social sustainability. Conversely, Dunphy *et al.* (2003: 3) use the term to mean corporate contribution to '. . . the continuing health of the planet, the survival of humans and other species, the development of a just and humane society, and the creation of work that brings dignity and self-fulfilment to those undertaking it'. These are just several examples of the wide variety of understandings stated and implied within the literature.

Such variation both speaks to the diversity of extant understanding (Bosshard 2000; Phillis and Andriantiatsaholiniaina 2001), and highlights its worthiness for further research. We propose that rather than adding to the plethora of existing definitions, a deeper appreciation of how people understand the concept is required. We follow Kidd's (1992) and van Marrewijk's (2003) suggestions and assume there to be differences in the way individuals understand corporate sustainability. Consequently, our overarching research question is 'How is corporate sustainability understood?'

Public and private sector organizations differ in their raison d'être, and are governed by different structures. Governance structures refer to '. . . all those arrangements by which field-level power and authority are exercised involving, variously, formal and informal system, public and private auspices, regulative and normative mechanisms' (Scott *et al.* 2000 as quoted by Scott 2001: 140). They include a wide variety of mechanisms and relationships, the arrangement of which differs between sectors (Scott 2001; van Marrewijk 2003). For example, the state, business, and society each have specific mechanisms that coordinate their behaviour and fulfil their roles (van Marrewijk 2003).

More specifically, governments are described as regulators, and are responsible for developing and maintaining legislation (Scott 2001). Government roles have been said to include social betterment (Murray 1995), securing and maintaining stability and order (Holmer 1968), and a debatable amount of economic intervention (Levitan and Johnson 1983; Ogata 1990; Marshall 1992; Shin 2001). Conversely, businesses are regulated by government and seek legitimacy by complying with regulation (Powell and DiMaggio 1991) in order create economic wealth in the market (van Marrewijk 2003). The primary role of private organizations is, however, debated. This debate is largely polarized around whether the purpose of business is to maximize profit and returns to shareholders (Friedman 1970), or whether it extends to other roles relating to social responsibilities (Margolis and Walsh 2003).

Governments have become increasingly interested in corporatization and modernization. This has led some public organizations (known variously as public corporations, government-owned corporations (GOCs), government companies, government-owned companies) to act more like regular businesses (Meklin and Ahonen 1998). These organizations exist pursuant to a variety of regulatory arrangements, ranging from those identical to private business, to those operating under their own hybrid public–private legislative arrangement, and to those remaining under the legislation under which the parent government organization exists (Fisher 1982; Kole and Mulherin 1997; Meklin and Ahonen 1998). Government-owned corporations, as we term them, have been said to be less profitable than private firms (Fisher 1982) as a result of a reduced focus on profitability by State owners. In contrast, some have also been shown to perform similarly to other organizations in the same industry (Kole and Mulherin 1997).

Empirical research suggests that the relationships between public and private organizations are growing in importance as regulation becomes more flexible (Fineman 2000; Darnall 2002). For example, Fineman's (1998) and Fineman and Sturdy's (1999) studies of the Environment Agency of England and Wales found that the organization–regulatory relationship plays a large part in ensuring compliance and ongoing environmental sustainability. Fineman describes regulatory inspectors as 'street-level bureaucrats' (1998), and suggests that their perceptions play a significant role in the relationship between the regulatory agency and regulated organizations.

Fineman (1998) also demonstrates that regulation is often ambiguous and essentially socially constructed. He suggests that it is through the relationship between the regulator and the regulated organization that the meaning of regulation is decided. Statements from Scott, such as 'All laws are subject to variable interpretation . . .' (2001: 170) and '. . . laws and regulations are socially interpreted and find their force and meaning in interactions between regulators and the regulated . . .' (Scott 2001: 169) support Fineman's (1998) argument. This also provides support for our theses that public and private organizations have differing interpretations of corporate sustainability.

Further evidence of our thesis is evident in the work of Banerjee (2001) and Fineman (1997), who examined the perspectives of private industry managers in terms of environmental issues. Banerjee's (2001) findings suggest individual perceptions of corporate environmentalism are largely based on the organization's institutional framework for interpreting environmental issues. Similarly, in his study of managers in the UK automotive industry Fineman (1997: 31) found that interviewees often interpreted environmental issues based on the 'institutionalized and bureaucratized' interpretations of their organizations. From these studies it appears that there are likely differences in individual understanding of environmental issues, based on the organization to which the individual belongs.

The previous review has demonstrated the complexity surrounding the public–private flexible regulatory and commercial arrangements, and suggests that differences in governance structures between public and private sector organizations yield differences in their members' understandings of corporate sustainability, thus leading to our second research question: 'What are the differences in understanding corporate sustainability between members of public and private organizations?'

RESEARCH DESIGN AND METHODOLOGY

Our research questions aimed to grasp how people understand and enact corporate sustainability in different contexts. We therefore considered a qualitative approach the most appropriate methodology as it seeks to analyse phenomena, such as people and situations, in their temporal and local context (Flick 2002). Within our qualitative framework we employ a phenomenographic methodology. The use of this methodology is based on the assumption that person and world are inextricably related through the person's lived experience of their world (Marshall and Rossman 1999).

In order to explore the variation in understanding of corporate sustainability we initially selected participants from the theoretical categories of public, private and government-owned corporations. Participants were recruited from organizations we identified as meeting essentially one of three criteria. We first recruited participants from public organizations and agencies that had a stated sustainability focus in their operations. In recruiting private sector participants we targeted organizations that had an interest and some strategic focus on corporate sustainability. We selected organizations from the Australian *National Pollutant* Inventory, which provided the names of companies that emit pollutants.

We sought to recruit a wide range of participants with the aim to achieve the greatest variation in understanding, a core element of the phenomenographic approach (Marton 1981). We continued to recruit participants until we were certain we had reached theoretical saturation (Eisenhardt 1989), or the point at which adding new data was unlikely to produce new insights (Eisenhardt 1989; Lee 1999). This sampling method led to a total sample of 38 individuals. A summary of the demographic attributes of these participants is detailed in Table 2.1.

Data collection and analysis

Participants took part in a single, one-on-one interview with one of the three researchers conducting the study, over a period of seven months. We asked participants four open-ended questions: 'What do you do to bring about corporate sustainability?'; 'What are the most important aspects of corporate sustainability?'; 'What is corporate sustainability to you?'; and 'How do you think government sees sustainability?' or 'How do you think business sees sustainability?' Follow-up questions were used to encourage participants to elaborate on their comments and to garner the personal understanding of corporate sustainability (Kvale 1989). Such questions included: 'What do you mean by that?'; 'Can you explain that further?'; and 'Can you give an example?' Each researcher independently coded the transcripts and searched for *what* the participants considered corporate sustainability to be and *how* they enacted this understanding in practice.

RESULTS

Our analysis produced four categories of how corporate sustainability is understood. Specifically, we found corporate sustainability to be understood as: (1) a corporation working towards long-term economic performance; (2) a corporation working towards positive outcomes for the natural environment; (3) a corporation that supports people and social outcomes; or (4) a corporation with a holistic approach. A summary of the results is provided in Table 2.2, which includes key themes and illustrative quotes for each category of understanding.

Table 2.1 Summary of participant demographics

		Organization type (%)			Gender (%)		Age (%)			Highest level of education (%)			Tenure (%)			Level of manager (%)		
Category	*Total (%)*	*Public*	*Private*	*GOC*	*Male*	*Female*	*<40*	*40–49*	*50+*	*Secondary*	*Tertiary*	*Post-grad*	*<5 years*	*5–9 years*	*>10 Years*	*Senior*	*Middle*	*Lower*
Economic	16	0	100	0	83	17	33	33	33	50	33	17	33	33	33	17	17	67
Natural environment	42	44	44	13	75	25	50	38	12	0	31	69	44	25	31	25	56	19
Social	29	36	55	9	73	27	55	27	18	0	64	36	18	55	27	18	55	27
Holistic	13	60	0	40	80	20	20	40	40	0	20	80	40	20	40	40	60	0
Total	100	37	50	13	76	24	45	34	21	8	39	53	34	34	32	24	50	26

Table 2.2 *Categories and themes*

Understanding 1: a corporation working towards long-term economic performance

Themes
- Priority is long-term profitability and growth of the organization
- Compliance with legislation; and
- Government's role is as a tax collector

Understanding 2: a corporation working towards positive outcomes for the natural environment

Themes
- Priority is conservation of the natural environment and eco-efficiency
- Social aspects are recognized but subordinate to the natural environment; and
- Strong personal commitment

Understanding 3: a corporation that supports people and social outcomes

Themes
- Priority is understanding and valuing people
- Taking care of people leads to positive ecological outcomes; and
- Strong personal commitment

Understanding 4: a corporation with a holistic approach

Themes
- Priority is understanding the interconnectedness of the system and the organization's role in the system
- Understanding the context in which the organization exists and decisions are made; and
- Intervening in systems can improve them

Understanding 1: a corporation working towards long-term economic performance

Those who demonstrated this category of understanding suggested that the dominant purpose of the organization was to work towards long-term economic performance. This was framed in terms of the longevity of corporate profitability and growth. Participants communicated the need for their organizations to comply with existing legislation, and saw the role of government as a tax collector. Of the six participants who expressed this category of understanding all were members of private organizations. The majority noted their highest level of education as a high school certificate, and were predominantly at the lower level of management participants in our study (see Table 2.1).

Within this category there was a strong focus on sustainability as meaning the viability of the organization to remain in business for the long term, or 'keeping the business alive' (IV25). For example, one participant responded, 'What is corporate sustainability? Well it's the ability for a company to . . . to stay in business for a long run' (IV16). Another participant responded similarly and suggested, 'In terms of what I think corporate sustainability is for [this organization] it's strategies and policies that will get us being [this organization] in twenty years' time and not a defunct business . . .' (IV38).

Within this category there was a strong theme of the need for the organization to be compliant with existing legislation. There was no particular focus on one type of legislation, but rather a wide range of compliance issues was raised. For example participants mentioned the need for compliance with environmental legislation, occupational health and safety legislation, hygiene standards, and the need to meet minimum standards from local government to international bodies. For example, 'More regulation to ensure the environment stays as best as it can basically' (IV18) and 'For [this organization] and for the waste business those things are being a waste manager, being compliant, being environmentally friendly, for the want of a better word. We call it compliance here . . .' (IV38). Further,

> And at the end of the day leave the project area, albeit with some impact, but with the minimal amount of impact as possible and comply to all the standards that are set down, whether they be by the local authorities, government, World Bank, whatever . . .
>
> (IV16)

Another theme that emerged from within this category concerned the role of government. When asked 'How do you think government sees sustainability?' participants predominantly focused on the role of government as a tax collector. For example, 'Treasury just wants the money to roll in . . .' (IV16) and '. . . they see the tax coming in I suppose . . .' (IV27). Other roles of government were offered; however, tax collection was dominant throughout this category of understanding. One participant suggested it was the role of government to address social issues using tax revenue,

> . . . that's the main point in why government is there is to collect taxes at the end of the day. And hopefully get better roads, hospitals, and schools and et cetera like that so, bit of luck that'll happen, in most cases.
>
> (IV27)

Understanding 2: a corporation working towards positive outcomes for the natural environment

Participants expressing this category of understanding were primarily concerned with organizational achievement of positive ecological outcomes and generally focused on conservation or ecoefficiency behaviours. In describing their understanding, participants also identified social aspects of corporate sustainability, but considered these subordinate to natural environment issues. They also identified a strong personal commitment to the achievement of natural resource conservation. Participants in this category were predominantly at middle levels of management, but were quite evenly distributed in terms of tenure and organizational type (see Table 2.1). While male participants were quite evenly distributed across the four categories, most female participants in our study attributed their understanding of corporate sustainability to this category.

Within this category there was a strong focus on the ultimate goal being conservation of the natural environment, through 'maintaining natural biodiversity' (IV1). For example, IV1 suggested that '. . . it's about . . . protecting areas of bushland', and IV8 mentioned, '. . . well obviously the koala conservation area you should have this zoned no cats and dogs, they're the biggest threat [to native wildlife] . . . second to trees being taken away'. Another example was provided by IV29 when describing the organization's ownership of land:

> . . . some of those leases might be 10 years, might be five years, so we need to make sure that we're going to get that land back at the end of the day. So we have, sort of, ultimate control, I suppose over all the lands out here . . . that's significant because on two fronts we border [a marine park]. Um, and that's fairly significant obviously because it has high ecological and conservation value . . .
>
> (IV29)

The emphasis on conserving natural resources was balanced by descriptions of eco-efficient behaviours. Participants described eco-efficiency as about producing goods and services, or conducting business as usual, while reducing the consumption of natural resources. IV9 suggested that '. . . from a personal point of view to me . . . it's about saving resources'. Similarly, an example was given of eco-efficient design,

> The building we're sitting in at the moment . . . when we decided to design it, we sort of looked at lighting principles . . . the facility uses natural air conditioning, natural cooling systems. It's orientated to take advantage of the light. It's a great model for us to bring proponents down here and say, if you're going to build something [here], this is the sort of thing we're talking about. Water-sensitive urban design in the car park, take that back to yours. So sustainability for us, is, has really been about the, the building of a sustainable asset . . .
>
> (IV29)

Eco-efficiency was also described as a way to conserve resources and simultaneously create value and save money for the organization. For example, it was suggested that 'being more sustainable [the organization] can in fact save money or become more profitable. And that's the reality, it's not . . . something that they have to do to be good corporate citizens. They can actually benefit from it' (IV11). This was also demonstrated by IV23 when describing their role, 'they look at me really as being a person I guess who can save them money by doing things a different way. And I do that through environmental practices'.

A further theme emerging from the data in this category of understanding was the link between ecological and social outcomes. Several participants expressed an awareness of social issues, however, in all cases these were acknowledged as subordinate to their environmental understanding. For example, one participant spoke of trying to increase the environmental awareness of others, '. . . a lot of it is just really . . . when I'm talking to people I'm letting them know of the impact they have on the environment' (IV12). Alternatively, one participant suggested that using eco-efficiency would lead to happier employees, 'Here's an energy-efficient building that doesn't cost much to run and the people inside it are happy' (IV31). Another participant described corporate sustainability as:

> More about eco-efficiency; but also, you know providing a good safe work environment, sponsoring the local soccer team; so having a role in a community commensurate with the size of the business and capability of the business, so still those social kind of aspects.
>
> (IV13)

There was also evidence within this category of a strong sense of personal commitment towards the natural environment. Participants often demonstrated this by recounting measures they had taken in working towards their goal of creating positive ecological outcomes. An example of this was:

> One of the things I wanted to do was to start getting myself sustainable before I really started preaching sustainability to anybody else because I don't believe unless you walk the talk you have any right to talk, or really jump up and down and tell people that they're unsustainable.
>
> (IV2)

Similarly,

> What I try and do is act on behalf of 6 billion people, so if I've . . . if I've got a bottle or something like that in my hand it could be recycled but there's no recycling bin around I think I could just throw it in the bin, what I do is ask myself what if 6 billion people threw this into the bin. I'll treat it like that. I'll multiply my actions by six billion I guess is a summary of how to say it. So that makes me, that motivates me and inspires me to make a difference.
>
> (IV6)

Understanding 3: a corporation that supports people and social outcomes

Participants who demonstrated this understanding strongly emphasized the need to understand and value people, both within and external to the organization. There was also acknowledgement of issues concerning the natural environment in this category;

however, these were considered subordinate to social issues. A third theme, similar to that which emerged from the natural environment category, was the identification of a strong personal commitment to the achievement of sustainability. Of the eleven participants within this category of understanding, most were at middle levels of management and had been working in their organization for more than five years. Participants were quite evenly distributed in terms of the other demographic variables of gender, age, education and industry type (see Table 2.2).

Participants with this understanding emphasized the importance of people. This was demonstrated in statements such as '. . . we've got a really good understanding of our people', (IV28) and 'Our people are very very important . . . we try and look after the people we've got. I think our people are very very important to us. That's the way I see it' (IV34). Other participants also recognized the importance of people outside the organization. For example:

> . . . my vision of corporate sustainability is where there is active involvement of people who work there, the support for what the organisation is trying to achieve, the support not only among the people who work in the organisation but people who are affected by that organisation.
>
> (IV4)

There was also a focus on the need to connect people in order to progress sustainability. Participants spoke of 'bringing people together' (IV12) and finding opportunities to network with other people who are interested in sustainability. For example,

> . . . and right now I'm looking at . . . more on the social side of . . . sustainability . . . and that's taking the form of a newsletter . . . it's more about . . . connecting people at a non-work level . . . not so much the daily grind material, more what's the interests, you know, getting to know who we're working with more . . . this is the angle on sustainability that I wanna get into more.
>
> (IV6)

While the social aspects of sustainability were given priority in this category, the natural environment was also acknowledged. In contrast to the natural environment understanding where the end goal was seen as natural resource conservation, the goal here was focused on taking care of the welfare of human society which would then lead to improved outcomes for the natural environment. For example,

> That, you know, social equity, this thing about poverty that I was talking about a minute ago, is part and parcel of it. That we can't . . . be sustainable . . . in an ecological sense if in the process we are raping and pillaging different parts of the human society of the planet.
>
> (IV7)

Additional evidence of a link between social outcomes and improved natural environmental outcomes is demonstrated by statements such as 'I think it starts with people . . . the next step is probably people's involvement with the environment . . . it's a very close end tie' (IV4) and '. . . how much we impact on the environment . . . is a product of how much . . . how we feel as a group, you know within this division' (IV6).

The final theme that emerged from this category of understanding was similar to the natural environment category, in that participants with this understanding demonstrated a feeling of personal commitment towards sustainability. For example,

> . . . it's becoming more and more important for the community to, you being seen as environmentally minded. And I find I get very proud when I put a system in place and the company is seen as, we follow those, that system and we don't impact. What we do every day doesn't impact on the people around us.
>
> (IV22)

This was further demonstrated by IV6, who described how they had organized and attended an informal sustainability group with other like-minded people in order to progress their own conception of sustainability. Similarly, IV4 described their involvement in workshops to educate and encourage businesses to take on more sustainable practices. Another example included a description of the role of a participant being '. . . an advocate for sustainable development . . . most of my contribution has been through public leadership on issues to do with . . . sustainable development' (IV7).

Understanding 4: a corporation with a holistic approach

Participants exhibiting this understanding emphasized a systems thinking approach to corporate sustainability. This was expressed through a description of the organization as part of system and the need to appreciate the context in which the organization operates and in which decisions are made. Another theme which emerged from this understanding was recognition that interventions could improve the overall system. Of the five participants who expressed this understanding, all were members of public organizations or GOCs; with no members of private organizations expressing this understanding. Furthermore, those within this category tended also to be highly educated, with most having a post-graduate qualification. Participants in this category were also predominantly in high organizational positions; no operational level management participants expressed this category of understanding (see Table 2.1).

There was strong evidence of systems and holistic thinking in this category of understanding. For example, when asked to describe the most important aspects of corporate sustainability IV5 responded,

> I'll be really reluctant to do that . . . because it's a bit like sort of looking at an animal's body and saying that its skin is more important than its intestines, you know, and

> basically you need the whole lot working well in order to have a healthy system. So, I think if you were looking at important areas, you know, would be the degree to which you can understand how the system works, and how it can be sort of a fully functional system and be sustaining . . .
>
> (IV5)

The idea of systems and holistic thinking was reiterated in all interviews in this category of understanding. Participants often described 'a way of thinking' (IV37), 'applying systems thinking' (IV30) or 'taking a holistic approach' (IV30). This was reiterated similarly by IV30, who suggested, 'I guess true to sustainability, they're all intermeshed, as they're, in terms of what's most important . . .' (IV30). This idea of interconnections and systems thinking was also demonstrated by IV37, who succinctly stated his understanding as 'For me corporate sustainability is . . . achieving positive outcomes out of . . . balancing workplace, marketplace, environment and community' (IV37). Similarly, IV3 articulated corporate sustainability as:

> . . . when everything comes together and it fits . . . when you've got an organizational fit in terms of the organization's fit within its marketplace context; when you've got an organizational fit in relationship to its stakeholders and its sphere of influence; when you've got an organizational fit in terms of, you know, um connectivity within the context, within which its operating . . . fit in terms of business fit in terms of values, direction and its that sort of compass and gyroscopes stuff that's sort of like, making sure that you're headed in the direction that the rest of society is . . .
>
> (IV3)

A further theme that emerged from within this understanding was the need to understand the context in which the organization operates and decisions are taken. This was articulated in statements like '. . . I think you've got to really be able to, put your, your views in context . . .' (IV37) and the example:

> Well you can be working flat out on a recovery plan for a particular species, for instance, say someone's identified that . . . the hairy nosed wombat is in decline as a species so we've got to get in there and do a recovery plan. The reality is that if another agency has actually approved land clearing for that whole region and that, you know . . . you've got a . . . breeding programme it just doesn't translate into effective work because you've actually already lost if you're actually engaging in that issue that far down the track. Whereas you've actually got to be cognizant of the full context and actually work out where the strategic interventions would be.
>
> (IV3)

The latter quote also indicates another theme which emerged from this category, which was the belief that system interventions could be put in place to correct or optimize an organizational system if necessary. This was also demonstrated by IV5, who stated:

> . . . we were reading . . . about how and when . . . to intervene in systems that aren't working well . . . instead of basically saying uh, we gotta start again . . . if you can see how a system's working then you can look at . . . the interventions which . . . have clear intent . . . and are timed in a way that they will work with the dynamics of the organisation rather than contrary to them . . .
>
> (IV5)

Relationships between categories

Our analysis also revealed that there was a notable relationship between the four categories of understanding. A graphical representation of this is provided in Figure 2.1. As illustrated, Understanding 1, which prioritizes economic performance, was distinctly different from the other understandings. Those who demonstrated this understanding prioritized economic outcomes over any other considerations, and there were few similarities between participants with this understanding and participants in the other categories. We represent this as a category sitting primarily at the lower end of the vertical axis.

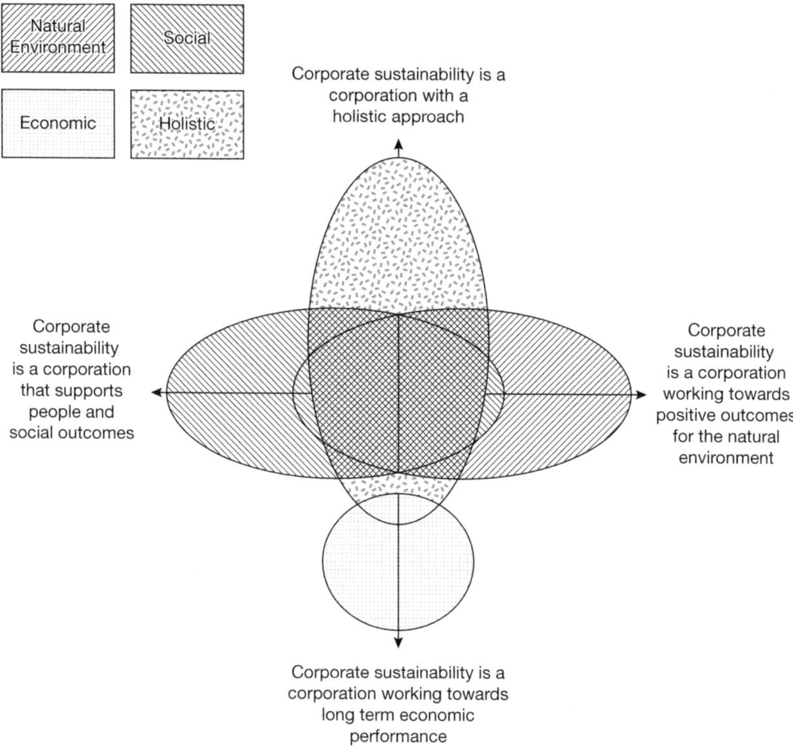

Figure 2.1 Representative relationships between understandings

In contrast, we found a number of similarities between the natural environment and socially focused understandings. Participants in both these categories of understanding acknowledged the importance of economic outcomes, thus acknowledging Understanding 1. Participants with these understandings framed economic issues in terms of their priority for either the natural environment, or social issues. We illustrate this by overlapping these two categories with the economic understanding. Additionally, individuals who demonstrated either of these two categories of understanding also acknowledged the presence of different understandings, as illustrated by the overlapping categories on the horizontal axis. For instance, those with a natural environment understanding acknowledged social issues, and those with a socially focused understanding also acknowledged the natural environment.

Participants who demonstrated a holistic understanding acknowledged a range of issues around the concept of corporate sustainability. As described above, their discussions centred around a need to balance economic, social and natural environment issues, and suggested a need to understand the system and the interconnections between each element in the system. Thus, these participants also acknowledged the existence of all three alternative understandings. We have represented this understanding in Figure 2.1 as being primarily at the holistic end of the vertical axis, but also crossing each of the other categories of understanding.

DISCUSSION AND CONCLUSION

In discussing our results we focus on addressing our two research questions. We first discuss our findings in relation to the question 'How is corporate sustainability understood?', namely evidence of four distinct categories of how corporate sustainability is understood. Until now this finding has been implied in the literature, though not empirically supported. The distribution of participants across the different understandings is illustrated in Figure 2.2. Our second discussion point relates to our research question 'What are the differences in understanding corporate sustainability between members of public and private organizations?' In answering this question we suggest that the dominant governance system of an organization appears to influence participants' understanding of corporate sustainability.

Distinct understandings of corporate sustainability

Our results provide empirical evidence that there are multiple ways in which corporate sustainability is understood. The existence of Understanding 1, which prioritizes economic outcomes supports Diesendorf's (2000) thesis that corporate sustainability means a long-lived corporation. Descriptions of orthodox management theory also reflect this understanding which is largely focused on economic sustainability (Gladwin *et al.* 1995; Banerjee 2001; Dyllick and Hockerts 2002). While scholars

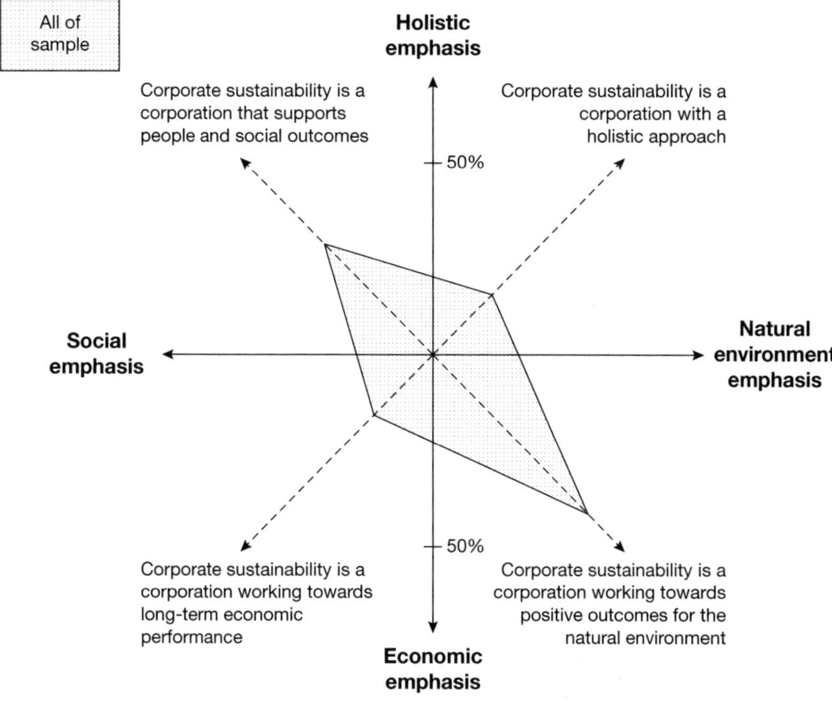

Figure 2.2 *Distribution of understandings of all participants*

acknowledge the presence of this understanding, many suggest the continued progression of corporate sustainability requires a movement away from such economic prioritization (Gladwin *et al.* 1995; Shrivastava 1995; Stead and Stead 2004).

Understandings 2 and 3, which prioritize the natural environment and social aspects respectively, are well supported in the literature. For example, Blum-Kusterer and Hussain (2001) align corporate sustainability with environmental outcomes. Similarly, van Marrewijk's (2003) description of more humane and ethical business reflects our finding of a socially focused understanding. Ongoing research in the ONE interest group and the Social Issues in Management division of the Academy of Management provides further support for these two categories of understanding (Sharma and Ruud 2003). The connection between these two categories and the sharing of similar themes (see Table 2.2), is also reflected in the work of Dunphy *et al.* (2003) and van Marrewijk (2003), citing the natural environment and social issues as important elements of corporate sustainability.

Understanding 4, which demonstrated a holistic approach to corporate sustainability, was also supported in the literature. For example, Gladwin *et al.* (1995) describe a 'sustaincentric' management paradigm as a way to embrace 'the full conceptualization of political, civil, social, economic, and cultural human rights'. Similarly, Starik and

Rands (1995) propose a systems view of the organization, which reflects our findings in this category. Our study contributes to this literature and provides support for the theoretical discussion of a holistic approach.

While literature has previously alluded to differences in understanding of corporate sustainability, our findings provide empirical evidence of four different understandings. These results have several implications for researchers and managers. The existence of multiple understandings signals the need to cancel subscriptions to homogeneous notions or delimited definitions of what corporate sustainability means (Kidd 1992; van Marrewijk 2003). Rather it implies the need to appreciate the variation between individuals, organizations and industries. Second, appreciating that variation exists comes with a prompt to ensure differences in understanding are clarified and managed; particularly where policy may be interpreted differently (Scott 2001). This will likely facilitate managers and public officials to work together more effectively towards commonly understood goals (Bosshard 2000).

Understandings in public and private organizations

In answering our second research question, 'What are the differences in understanding corporate sustainability between members of public and private organizations?', we found there to be noteworthy differences between the understandings that exist within the types of organizations that participated in our study. In order to illustrate these differences we plotted the percentage of individuals in each organizational type based on their category of understanding in Figure 2.3. For example, of the individuals within public organizations 50 per cent demonstrated the natural environment understanding, 29 per cent the socially focused understanding, 21 per cent the holistic understanding; with none demonstrating an economic understanding.

Figure 2.3 also illustrates that GOCs in our sample reflected a pattern of understanding comparable to public organizations. This suggests that GOCs may be influenced by the same or similar governance structures as public organizations (Scott 2001). Following this, Scott's (2001) and Oliver's (1997) arguments regarding institutional influence of strategic action, and the isomorphism found by Dacin (1997), suggests these organizational types may act similarly in respect of sustainability issues, and possibly achieve similar outcomes. This is a direction worthy of further research.

Our findings of differences in collective understandings across organizational types supports inferences and statements present in the literature. For example, Scott (2001) and van Marrewijk (2003) make explicit such differences in governance structures and roles of these organizational types. It does ensue that institutions governing a sector will affect how things are understood by its members. We already know, for example, that interpretation is embedded in the institutional environment (Berger and Luckmann 1967), and that institutional forces have an isomorphic influence on tastes and preferences (Dacin 1997). This suggests that members of similar organization types or industries might tend to exhibit similarities in their tastes and preferences, or perhaps

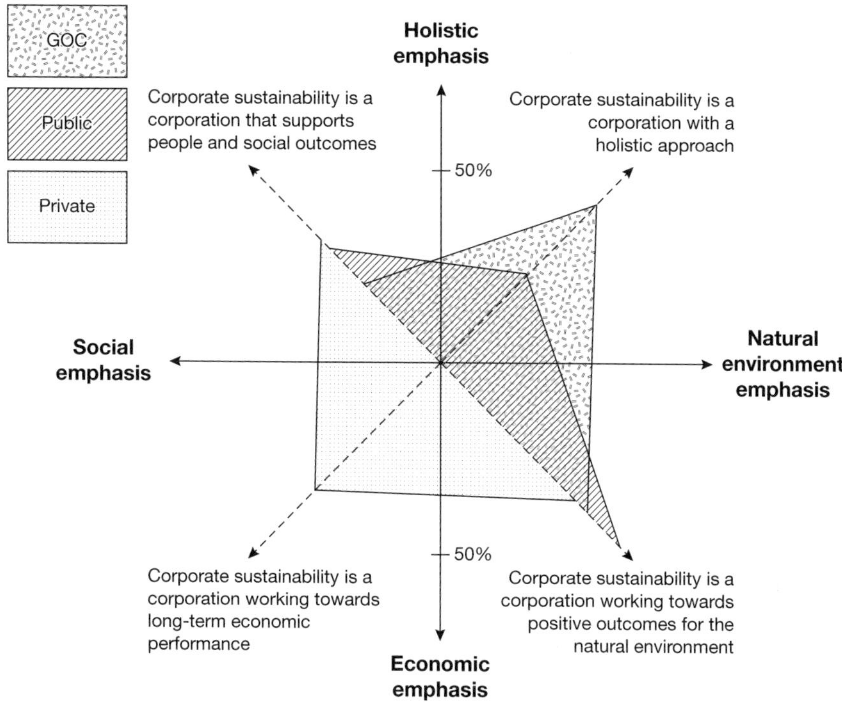

Figure 2.3 *Comparison of understandings by organization type*

understandings, and these influences also shape the strategies that firms can put in place (Oliver 1997; Scott 2001). We make a contribution to this literature by demonstrating this difference with empirical data.

These findings have a number of important implications in the pursuit of corporate sustainability. For instance, Figure 2.3 demonstrates a polarization of public and private understandings, with private organizations tending towards economic priorities and public organizations taking a more holistic perspective. This suggests that regulation is written by individuals with an understanding which is likely to be different from those to which it is applied. This presents problems for relationships between public and private organizations, as well as for the interpretation and enforcement of regulation (Fineman 2000). We suggest that further research could investigate this issue and examine the effects of different understandings on public–private partnerships, self-regulation and compliance issues.

We also suggest that an additional area worthy of future research would be an examination of whether and how individuals and organizations progress through the different categories of understanding. We note that many researchers have prescribed a need to move towards a more holistic understanding of corporate sustainability (Gladwin *et al.* 1995; Shrivastava 1995; Stead and Stead 2004). However, there is a lack of empirical research that examines how this is to occur. We suggest that the development of a tool to quantitatively measure current organizational understanding may facilitate organizations in this process.

We make a unique contribution to literature on corporate sustainability by providing empirical evidence of how corporate sustainability is understood in a variety of industries, and across the private–public organization divide. We found four distinct categories of understanding, namely that corporate sustainability is: (1) a corporation working towards long-term economic performance; (2) a corporation working towards positive outcomes for the natural environment; (3) a corporation that supports people and social outcomes; or (4) a corporation with a holistic approach. We also found different understandings of corporate sustainability across the public–private organization divide, which appear related to differences in the arrangement of governance structures for these organization types. Our results have implications for both management research and practice, perhaps the most important of which is the need for awareness and discussion of how individuals understand corporate sustainability.

REFERENCES

Banerjee, S.B. (2001) 'Managerial perceptions of corporate environmentalism: interpretations from industry and strategic implications for organizations', *Journal of Management Studies*, 38(4): 489–513.

Bebbington, J. (2001) 'Sustainable development: a review of the international development, business and accounting literature', *Accounting Forum*, 25(2): 128–57.

Berger, P.L. and Luckmann, T. (1967) *The Social Construction of Reality: A Treatise in the Sociology of Knowledge*, London: Penguin.

Blum-Kusterer, M. and Hussain, S.S. (2001) 'Innovation and corporate sustainability: an investigation into the process of change in the pharmaceuticals industry', *Business Strategy and the Environment*, 10(5): 300–16.

Bosshard, A. (2000) 'A methodology and terminology of sustainability assessment and its perspectives for rural planning', *Agriculture, Ecosystems and Environment*, 77(1–2): 29–41.

Dacin, M.T. (1997) 'Isomorphism in context: the power and prescription of institutional norms', *Academy of Management Journal*, 40(1): 46–82.

Darnall, N. (2002) 'Motivations for participating in a US voluntary environmental initiative: the multi-state working group and EPA's', in S. Sharma and M. Starik (eds) *Research in Corporate Sustainability: The Evolving Theory and Practice of Organizations in the Natural Environment*, Cheltenham: Edward Elgar, 123–54.

Diesendorf, M. (2000) 'Sustainability and sustainable development', in D.C. Dunphy, J. Benveniste, A. Griffiths and P. Sutton (eds) *Sustainability: The Corporate Challenge of the 21st Century*, St Leonards: Allen & Unwin, 19–37.

Dunphy, D.C., Griffiths, A. and Benn, S. (2003) *Organizational Change for Corporate Sustainability: A Guide for Leaders and Change Agents of the Future*, Understanding Organizational Change, London: Routledge.

Dyllick, T. and Hockerts, K. (2002) 'Beyond the business case for corporate sustainability', *Business Strategy and the Environment*, 11(2): 130.

Eisenhardt, K.M. (1989) 'Building theories from case study research', *Academy of Management Review*, 14(4): 532–50.
Fineman, S. (1997) 'Constructing the green manager', *British Journal of Management*, 8(1): 31.
Fineman, S. (1998) 'Street-level bureaucrats and the social construction of environmental control', *Organization Studies*, 19(6): 953–74.
Fineman, S. (2000) 'Being a regulator', in S. Fineman (ed.) *The Business of Greening*, London: Routledge, 97–133.
Fineman, S. and Sturdy, A. (1999) 'The emotions of control: a qualitative exploration of environmental regulation', *Human Relations*, 52(5): 631.
Fisher, P.S. (1982) 'Alternative institutional structures for state and local government ownership of railroads', *Logistics and Transportation Review*, 18(3): 235–54.
Flick, U. (2002) *An Introduction to Qualitative Research*, 2nd edn, London: Sage.
Friedman, M. (1970) 'The social responsibility of business is to increase its profits', *New York Times Magazine*, 13 September, 32–3.
Gladwin, T.N., Kennelly, J.J. and Krause, T.-S. (1995) 'Shifting paradigms for sustainable development: implications for management theory and research', *Academy of Management Review*, 20(4): 874–907.
GRI (2002) *Sustainability Reporting Guidelines*, Global Reporting Initiative.
Holmer, F. (1968) 'Management research in state and local governments', *Operations Research*, 16(6): 1093–99.
Jennings, P.D. and Zandbergen, P.A. (1995) 'Ecologically sustainable organizations: an institutional approach', *Academy of Management Review*, 20(4): 1015.
Kidd, C. (1992) 'The evolution of sustainability', *Journal of Agricultural and Environmental Ethics*, 5: 1–26.
Kole, S.R. and Mulherin, J.H. (1997) 'The government as a shareholder: a case from the United States', *Journal of Law and Economics*, 40(1): 1–23.
Kvale, S. (1989) 'To validate is to question', in S. Kvale (ed.) *Issues of Validity in Qualitative Research*, Lund: Studentlitteratur, 73–91.
Lee, T.W. (1999) *Using Qualitative Methods in Organizational Research*, Thousand Oaks: Sage.
Levitan, S.A. and Johnson, C.M. (1983) 'The contradictions of industrial policy', *Journal of the Institute for Socioeconomic Studies*, 8(4): 48–64.
Margolis, J.D. and Walsh, J.P. (2003) 'Misery loves companies: rethinking social initiatives by business', *Administrative Science Quarterly*, 48: 268–305.
Marshall, C. and Rossman, G.B. (1999) *Designing Qualitative Research*, London: Sage.
Marshall, R. (1992) 'The future role of government in industrial relations', *Industrial Relations*, 31(1): 31–50.
Marton, F. (1981) 'Phenomenography – describing conceptions of the world around us', *Instructional Science*, 10: 177–200.
Meklin, P. and Ahonen, P. (1998) 'Government-owned companies in Finland: pragmatic change and modernization', *Public Administration and Development*, 18(3): 265–73.
Munda, G., Nijkamp, P. and Rietveld, P. (1994) 'Qualitative multicriteria evaluation for environmental management', *Ecological Economics*, 10(2): 97–112.
Murray, S. (1995) 'The roles of government and the public administrator', *Public Manager*, 24(3): 46–8.
Ogata, S. (1990) 'Government's role in the market economy', *Management Japan*, 23(1): 17–22.
Oliver, C. (1997) 'Sustainable competitive advantage: combining institutional and resource based views', *Strategic Management Journal*, 18(9): 697–713.

Phillis, Y.A. and Andriantiatsaholiniaina, L.A. (2001) 'Sustainability: an ill-defined concept and its assessment using fuzzy logic', *Ecological Economics*, 37(3): 435–56.

Powell, W.W. and DiMaggio, P.J. (1991) *The New Institutionalism in Organizational Analysis*, Chicago: University of Chicago Press.

Scott, W.R. (2001) *Institutions and Organizations*, 2nd edn, Thousand Oaks: Sage.

Sharma, S. (2002) 'Research in corporate sustainability: what really matters?' in S. Sharma and M. Starik (eds) *Research in Corporate Sustainability: The Evolving Theory and Practice of Organizations in the Natural Environment*, Cheltenham: Edward Elgar, 1–29.

Sharma, S. and Ruud, A. (2003) 'On the path to sustainability: integrating social dimensions into the research and practice of environmental management', *Business Strategy and the Environment*, 12(4): 205.

Shin, R. (2001) 'Strategies for economic development under decentralization: a transformation of the political economy', *International Journal of Public Administration*, 24(10): 1083.

Shrivastava, P. (1995) 'The role of corporations in achieving ecological sustainability', *Academy of Management Review*, 20(4): 936.

Starik, M. and Marcus, A.A. (2000) 'Introduction to the special research forum on the management of organizations in the natural environment: a field emerging from multiple paths, with many challenges ahead', *Academy of Management Journal*, 43(4): 539.

Starik, M. and Rands, G.P. (1995) 'Weaving an integrated web: multilevel and multisystem perspectives of ecologically sustainable organizations', *Academy of Management Review*, 20(4): 908.

Stead, W.E. and Stead, J.G. (2004) *Sustainable Strategic Management*, New York: M.E. Sharpe.

van Marrewijk, M. (2003) 'Concepts and definitions of CSR and corporate sustainability: between agency and communion', *Journal of Business Ethics*, 44(2–3): 95–105.

WCED (World Commission on Environment and Development) (1987) *Our Common Future*, Oxford: Oxford University Press.

Part II

Limitations of existing models of corporate governance

Chapter 3

Why corporate governance rankings do not predict future value

Evidence from Toronto Stock Exchange listings 2002–5

David Wheeler and Rachel Davies

INTRODUCTION

In the study of strategic management, the assumed drivers of competitiveness and ultimately the economic value of the firm have historically been grounded either in traditional theories relating to market and industry structure (Porter 1980, 1985) or in more contemporary theories relating to specific capabilities of the firm – the so-called 'resource-based view' or RBV (Wernerfeld 1984; Barney 1991). In the RBV, firms that have resources that are rare, valuable, hard to imitate or substitute will achieve sustained competitive advantage notwithstanding changes in market and industry conditions (Grant 1991). There have been attempts to bridge these two perspectives. For example Mintzberg and co-workers have argued that all schools of strategic management have merit in different contexts (Mintzberg *et al.* 1998) and thus the real source of competitiveness in business lies in knowing which approach best fits the particular circumstances, and the key role of managers is to *think* strategically at all times (Mintzberg 1991). Nonetheless, the active debates continue between protagonists defending alternative paradigmatic assumptions about strategic management, competitiveness and the value-creation process (Priem and Butler 2001; Makadok and Coff 2002).

Scholars interested in questions of firm competitiveness and sustainability (or corporate social responsibility) have tended to rely more on resource-based arguments, partly because they do not necessarily subscribe to economically rationalist approaches to business strategy and partly because resource-based approaches provide richer descriptions of the *intangible* assets that allow firms to succeed, for example firm capabilities, social capital, human capital, reputation, management values, corporate culture, etc (Hart 1995; Wheeler and Sillanpää 1997, 1998; Sharma and Vredenburg 1998; Clarke and Clegg 2000; Aragón-Correa and Sharma 2003). These intangible resources or assets are undoubtedly of growing importance to firm valuation (Wheeler and Davies 2004) and thus they seem highly relevant to the so-called 'business case' arguments for sustainability and/or corporate social responsibility so often debated by practitioners and academics alike.

The argument is that firms that focus on harnessing and leveraging their intangible assets – either for reasons of corporate values or straight competitiveness – are more likely to be sensitive to stakeholder and broader societal interests and therefore a virtuous cycle is created between socially responsible or sustainable behaviours and firm success (Wheeler 2003). Simply stated, when stakeholders – be they investors, customers, workers, value chain partners or society at large – get what they want from the firm they come back for more. This somewhat uncontestable proposition has been advanced by Professor Edward Freeman and his co-workers for more than two decades (Freeman 1984; Freeman and McVea 2001).

One way of characterizing the competing prescriptions for competitiveness, value creation, sustainability and corporate social responsibility within the RBV is to think of the modern corporation less as a monolithic, fixed structure and more as an entity presiding over a kind of business ecosystem or a set of interlocking 'value based networks' where value is defined by the firm and its different stakeholders according to the nature of the relationship (Wheeler *et al.* 2003). The successful maintenance and extension of these self-reinforcing networks then becomes a very important corporate resource or intangible asset, as does the reputation associated with this capability.

As with most reputational phenomena, 'social responsibility' is socially constructed and emerges when people associated with the firm are happy. Empirical evidence for this proposition has been accumulated in a large number of studies exploring the link between corporate social performance (CSP) – variously defined, but usually based on proactive attention being paid to one or more defined stakeholders – and corporate financial performance. Margolis and Walsh (2001) described 80 such empirical investigations, approximately half of which provided direct evidence of a correlation between financial performance and CSP (as the independent variable). A negative relationship was found in only 5 per cent of studies and no relationship or a mixed relationship was found in the remainder.

Based on this kind of evidence as well as some moral reasoning, a number of authors have advocated a pragmatic 'stakeholder approach' to corporate governance (Freeman and Evan 1990; Freeman *et al.* 2004; Solomon and Solomon 2004). This is entirely consistent with the resource-based view, and may indeed be considered a special version of the RBV which acknowledges that stakeholders external to the firm often control access to resources or at least their ability to be leveraged (Pfeffer and Salancik 1978).

In contrast to the dominant theory of corporate governance, i.e. a normative and somewhat narrow version of agency theory long associated with Professor Michael Jensen (Jensen and Meckling 1976; Jensen 2005), some corporate governance theorists have also based their conceptions of the role of directors and boards on a version of RBV. These commentators argue that one of the most important roles of directors (rather than the firm as a whole) is to act as effective links between the firm and its external environment, thereby securing preferential access to financial and other resources (Hillman *et al.* 2000). This has been shown to be especially important to firms seeking financial support for public offerings (Certo 2003). Stewardship theory has also been advocated (Davis *et al.* 1997; Sundaramurthy and Lewis 2003) to better describe a reality that acknowledges that corporate executives are not constantly motivated by a temptation to steal from shareholders, but often find good social and financial reasons to align their interests with investors.

Applying this thinking to corporate governance and building on a broad interpretation of agency theory (Eisenhardt 1999) and the stakeholder-agency arguments of Hill and Jones (1992) and Aguilera and Jackson (2003), we have argued that:

> One of the main roles of the board, and corporate governance processes more generally, is stewardship over resources. Consistent with resource dependency theory and the resource-based perspective of strategic management, we might characterise this duty as one of protecting, growing and helping gain access to resources that might benefit the firm and its ability to create value.
>
> (Wheeler and Davies 2004)

We have also proposed a conceptual model for sustainable value creation within a resource stewardship and stakeholder-agency notion of corporate governance informed both by a 'sustainability mission' and a 'stakeholder approach' to strategic management. See Figure 3.1 below.

The challenge of course is to identify what corporate governance metrics may be relevant to generating value through such a model. What can boards and individual directors do to demonstrate to an objective observer that intangible assets such as human and social capital (goodwill) and reputation are being proactively managed for tangible value outcomes such as increased sales, increased market share or increased market capitalization, let alone less tangible outcomes? We will now explore the evidence for *tangible outcomes* (principally market and economic value) being associated with conventional corporate governance norms since this is what drives most of the discourse around corporate governance reform.

CORPORATE GOVERNANCE AND FIRM PERFORMANCE

There is relatively little evidence that best practices in corporate governance *as currently defined* have any direct and predictive association whatever with even basic tangible performance measures, for example increase in prosperity for investors as represented by increased market capitalization of the firm over time.

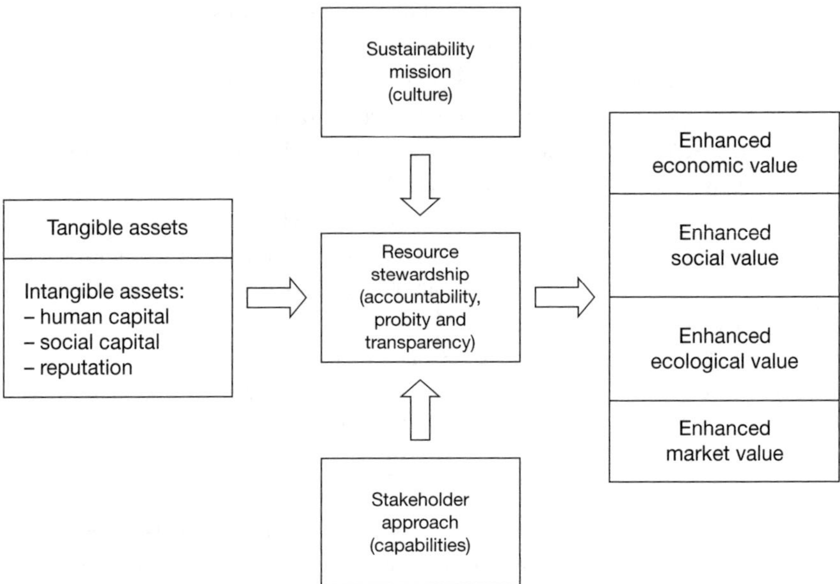

Figure 3.1 *A sustainable resource-stewardship model for corporate governance (Wheeler and Thomson 2006)*

Sonnenfeld (2002), Lynall *et al.* (2003) and Solomon and Solomon (2004) have reflected on some of the difficulties of establishing unequivocal correlations between good corporate governance and firm performance, finding mixed or only weak evidence for such links and no evidence of causality. Colley and co-workers (2003) cite the results of *Business Week* corporate governance rankings over the period 1997–2002 based on a number of factors relating to (1) director independence; (2) collective and individual director quality; and (3) accountability. They noted that a company featuring on the 'worst boards' list was twice as likely to under-perform compared to the SandP 500 Index than one on the 'best boards' list. In contrast, companies on the 'best boards' list were three times as likely to outperform the SandP 500 compared with firms on the 'worst boards' list. However, the authors note that because of the small sample size these data could not be considered conclusive evidence for a causal link between board effectiveness and company performance.

Two more recent reviews of the evidence for links between good corporate governance practices (variously defined) and firm performance (also variously defined) have been provided by Leblanc and Gillies (2005) and Brown and Caylor (2004).

Leblanc and Gillies draw attention to the fact that much of the academic research describes measures of corporate governance related to structural and other fixes designed to address the so-called 'agency problem' – the notion that executive leaderships need to be controlled to prevent them diverting corporate resources from activities that add to shareholder wealth rather than personal wealth and prestige. They cite a range of authors who now question the usefulness of such measures of good corporate governance and the deliberations of a special topic forum of the Academy of Management which concluded 'were independent governance structures clearly of superior benefit to shareholders, we would expect to see these results reflected in the results of scholarly research. Such results, however, are not evident': Daily *et al.* 2003.

Brown and Caylor (2004) cite a number of empirical studies of largely US firms that failed to find an association between board independence and a range of measures of firm performance, including firm valuation. They also cite other studies, including their own, that claim links between the appointment of independent board members and a number of measures, for example, return on equity and dividend yields, but not necessarily firm value. Brown and Caylor go on to list a range of contradictory studies on the issue of audit committee and auditing independence and firm performance. They find some evidence for firm valuation being linked to the separation of chairman and CEO roles and they cite Gompers *et al.* (2003) in establishing a link between firm valuation and 'shareholder rights' based on data from the Investor Responsibility Research Center. We will return to a more detailed discussion of the Brown and Caylor study later in the chapter.

The absence of clear correlations between something as basic as board independence and shareholder value must be perplexing for traditional followers of normative or 'narrow' agency approaches to corporate governance. It implies that notwithstanding all of the doubtless very worthy and well-intended activity by corporate governance reformers and legislators around the world, aimed at protecting investors through structural and other fixes, current best practice codes and even draconian legislation such as the United States Sarbanes–Oxley Act 2002 have not delivered unequivocal economic gains for investors in companies that take such codes seriously. Davis (2005) has applied a sociological frame to this self-evident truth, noting that 'compliance with external demands often takes the form of cynical adoption of token structures decoupled from actual practice; moreover, when structures are not decoupled, they can often produce unintended consequences that are worse than the problem being addressed'.

Simply stated, current apparent norms of corporate governance with their over-reliance on questions of investor rights or structural control of management do not automatically guarantee better stock performance either over the shorter or longer terms. There may be several reasons for this. Of course there are significant variables with respect to firm sector, firm size and jurisdiction with which to contend. Studies based on a basket of sectors may blur the very real differences in governance style and board effectiveness that may pertain in industries as different as, say, entertainment and mining. Studies conducted on US firms may not be generalized to Europe and *vice versa*. However, one emerging confounding variable that is attracting increasing attention from corporate governance theorists is the issue of board culture and competence.

Writing from a US standpoint, Colley and co-workers (2003) note that 'the functioning of a company's board of directors is somewhat indescribable in that it draws on the unique amalgamation of the skills, experiences, and motivations of the individual directors'. These authors also identify a number of potential deficiencies that boards must avoid, including several that relate to board culture, including toleration of legal violations, lack of board leadership and internal political or personality conflict problems. This theme has been developed in some detail by Leblanc and Gillies (2005) who postulate ten director stereotypes that may be associated with functional and dysfunctional boards. They also suggested a model for designing effective boards based on the acronym CBSR: competency, behaviour, strategy and recruitment.

Clearly if two of the major variables in board effectiveness are culture and competence, then all of the attention devoted to structure and form in corporate governance rankings may fail to capture two major drivers of firm performance (or lack of it). In the past we illustrated this point with preliminary data from the Toronto Stock Exchange, seeking – and failing – to find evidence that high scores in a well-respected annual governance ranking of firms in the exchange are associated with higher than average short-term stock returns in the year following the publication of the ranking (Wheeler and Davies 2004). We are now able to elucidate this phenomenon in more detail, given the availability of more years' data.

STUDIES ON CORPORATE GOVERNANCE RANKINGS AND THE TORONTO STOCK EXCHANGE

To demonstrate the level of association between governance norms and firm performance (simply defined as increase in market capitalization over time) we took the Canadian 'Report on Business' (ROB) annual ranking of corporate governance performance for 2002, 2003 and 2004 and compared shifts in the rankings for firms with shifts in market capitalization in the same time frame. We then performed a number of simple linear regression analyses on the data.

The ROB annual corporate governance ranking is compiled and published annually, typically emerging in October of each year. Corporate governance is evaluated against 'best practice' criteria as recommended by a variety of major institutional investors, academics and industry associations. The criteria are revised each year as standards shift and views on corporate governance mature.

A total score, out of 100, is based on four broad categories with a range of measures included for each. The broad categories are: Board Composition, Shareholding and Compensation, Shareholder Rights and Disclosure. Data is obtained from the most recent proxy circulars of 218 companies included in the S&P/TSX composite index as of 15 June of each year. Some companies did not receive marks in 2003 or 2002, because they were not members of the S&P/TSX index group at that time.

A number of changes to the ranking system have been made since its inception in 2002 (Report on Business 2003, 2004). Based on investor feedback, ROB increased or decreased the maximum possible score for several questions. For example, in order to recognize growing emphasis on equal voting rights for all shareholders, ROB awarded more marks to companies that did not have dual-class shares. Although marks for these questions are not completely comparable with results from previous years, ROB included prior results to examine the performance of various companies on a relative basis.

In addition to these modest adjustments, a number of more significant changes have been made. They include:

1 To address the concerns of some of the lower-scoring companies, ROB opted to consider each company's historic financial performance. The five-year return (as of 31 August) for each firm was therefore included in 2003. From our perspective this inclusion risks introducing tautology to the ranking system by implying that good governance is a priori restricted to maximizing shareholder returns rather than a broader model of value creation. We will discuss this point later.
2 The addition of a new category to assess whether companies grant shareholders the right to vote for each director nominee individually or the board as a whole. ROB added this question in 2004 in response to heightened investor interest in being able to approve or reject individual directors without withholding votes for the others. Inadequate attendance records and share ownership were the most frequently cited reasons for rejecting board nominees.
3 Two questions that were included in previous years were dropped in 2004 as they were no longer considered useful measures. The first question assessed companies based on their election terms for directors (i.e. annually versus staggered terms), while the second looked for the inclusion of corporate governance practices in shareholder proxy circulars. Because these practices have been nearly universally adopted, ROB excluded these questions in 2004.

Since inception in 2002 the ranking has seen some significant shifts in governance scores for individual corporations but this has not necessarily been followed by equivalent shifts in market capitalization. For example, the Bank of Nova Scotia, Canada's second largest corporation by market capitalization in 2002, rose from a score of 78 to one of 93 between 2002 and 2004 (15 point increase). The value of the company rose by a compound rate of 27.3 per cent over this period. In contrast, Barrick Gold was also one of the highest risers, adding 26 points to its 2002 governance score to achieve a score of 75 in 2004. However, compound growth for Barrick Gold over the period was just 2.8 per cent. Ten of our sample of companies saw small declines in their governance ranking, for example Dofasco, which lost 9 points between 2002 and 2004 (from 90 to 81) whilst at the same time as achieving a compound growth in market capitalization of 24.4 per cent.

Partly because of the danger of bias arising from changes in the ranking system (driven by the complaints of apparently poorly governed but high-performing smaller companies), we elected to explore changes in ROB rankings for the TSX60 (i.e. the top 60 companies by market capitalization). From the TSX60 we ended up with a subset of

55, as some firms became members of this index after the first governance scores were released (for example, Kinross Gold and Research in Motion). In addition, ROB excluded a few companies from the annual rankings as they had not issued proxy circulars.

The graphical depiction of all the raw comparative data (numeric shift in governance ranking between 2002 and 2004 versus shift in market capitalization in the 34 months between October 2002 and August 2005) for the 55 companies in our sub-sample is shown below (Figure 3.2). The figure shows a positive slope but no statistically significant relationship.

Expressing the shift as a percentage of the original score (out of 100) yields a very similar picture: a positive slope but no statistically significant relationship. See Figure 3.3 below.

It would be theoretically possible for changes in scores and changes in market capitalization not to be correlated but for absolute scores in one year to be predictive of future performance over subsequent years. So we also explored whether the specific governance scores for companies in one year could be correlated with market capitalization over time.

We found that for the 2002 and 2003 scores there was no correlation between specific governance scores and short term shifts in market capitalization in the one year period immediately following publication of the score. For the 2002 scores there was actually a negative slope but no correlation and for the 2003 scores there was a positive slope but again no correlation. See Figure 3.4 below.

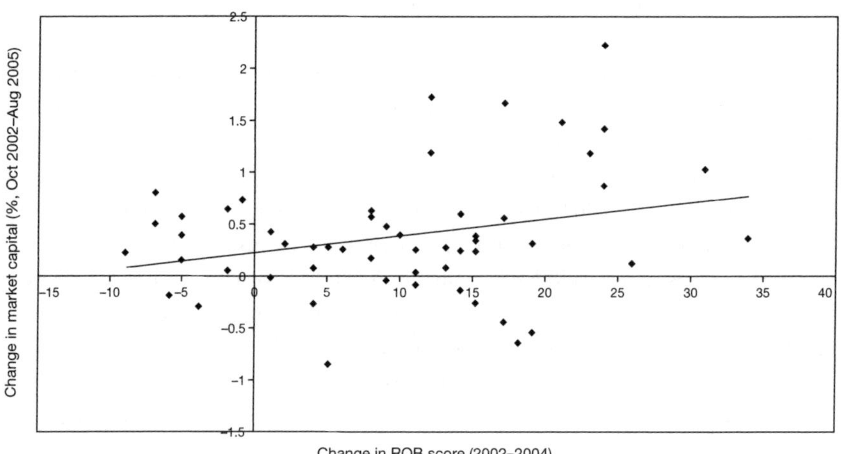

Figure 3.2 *Change in numeric corporate governance ranking (ROB score) 2002–4 for 55 of the top 60 companies on the Toronto Stock Exchange versus change in market capitalization 2002–5 ($p = 0.131$, $r^2 = 0.043$)*

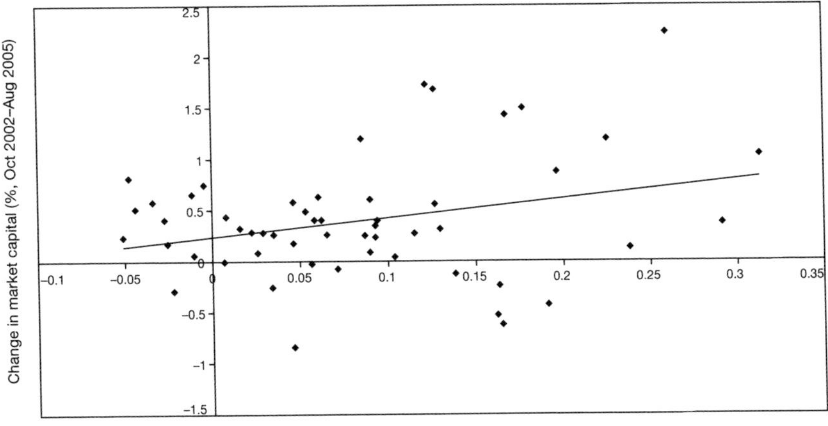

Figure 3.3 *Change in percentage corporate governance ranking (ROB score) 2002–4 for 55 of the top 60 companies on the Toronto Stock Exchange versus change in market capitalization 2002–5 ($p = 0.204$, $r^2 = 0.030$)*

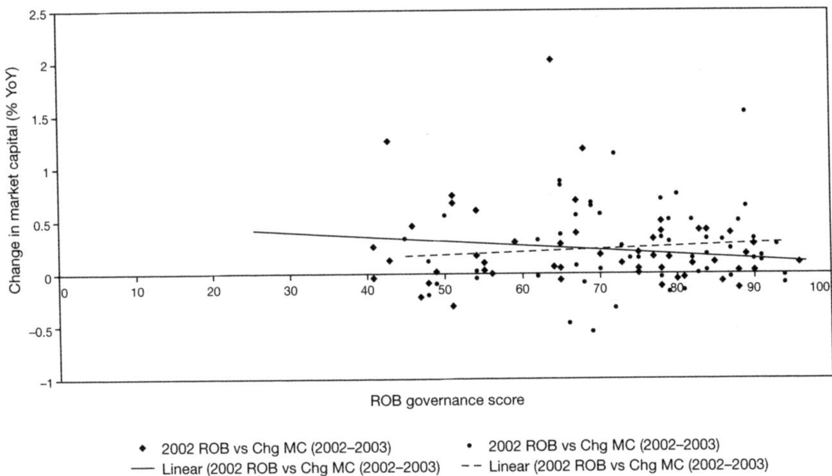

Figure 3.4 *Corporate governance rankings (ROB governance score) for 2002 and 2003 versus short-term (one-year) changes in market capitalization for 55 of the top 60 companies on the Toronto Stock Exchange (2002: $p = 0.247$, $r^2 = 0.025$; 2003: $p = 0.468$, r^2 0.010)*

We then sought to give the maximum possibility for the ROB governance rankings to correlate with shareholder value added by exploring whether the 2002 and 2003 rankings were at all predictive of longer-term shifts in market capitalization. We explored periods of 34 months and 22 months respectively for the 2002 and 2003 rankings

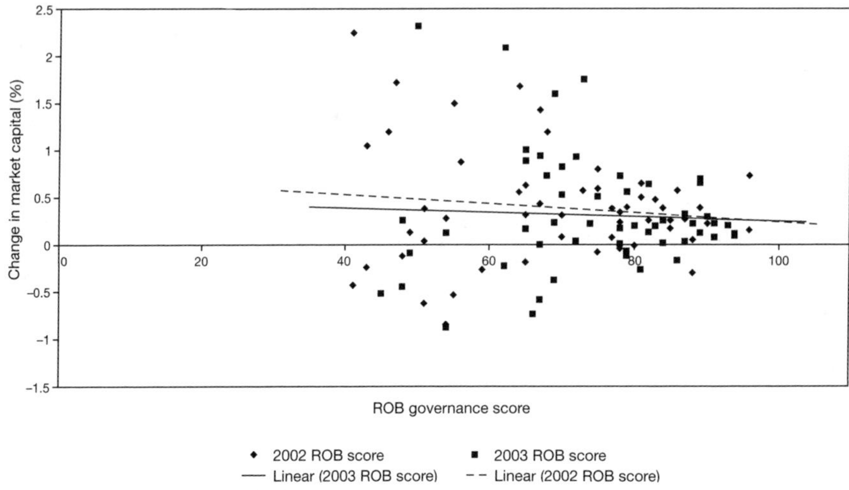

Figure 3.5 *Corporate governance rankings (ROB governance score) for 2002 and 2003 versus longer-term (34-month and 22-month) changes in market capitalization for 55 of the top companies on the Toronto Stock Exchange (2002:* $p = 0.163$, $r^2 = 0.036$; *2003:* $p = 0.769$, $r^2 = 0.002$*)*

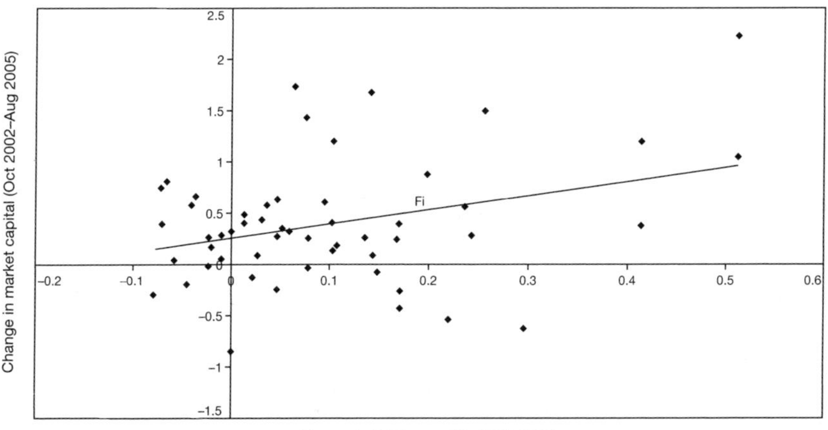

Figure 3.6 *Change in corporate governance rankings (ROB governance score) between 2002 and 2003 (per cent) versus longer-term (22 month) changes in market capitalization for 55 of the top 60 companies on the Toronto Stock Exchange (*$p = 0.015$, $r^2 = 0.106$*)*

(October 2002 to August 2005 and October 2003 to August 2005). We found that neither ranking was correlated with longer-term changes in market capitalization (see Figure 3.5 above). Indeed in both cases the curve was negative, implying a moderately inverse relationship between longer-term market capitalization and ROB rankings for the two years in question (albeit again with no statistical significance).

We then took the percentage change in ROB scores between 2002 and 2003 and did establish a significant correlation with longer term change in market capitalization (22 months from the 2003 ranking). In this case we found both a positive slope and a statistically significant relationship, implying that investors who invested selectively in firms whose ROB scores changed positively between 2002 and 2003 would have seen their portfolios outperform those of passive investors in the TSX (see Figure 3.6 opposite).

DISCUSSION OF FINDINGS

Building on our prior theoretical and empirical work (Wheeler and Davies 2004; Wheeler and Thomson 2006), and the arguments of Sonnefeld (2002), Colley *et al.* (2003), Letendre (2004) and Leblanc and Gillies (2005), we were unsurprised to find no predictive value in the ROB corporate governance scores and either short term or longer term shifts in market capitalization of the firms in question. As noted above we found no statistically significant relationships between absolute scores and short-term (one year) or longer-term (22–34 month) shifts in market capitalization. Our assertions in those earlier papers that corporate governance norms and rankings were in danger of addressing and measuring largely irrelevant factors – even from the perspective of shareholder value – seems to have been further borne out in this study, at least for larger firms in Canada.

As noted earlier, in a detailed empirical study of correlations between a wide range of corporate governance attributes and a number of performance measures, Brown and Caylor (2004) identified a number of factors that have potential salience from an investor's perspective. They also claimed that the metrics they employed (based on the analyses of Institutional Shareholder Services) were more comprehensive and more predictive of performance than the well-recognized indicators employed by Gompers *et al.* (2003) – based on the analyses of the Investor Responsibility Research Centre. The Brown and Caylor 'Gov-Score' comprised 51 separate metrics arranged in eight categories relating to corporate governance with respect to (1) audit practices, (2) Board of Director factors, (3) corporate charter and bylaws, (4) director education; (5) executive and director compensation; (6) ownership, (7) 'progressive practices'; and (8) jurisdictional state of incorporation. The six industry-adjusted performance measures were: return on equity, net profit margin, sales growth, Tobin's Q (firm valuation broadly based on assets and market valuation), dividend yield and share repurchasing.

In many cases Brown and Caylor found that corporate governance practices founded on conventional wisdom (as represented by governance codes, legislation or listings requirements) were either not correlated with any of the six measures of performance or they were negatively correlated. For example where consulting fees to auditors were less than audit fees paid to auditors, there was a strong negative correlation with four of the six performance measures (though not with firm valuation). Specifically related to firm valuation (the main variable discussed in this chapter), there was a strong negative correlation between Tobin's Q calculation of firm value and a generally supposed good practice in corporate governance which is Board control by outside directors.

Strong positive correlations (95 per cent or 99 per cent confidence limits) existed between firm valuation and *only six* of the 51 factors examined. These were: (1) all directors attend 75 per cent board meetings or had a valid excuse; (2) board members are elected annually; (3) the company either had no 'poison pill' provision or had one with shareholder approval; (4) shareholders could act with written consent and the consent was non-unanimous; (5) average share options granted in the previous three years did not exceed 3 per cent of outstanding shares; and (6) the firm was incorporated in a state without anti-takeover provisions. Forty-five of the potential good practice criteria yielded no significant correlation with the Tobin's Q definition of firm valuation.

In contrast, on the question of a second factor of direct relevance to investors, dividend yield, positive correlations were obtained with 23 of the 51 criteria (including all four criteria relating to stock ownership and all seven criteria 'progressive practices'). However, eight of the criteria yielded negative correlations, many of which related to bylaw and charter issues deemed important by other analysts such as IRRC.

From Brown and Caylor's work we may observe that investors in US stocks who are interested mostly in dividends are likely to have their expectations met where (1) all directors with more than one year of service own stock; (2) officers' and executives' stock holdings exceed 1 per cent but are less than 30 per cent of all stock holdings; (3) both executives and directors are subject to stock ownership guidelines; (4) there is a mandatory retirement age for directors; (5) performance of the board is reviewed regularly; (6) a board-approved CEO succession plan is in place; (7) the board has outside advisors; (8) directors are required to submit their resignation on change of job status; (9) outside directors meet without the CEO and disclose the number of times this happens; and (10) there is a director term limit. But not a single one of these criteria is correlated with firm valuation.

In the context of our observations and prior reasoning, it is relatively simple to describe the contrast between results for dividends and results for firm valuation found by Brown and Caylor. Where decisions and outcomes are determined by board directors and senior officers of the firm (for example, dividend policy), corporate governance 'good practices' aimed at aligning interests of directors and executives with those of investors are more likely to be correlated. Where outcomes are determined more by the marketplace, they are less likely to be correlated.

Possible explanations for Brown and Caylor's six (of 51) criteria being correlated with firm valuation are more challenging, partly because of the use of Tobin's Q as the firm valuation measure (rather than straight market capitalization). Nevertheless we may observe the following: three of the criteria are associated with what we might describe as board 'self-confidence and sensitivity' with respect to externally imposed discipline: the company either had no 'poison pill' provision; shareholders could act with written consent; and the firm was incorporated in a state without anti-takeover provisions. Three are associated with individual self-confidence and sensitivity with respect to their own roles: directors attend 75 per cent of board meetings; board members are elected annually; and directors and executives are not excessively motivated by options. The common threads here seem to be collective and individual self-confidence, sensitivity and discipline.

We may now turn to an explanation of our observations from the TSX data. Clearly the ROB rankings for 2002–4 provided little or no predictive value for increases or decreases in market capitalization of firms in the index in either the short or longer term. Indeed, a number of our regressions had negative slopes, implying inverse relationships. However, the shifts in scores between 2002 and 2003 were strongly correlated with longer-term market valuation.

It is axiomatic that firms that acknowledge and respond to external signals quickly – including changes in corporate governance norms – have a dynamic capability for such changes (Teece *et al.* 1997). Responding to the 2002 ROB rankings within one year to improve that ranking by as much as 10 or 15 per cent by the following year demonstrates (1) a very high level of sensitivity to reputational factors and/or (2) a capability for change that can only be achieved in relatively high trust environments, i.e. where there is general goodwill (i.e. social capital) among actors. Such manifestations of effective management of two key intangible resources (reputation and social capital) are precisely the type of predictors of future value creation that we have identified in earlier work on organizational sustainability (Wheeler 2003) and corporate governance (Wheeler and Davies 2004). These future value predictors are also consistent with many of the claims of advocates of socially responsible investment (SRI) who believe that indicators of 'best in class' social and environmental performance are simply a proxy for good management (Wheeler and Thomson 2006).

Thus it is perhaps no great surprise that our evidence is wholly consistent with Davis' plea for a sociological approach to corporate governance in which he draws attention to the failure of what he describes as 'contractarian' mechanisms to address and accommodate the idea that corporations are human institutions embedded in social structures that will largely determine how they behave (Davis 2005). As Davis notes, 'Investors may require credible evidence of transparency and accountability in corporate governance, but what is credible is a matter of rhetoric – that is, what does it take to convince others of the validity of one's assertions'. Our data support Davis' position empirically in that we have shown that companies with higher corporate governance scores may be good at demonstrating acceptable behaviour and standards to the institutions that track them, but they do not necessarily deliver superior returns to shareholders in terms of market capitalization.

So perhaps now we may be a little closer to identifying the ways in which the presence of value-creating intangible resources can be detected and even measured. Consistent with our sustainable resource-stewardship model for corporate governance (Wheeler and Thomson 2006) we might suggest that investors and analysts look for direct and indirect evidence of stewardship approaches to corporate resource management aimed at the effective and proactive conversion of intangible assets into both tangible and intangible outcomes for all stakeholders, including investors. Candidate direct and indirect indicators of such capabilities could then be subject to empirical testing. For example, we have demonstrated that *the capability to respond* to a well-respected, if somewhat flawed, ranking system and change structures and appearances *very rapidly* may be vicariously indicative of future superior value-creating potential.[1] Other such tests of board sensitivity and management of intangible assets could be developed and tested.

We might also gently propose to those responsible for the ROB ranking and indeed other such ranking systems that they (1) strip out criteria where there is little or no evidence of value to investors or other stakeholders arising from such criteria (shareholder rights, various structural factors); (2) broaden those criteria that reflect on the self-confidence, sensitivity to outside influences and discipline exhibited by boards and individual directors; and (3) avoid building in potentially tautological criteria such as historic five year returns to shareholders which may further re-enforce unhelpful and narrow agency assumptions about good corporate governance and how to measure it.

Finally, we believe we have found some indirect empirical evidence for the theoretical arguments of advocates of the resource based view and its implications for stakeholder inclusiveness and corporate social responsibility or 'sustainability'. From an investor's perspective, boards and senior management teams that demonstrate they understand their sociological, as well as their financial roles, may well be the ones to back.

NOTE

1 It is not necessarily the case that having identified a potentially predictive factor in the ROB governance ranking (i.e. the change from 2002 to 2003), this may have ongoing relevance. It is possible that future shifts in ranking may already have been arbitraged and that this was a one off phenomenon associated with the first publication of the ranking. All significant benefits associated with responsiveness to the ROB ranking may already have been taken.

REFERENCES

Aguilera, R.V. and Jackson, G. (2003) 'The cross-national diversity of corporate governance: dimensions and determinants', *Academy of Management Review*, 28(3): 447–65.

Aragón-Correa, J.A. and Sharma, S. (2003) 'A contingent resource-based view of proactive corporate environmental strategy', *Academy of Management Review*, 28(1): 71–88.

Barney, J.B. (1991) 'Firm resources and sustained competitive advantage', *Journal of Management*, 17: 99–120.

Brown, L.D. and Caylor, M.L (2004), 'Corporate governance and firm performance', Working Paper, Georgia State University. Online. Available at: http://ssrn.com/abstract=586423 (accessed 3 January 2006).

Certo, S.T. (2003) 'Influencing initial public offering investors with prestige: signalling with board structures', *Academy of Management Review*, 28(3): 432–46.

Clarke, T. and Clegg, S. (2000) *Changing Paradigms*, London: Trafalgar Square.

Colley Jr., J. L., Doyle, J. L., Logan, G. W. and Stettinius, W. (2003) *Corporate Governance*, New York: McGraw-Hill.

Daily, C.M., Dalton, D.R. and Cannella Jr., A.A. (2003) 'Corporate governance: decades of dialogue and data', *Academy of Management Review*, 28(3): 371–82.

Davis, G.H. (2005) 'New directions in corporate governance', *Annual Review of Sociology*, 31(8): 143–62.

Davis, J.H., Schoorman, F.D. and Donaldson, L. (1997) 'Toward a stewardship theory of management', *Academy of Management Review*, 22(1): 20–47.

Eisenhardt, K. (1999) 'Agency theory: an assessment and a review', *Academy of Management Review*, 14: 57–74.

Freeman, R.E. (1984), *Strategic Management: A Stakeholder Approach*, Boston: Pitman.

Freeman, R.E. and Evan, W. (1990) 'Corporate governance: a stakeholder interpretation', *Journal of Behavioral Economics*, 19(4): 337–59.

Freeman, R.E. and McVea, J. (2001) 'A stakeholder approach to strategic management', in M.A. Hitt, R.E. Freeman and J.S Harrison (eds) (2001) *Handbook of Strategic Management*, Oxford: Blackwell, pp.189–207.

Freeman, R.E., Wicks, A.C. and Parmar, B. (2004) 'Stakeholder theory and "the corporate objective revisited"', *Organization Science*, 15(3): 364–69.

Gompers, P., Ishii, J. and Metrick, A. (2003) 'Corporate governance and equity prices', *Quarterly Journal of Economics*, 118: 107–55.

Grant, M. (1991) 'The resource-based theory of competitive advantage: implications for strategy formulation', *California Management Review*, 33(3): 114–35.

Hart, S.L. (1995) 'A natural-resource-based view of the firm', *Academy of Management Review*, 20: 986–1014.

Hill, C.W. and Jones, T.M. (1992) 'Stakeholder-agency theory', *Journal of Management Studies*, 29: 134–54.

Hillman, A., Cannella, A. and Paetzold, R. (2000) 'The resource dependence role of corporate directors: strategic adaptation of board composition in response to environmental change', *Journal of Management Studies*, 37: 235–56.

Jensen, M.C. (2005) 'Value maximization, stakeholder theory, and the corporate objective function', in D.H. Chew and S.L. Gillan (2005) *Corporate Governance at the Crossroads: A Book of Readings*, New York: McGraw-Hill Irwin, pp. 7–20.

Jensen, M.C. and Meckling, W.F. (1976) 'Theory of the firm: managerial behavior, agency costs, and ownership structure', *Journal of Financial Economics*, 3: 305–60.

Leblanc, R. and Gillies, J. (2005), *Inside the Boardroom. How Boards Really Work and the Coming Revolution in Corporate Governance*, Ontario: Wiley.

Letendre, L. (2004) 'The dynamics of the boardroom', *Academy of Management Executive*, 18(1): 101–4.

Lynall, M.D., Golden, B.R. and Hillman, A.J. (2003) 'Board composition from adolescence to maturity: a multitheoretic view', *Academy of Management Review*, 28(3): 416–31.

Makadok, R. and Coff, R. (2002) 'The theory of value and the value of theory: breaking new ground versus re-inventing the wheel', *Academy of Management Review*, 27(1): 10–13.

Margolis, J.D. and Walsh, J.P. (2001) *People and Profits? The Search for a Link Between a Company's Social and Financial Performance*, Mahwah, NJ: Erlbaum.

Mintzberg, H. (1991) 'Strategic thinking as "seeing" ', in J. Nasi (ed.) *Arenas of Strategic Thinking*, Helsinki: Foundation for Economic Education. Cited in: Mintzberg, H., Ahlstrand, B. and Lampel, J. (1998) pp. 126–27.

Mintzberg, H., Ahlstrand, B. and Lampel, J. (1998) *Strategy Safari*, London: Prentice Hall.

Pfeffer, J. and Salancik, G. (1978) *The External Control of Organizations*, New York: Harper and Row.

Porter, M.E. (1980) *Competitive Strategy: Techniques for Analyzing Industries and Competitors*, New York: Free Press.

Porter, M.E. (1985) *Competitive Advantage: Creating and Sustaining Superior Performance*, New York: Free Press.

Priem, R.L. and Butler, J.E. (2001) 'Is the resource-based 'view' a useful perspective for strategic management research', *Academy of Management Review*, 26(1): 22–40.

Report on Business (2003) 'Board games: rating system revamped; feedback from last year's survey led to some changes in criteria, categories', *Globe and Mail*, 22 September.

Report on Business (2004) 'Board games: marking system goes well beyond mandatory rules; demanding set of criteria that embodies best practices are revised each year', *Globe and Mail*, 12 October.

Sharma, S. and Vredenburg, H. (1998) 'Proactive corporate environmental strategy and the development of competitively valuable organizational capabilities', *Strategic Management Journal*, 19: 729–53.

Solomon, J. and Solomon, R. (2004) *Corporate Governance and Accountability*. Chichester, UK: Wiley.

Sonnenfeld, J.A. (2002) 'What makes good boards great', *Harvard Business Review*, September: 106–13.

Sundaramurthy, C. and Lewis, M. (2003) 'Control and collaboration. Paradoxes of governance', *Academy of Management Review*, 28(3): 397–415.

Teece, D.J., Pisano, G. and Shuen, A. (1997) 'Dynamic capabilities and strategic management', *Strategic Management Journal*, 18(7): 509–33.

Wernerfeld, B. (1984) 'A resource-based view of the firm', *Strategic Management Journal*, 5: 171–80.

Wheeler, D. (2003) 'The successful navigation of uncertainty: sustainability and the organisation', in R. Burke and C. Cooper (eds) *Leading in Turbulent Times*, Oxford: Blackwell, pp. 182–207.

Wheeler, D. and Davies, R. (2004) 'Gaining goodwill: developing stakeholder approaches to corporate governance', *Journal of General Management*, 30(2): 51–74.

Wheeler, D. and Sillanpää, M. (1997) *The Stakeholder Corporation*, London: Pitman.

Wheeler, D. and Sillanpää, M. (1998) 'Including the stakeholders: the business case', *Long Range Planning*, 31(2): 201–10.

Wheeler, D. and Thomson, J. (2006) 'Business and sustainability: implications for corporate governance theory and practice', in M.J. Epstein and K.O. Hanson (eds) *The Accountable Corporation*, Greenwood: Praeger, 243–70.

Wheeler, D., Colbert, B. and Freeman, R.E. (2003) 'Focusing on value: reconciling corporate social responsibility, sustainability and a stakeholder approach in a network world', *Journal of General Management*, 28(3): 1–28.

Chapter 4

Synthesizing governance themes from political and management theory

Suzanne Benn, Dexter Dunphy and Andrew Griffiths

INTRODUCTION

In this chapter we explore, both theoretically and empirically, how the relationship between political systems and corporate governance practices can be used to progress corporate sustainability. We argue that corporate sustainability is facilitated by 'total responsibility management', as outlined by Waddock *et al*. (2002). Waddock *et al*. 2002 argue that corporate sustainability requires internal corporate governance to move beyond compliance to the holistic approach of 'total responsibility management'.

Specifically, the chapter explores the relative compatibility of the leading democratic systems of economic liberalism and social democracy with the kind of governance that enables and encourages corporate adoption and progressive development of a 'total responsibility management' system. An internal governance system of this kind is a set of values-based and interdependent management practices (Waddock *et al*. 2002) which incorporate corporate social responsibility, in terms of both human resource and community relations practices, and environmental sustainability.

For this new system of management to emerge and develop fully, a new societal and political system of governance is also required (see for example Sundaramurthy and Lewis 2003) that will support and encourage corporations to accord with the standards and demands of a range of stakeholders. We suggest the process of stakeholder engagement itself can lead to more reflexive and responsive corporate behaviour (Chapter 1). As a number of theorists and practitioners argue, participation in inter-organizational and multiple stakeholder arrangements and networks can encourage the development of a more-values based managerial approach to corporate sustainability (McIntosh 2002; Dunphy *et al*. 2003; Chapter 3, this publication). This philosophy stands in contrast to the current orthodoxy of shareholder primacy – a view which is based on agency theory and a philosophy of individualism (Sternberg 2000). Our argument is that because corporations now exercise social governance far beyond their economic function, they have an ethical responsibility to respond to the expectations of a variety of stakeholders (Stanfield and Carroll 2004). However changes in the political and societal systems of governance are necessary to generate the conditions which will support corporations adopting 'total responsibility management'.

A number of corporations are now moving to a stage of sustainability that can be termed 'compliance plus', defined as going beyond governmental regulation to a state of reaching compliance with conditions set by other stakeholders such as environmental organizations, industry associations, inter-sector alliances, partnership arrangements and community participation committees (Roome 1992; Dunphy *et al.* 2003). Fundamentally, 'compliance plus' is the condition of governance, or 'the structures, processes and relationships involved in exercising authority within an organization' (Stewart and Jones 2003: 11) that enable it to move towards 'total responsibility management'. The trend towards 'compliance plus' involves the emergence of new forms of governance external to the organization but yet affecting its internal codes of operation and behaviour. This raises the issue of which political traditions of representative democracy are best fitted to support this new stage of corporate sustainability and thus foster the widespread adoption of 'total responsibility management'?

ECONOMIC LIBERALISM, SOCIAL DEMOCRACY AND SUSTAINABILITY GOVERNANCE

The two leading forms of representative democracy in today's world are economic liberalism and social democracy; together they currently dominate Western political thought and compete for allegiance. Which of these democratic traditions provides the inter-organizational and multiple stakeholder conditions necessary for the widespread adoption of the holistic approach of 'total responsibility management'?

Economic liberalism is generally associated with a commitment to preserving individual freedoms and property rights, small government, free enterprise and market fundamentalism. As a philosophy, it is supported by the individualist principles of public choice theory (Pierson 1993; Giddens 1998). In this view, only 'limited government can be decent government' (Hayek quoted in Pierson 1993) and only the free market can respond adequately to the choices made by human beings as free, purposeful creatures (Bellamy 1999). As far as governance is concerned, economic liberalism argues that the state is legitimated through its creation and maintenance of the free market. As far as sustainability is concerned, the state is not based on a system of ethical principles that justify 'self-limitation' in order to reduce consumption, or that question the long-term effects of technologically driven capitalism (Bauman 1993).

Consequently proponents of economic liberalism do not see the state playing a major role in supporting sustainability – they expect private sector corporations to advance the cause of sustainability by using market mechanisms. The state is seen as having only a secondary role in supporting sustainability – its role is to ensure the maintenance of a free market. The achievement of a low-impact, decentralized society and empowered communities and employees is left to market mechanisms and therefore, logically, to actions by corporations.

In some ways, economic liberalism is compatible with a situation where corporations participate in an active civil society through the formation of inter-organizational and multiple stakeholder relationships. Ideologically, economic liberalism prioritizes the 'relationships and activities of civil society' (Beetham1993: 60). Political programmes based on this ideology also favour approaches designed to limit the state and to foster individualism and volunteerism. Such approaches encourage the development of corporate–NGO relationships. Yet economic liberals mount political, ethical and economic arguments against participatory, collaborative arrangements between NGOs and corporations, based variously on a critique of the accountability of NGOs and on corporate responsibility to shareholders.

In sum, the critical question for economic liberalism remains whether the market can effectively influence corporations to undertake actions which support what is, nominally at least, the shared goal of sustainability and whether the market can in fact deliver a sustainable society (Yearley 1996). In nearly a decade and a half since the ideal of global sustainability was given widespread support at Rio, this central question of the compatibility between the market-driven organization and sustainability remains unanswered (Jermier *et al*. 2006).

In contrast to economic liberalism, social democracy is critical of an unfettered free market system and advocates frequent monitoring by citizenry to ensure that market outcomes are just and equitable. Social democracy supports a more interventionist and proactive role for the state to protect collective interests. However these state activities can become bureaucratic, costly and cumbersome. In addition, as a political ideology, social democracy has to date often proved to be less supportive of ecological than human or social sustainability (Eckersley 1992). Neo-revisionist 'social democrats' have moved more recently to broaden the traditional left-wing focus on using state power to reduce class exploitation to protect against environmental exploitation (Giddens 1998; Wright 1999). However, social democracy still depends on bureaucratic rationality as outlined by Max Weber. Consequently, this model in practice can result in fragmented responsibility, lack of accountability, and the specialization of tasks. These factors undermine the interconnectedness that 'green' theorists argue is an essential feature of strong versions of sustainability (see for example Goodin 1992).

Some scholars argue that social democracy can provide the means for scientists, government, corporations and environmentalists to work together to restructure capitalist economies, with the outcome that both industry and the natural environment benefit (Hajer 1995; Mol and Sonnenfeld 2000). They believe that a more powerful, interventionist role for government will create reflexive legal frameworks and incentives to assist corporations to reorient towards both human and ecological sustainability (Orts 2002). Yet again there are limitations and we question whether such 'eco-modernist' perspectives can deliver the fundamental shift in mindset from mainstream business thought and practice required for organizations to support and renew, rather than exploit and degrade, society and the planet. Any reversion to the hard regulatory approach is also likely to result in antagonism from the private sector and can lead to shallow corporate responses, based on simplistic measures of performance, rather than a real change in corporate behaviour.

This short theoretical analysis leads us to the proposition that each of the traditional systems of representative democracy is limited in its capacity to ensure that corporations adopt the principles of 'total responsibility management'. Both forms of democratic political ideology are grounded in theoretical principles that appear incompatible with the organizational requirements of 'total responsibility management' and hence offer little promise for achieving a fully sustainable society.

So our theoretical analysis suggests that both governance systems and their wider politico-ideological bases have limitations when it comes to gaining corporate commitment to the pursuit of 'total responsibility management'. This raises the following question for empirical research: 'What form does the wider political system need to take if this preferred form of corporate governance is to be supported?'

CASE ANALYSIS

To answer this question we look to examples of corporations that are engaging with sustainability issues and, in the process, are involved in inter-organizational or multiple stakeholder relationships. Analysis of these situations should reveal the emergence of elementary forms of the governance systems needed to ensure corporate practices leading eventually to 'total responsibility management'. We may also be able to discern what changes in the wider political system would facilitate the development and adoption of these characteristics.

We summarize three case studies that we have researched in detail. Material for the case studies has been obtained through documentary analysis, semi-structured interviews and participant observation. Each of these case studies has been reported in more detail elsewhere (Benn 2002, 2004, Benn and Dunphy 2004; Benn and Onyx 2005). Here we examine in particular the corporate behaviour which progresses the organizations towards an internal governance system of 'total responsibility management'. The first case outlines how the Australian firm, Orica Pty Ltd, has gone about managing the largest stockpile in the world of the highly toxic organochlorine waste hexachlorbenzene or HCB. HCB is a suspected carcinogen and classified as a 'persistent organic pollutant' under the Stockholm Treaty. The second case describes a multiple stakeholder arrangement involving the Landcare organization in Australia, a network-based organization designed to contribute to environmental sustainability on the ground as well as lead to increased corporate awareness of sustainability criteria. The third is a study of how the executives of the Fuji Xerox Eco Manufacturing Centre in Sydney transformed their system of industrial production and, in particular, what part of this process involved developing new relationships with community organizations and government.

Case 1: Orica and toxic waste

The case of a massive stockpile of highly toxic waste stored on the shores of Botany Bay, Sydney, illustrates the difficulties that some organizations and industry sectors have in reaching the 'compliance plus' stage and implementing 'total responsibility management' systems. The case also highlights the challenges posed for democratic governance systems in managing complex environmental problems, many of which are associated with high levels of uncertainty.

For three decades controversy has raged about what to do with this huge stockpile of the highly toxic organochlorine waste HCB. Ten thousand tonnes of solid and liquid HCB is stored in 60,000 drums in a specially-built shed above ground and under the car park at the Botany plant of what is now Orica Pty Ltd. Orica acquired the HCB stockpile when it took over a substantial part of ICI Ltd Australia's Botany operations. The HCB was produced as a by-product of the manufacture of solvents during the period 1963–91. The Botany area was previously industrial but since the 1980s has become increasingly residential. By the mid-1980s enough public concern had been expressed about the dangers of the waste for ICI Ltd Australia to halt the production process at its Sydney plant responsible for generating the waste. By the late 1980s there had been many attempts to resolve the problem of such toxic organochlorine wastes. Industry, led by ICI Ltd, strongly supported high-temperature incineration as a solution (McDonell 1997). In this case, more than 30 failed attempts to site a high-temperature incinerator were made – and rejected by local communities.

Then an inter-governmental decision recommended that alternative, emerging technologies and decentralized solutions to the disposal of the toxic waste should be prioritized rather than the building of a centralized waste-disposal facility (McDonell 1997). There was extensive consultation and the government's wide reaching and detailed requirements for ongoing consultative decision-making included provision for a Community Participation and Review Committee (CPRC) (Lloyd-Smith 2001). The CPRC is a multiple-stakeholder arrangement, including local community groups, environmentalist organizations, local council and other corporations. Eventually carefully drawn-up Waste Management Plans were legislated for in 1996 by the national government, requiring the waste at Botany to be destroyed by 2006.

Orica now has responsibility for the HCB and its site manager has been named as Custodian of the Waste, although the CPRC was also legislated for to advise and review the decision-making on destruction of the waste. The role of this Committee is stipulated to facilitate communications between the community, the NSW Environment Protection Agency (EPA) and Orica and to advise them on relevant proposals, including the monitoring and evaluation of the management plan for the destruction of the waste. Since its formation in 1996, the Committee has met approximately three times per year and produces its own newsletter.

Orica's Environmental Impact Statement (EIS) proposal to destroy the waste on site using Geomelt technology was opposed by community representatives on the CPRC and prompted a large number of submissions in opposition. In response the government called a Commission of Inquiry, which recommended destruction on site. But after considerable protest from a number of stakeholders and with the issue gaining increasing publicity, another attempt was made to resolve the dispute by implementing an Independent Panel to examine the case. The Panel recommended that disposal at a regional site would be preferable to disposal at Botany (Frew 2005). At time of writing (2006) Orica is seeking expressions of interest from local governments outside metropolitan Sydney in the location of a plant to destroy the HCB and the firm has declared its intentions to improve its community consultation practices (Brown 2006).

In the meantime the waste remains stored at Botany in the anticipation of approval of a suitable destruction site. Nearly a decade after the Plan was drawn up, there has been no final decision made as to how and where the HCB is to be destroyed. How do we explain this stalemate and apparent failure of what was so widely seen as appropriate governance structures and policies to address the issue?

Initially, government, radical environmentalists and industry specialists in Australia applauded the Waste Management Plans as an unprecedented success (Brown 1999). Yet community representatives on the CPRC came to express considerable mistrust in both Orica and the government. A key issue explaining this shift in relations appears to be the lack of interest by NSW Government in CPRC matters and, in particular, its refusal to fund independent experts to sit on the CPRC. The expert advice given on relative merits of on- and offsite destruction technologies was paid for by Orica. Lacking equivalent financial resources, the community groups opposing the proposed technology were unable to draw on equivalent techno-scientific expertise to test the company's case (Brown 1999; Jensen-Lee 2003). However, the local community itself has developed considerable knowledge of the various suggested disposal technologies. Hence the community groups are suspicious of the conclusions reached, which favour Orica's position supporting disposal on site (Brown 1999). But underpinning and compounding this suspicion is a long history of mistrust between Orica and the local community, rooted in a record of non-transparency associated with a number of safety incidents at the Botany site (Benn 2002).

Greenpeace, also represented on the CPRC, has been somewhat silenced in the debate as a result of its long-term opposition to transportation of toxic waste and its resulting support of disposal on site, a position which the community opposes. We can see an attempt to implement appropriate governance measures for the disposal of the waste has been immobilized by the competing demands of community and corporation and by the scientific uncertainty associated with the disposal of such a large quantity of the HCB – a situation for which there is no precedent.

Although the NSW government did attempt to put new governance systems in place to manage the waste, its actions highlight the limitations of pluralist systems in terms of ensuring the equitable and inclusive decision-making across interest groups that is necessary if trusting multiple stakeholder or inter-organizational arrangements are to develop and such stalemates are to be avoided. There is a need for governments to resource community groups so that they can communicate in a more positive fashion with techno-scientific and corporate stakeholders. Only by giving citizens access to expertise so that they can challenge corporate/techno-scientific hegemony can some corporations be persuaded to move to compliance plus and a full range of technological solutions to such problems be effectively canvassed. The effect of treating unequals equally, a typical feature of both current systems of pluralist representative democracy, is not enough to ensure legitimate governance in these disputes (Jensen-Lee 2003). The 'community' will no longer give hired experts, or the other traditional institutions of authority, unlimited credibility (Beck 1992).

In summary, the Orica case shows up the broad shortcomings of pluralist forms of democracy, shared by both leading interpretations. We suggest that an alternative governance system which draws on the principles of deliberative democracy could enable more positive outcomes from such attempts at multiple stakeholder decision-making and dialogue. Luskin and Fishkin (2004: 1) define the processes of deliberative democracy as follows:

> Deliberating citizens seek relevant information, reflect on the issues, and exchange views with others. The most valuable kind of deliberation is balanced, taking account of information both convenient and inconvenient to given arguments and alternatives, although much naturally occurring deliberation is of course highly imbalanced.

These writers argue that the focus on deliberation makes citizens better informed and better able to contribute to the critical assessment of policy issues. In short, it increases their political efficacy. In practical terms, applying such decision-making principles to multiple stakeholder arrangements involving corporations and community stakeholders would involve all stakeholders considering relevant information from a number of different perspectives, being given opportunity for critical conversation on the issues in conditions of open and trusting dialogue and then opportunity to reconsider their original opinion (Habermas 1996; Carson 2001).

The Orica case study leads us to question the capacity of the leading forms of pluralist representative democracy to address the need for new forms of civil governance. It also highlights some of the challenges of this new form of governance as corporations attempt to move to 'compliance plus' (Roome 1992; Dunphy *et al.* 2003), and to accord with the standards and demands of a range of stakeholders beyond government. Other researchers have published empirical work indicating that such relationships between corporate and community or NGO groups can develop the capacity to deliver devolved governance and community participation in decision-making (Stewart and Jones 2003), a key requirement of the Rio Declaration. Our next case is a further exploration of the capacity of our traditional forms of pluralist democracy to foster these social processes for active grass roots community involvement in sustainability issues and thus drive the corporate change that will, over the long term, build the capacity of the corporation to achieve a more environmentally and socially responsible position.

Case 2: Landcare in Australia

Our second case involves the Landcare movement in Australia. Landcare is a social movement that fosters cooperation between land managers and farmers with the aim of developing more sustainable natural resource management practices and to restore degraded agricultural lands. Its origins lie in an unlikely partnership formed in the late 1980s between peak farmers' organizations and conservationist groups. The arrangement had strong government support. Since 1988 government funds from the sale of 50 per cent of the national telecommunications facility have been used to subsidize Landcare.

Federal Government funding covers the employment of coordinators for Landcare, whose responsibilities include networking and developing community understanding of environmental issues. State governments also exercise control through a Landcare funding delegation from the federal government. But the Landcare movement is largely volunteer-driven and the system of local Landcare Groups, area Landcare Networks and Landcare Regional Networks have to date remained autonomous organizations with the policy directions of the movement determined according to participatory voting practices at regional, state and national conferences. The local groups have also had considerable autonomy in selection and management, including management of funding, for their Landcare projects. There are 4,500 local Landcare Groups across Australia, and approximately 100,000 members in total.

This volunteer 'army' has widespread public recognition in Australia, and the Landcare logo of two linked green hands has generated strong interest from Australian corporates who see this as an important addition to their branding strategies. Some of the major corporate sponsors in Australia include Alcoa, BHP, Betta Homes, Amcor, Dow Agrosciences, Monsanto, Rio Tinto, Mitre 10, Rice Growers of Australia and Cotton Australia. Tradeoffs are made for the sponsorship arrangement and monitoring of the 'compliance plus' style bargain is done by a committee including a representative of the Australian Conservation Foundation, the peak environmental group in Australia. In one example of 'compliance plus', Mitre 10, a paint manufacturer, was required to place warning environmental health and safety labels on their paints before they could take part in sponsorship arrangements.

In some ways Landcare has been a great success story. It brings together previously diverse, even antagonistic, factions of society into networked relationships. Thus Landcare brings together farming and green interests, and also encompasses bush regeneration, 'tidy towns', Scouts, Rivercare, Dunewatch and numerous other locally understood approaches to sustainability. Landcare networks build new social capital through shared experiences in learning and communication and this form of social capital contributes to the success of networks, strengthening their contribution to ecological sustainability (Sobels *et al*. 2001).

But Landcare also has many critics, both internal and external to the organization. A key theme in the critique is that Landcare's voluntarist basis reflects the determination of an economic liberal regime at the federal level in Australia to shift responsibility away from the state, while providing little real support for local level change for sustainability (Lockie 1999). One result is the high 'burn-out' of local Landcare leaders (Lockie 1999). Our own research has indicated that many local groups see corporate support for Landcare as greenwash rather than a positive example of multiple stakeholder collaboration to support sustainability through a system of 'compliance plus'. The great majority of local Landcarers that we interviewed perceived corporates are only interested in high-visibility Landcare projects that have obvious branding and marketing benefits.

Others argue that the decentralization and local independence and autonomy of the movement have made it ecologically irrational, characterized by lack of planning and accountability (Cary and Webb 2000). In tune with this critique, the state governments in Australia (largely the Labor Party) have moved to bureaucratize and standardize the local Landcare group. Pressures have been placed on the local groups to be more accountable to the Landcare regional offices. The effect has been the emergence of two competing 'story lines' of Landcare (Hajer 1995; Benn and Onyx 2005). The discourses of the competing 'story lines' are contrasted in Table 4.1.[1]

Table 4.1 *The competing discourses of Landcare*

Discourse at the local level	*Discourse at the bureaucratic level*
Landcare Coordinator	Community Support Officer
Local	Regional, corporate
Landcare	Landcare
Holistic	Strategic
Farm	Catchment
Local awareness raising	Priority projects

The research in this case tracing the emergence of these 'story lines' indicates that the Landcare inter-organizational domain is in fact two quite distinctive decision-making arenas whose relationship is characterized by a number of tensions. The bureaucratic decision-making arena contains the formally constituted, tightly organized bureaucracies such as state and federal government departments, catchment management authorities and corporations, including the corporate marketing arm of Landcare, Landcare Australia Limited. These organizations are in a 'discourse coalition' with natural resource management professionals and a number of academics who have made the social and political aspects of natural resource management their academic sphere of expertise. This coalition has formed around the general argument that 'local' Landcare should only be an aspect of wider catchment management and planning.

The other arena is the local arena. It contains the members of looser community-based networks, the local Landcare groups and the local Landcare network coordinators, local government officers, local business organizations, academics and other actors who support the grass-roots approach. This coalition has formed around the perception that change for sustainability emanates from basic community-building processes that develop and recognize the success of small, local projects.

The discursive struggle between these two arenas expressed in the 'story lines' show Weberian bureaucratic practices challenging the participatory, bottom-up decision-making of the local Landcare groups. But the segmented Landcare arena also highlights the negative impacts that a purely market-driven approach can have on multiple stakeholder arrangements. Instead of Landcare networks bringing corporations into a learning situation through grassroots contact with sustainability initiatives, corporate relations with the community are filtered through the marketing arm of the organization. As a result, the large corporations find themselves restricted to the bureaucratic arena even if they wish to engage with local Landcare. In the words of one senior manager of Fuji Xerox, a leading sponsor of Landcare: 'we found it hard to get down to the local groups; in the end we were disappointed that more of our staff did not get involved' (Cavanagh-Downs in Benn 2002).

This case illustrates the limitations of governance principles associated with both systems of pluralist democracy in managing ecological issues. Interventionist and bureaucratic intent by government has marginalized local landcarers and polarized expert and lay knowledge and in so doing negated some of the initial success of Landcare in building the social capital so necessary in rural communities. At the same time, the voluntarist and privatization policy-making of the Australian federal government has 'burnt out' and further marginalized the community base of Landcare. As with the Orica case, issues of lack of trust again emerge to prevent better outcomes in terms of opportunities for corporate learning and sustainability from potential 'compliance plus' style arrangements.

We argue that Landcare is an example of the multi-faceted collaborative arrangement which has real potential to facilitate corporations moving towards 'total responsibility management'. However we see that both the neo-liberal and social democratic intentions for Landcare are inappropriate to the long-term survival of a grass-roots based inter-organizational arrangement which has major potential to deliver change for sustainability in the corporate partners. Neither appears to deliver conditions enabling more trusting relations between diverse stakeholders. As well, both Orica and Landcare examples raise the issue of the role of autonomous organizations such as community-based groups and NGOs in democracies. Landcare, for example, supplies essential structural support for sustainability at the grass-roots level, and may facilitate learning and awareness raising, leading to corporate sustainability.

Our next case deals with the issue of relationships between corporates in the inter-organizational domain. What political systems facilitate learning or dialogue concerning sustainability between corporates across this domain, enabling them to implement 'total responsibility management'? What role do other organizational forms play in this process?

Case 3: Fuji Xerox Eco Manufacturing Centre, Sydney

According to the Dunphy *et al.* phase model (2003), the Fuji Xerox Eco Manufacturing Centre in Sydney clearly demonstrates the characteristics of Proactive Strategic Sustainability – that is, successful implementing of product and process redesign that accords with pollution prevention and product stewardship (Benn and Dunphy 2004). It is, of course, only one plant within the large multinational Fuji Xerox company but there are seven similar plants worldwide which are an integral part of the company's push for sustainability. Fuji Xerox took the decisions to lease not sell its equipment, to produce only waste-free products and to develop manufacturing processes that dramatically reduce its environmental footprint. The Sydney plant represents the leading edge of these reforms.

The company leases rather than sells office equipment and services it. As component defects occur, service personnel return the equipment to the plant, where parts are replaced, often with remanufactured and redesigned components. There is no waste to landfill; any unusable parts are recycled. By retrieving virtually all their products, not only is valuable equipment reused rather than thrown away, but systematic performance data are gathered and used to improve product design. For example, the redesign of a five cent spring on a roller doubled the roller's life, saving the company millions of dollars worldwide. What was once waste, for example carbon retrieved from machines, is now extracted into sealed canisters and used by BHP Steel in the steelmaking process. Rather than the new plant and processes being an expensive luxury, savings in the plant (after amortization of the plant and equipment) were $22.5m in 2000–2001 and have increased in each subsequent year. The plant is now exporting to seven other countries in Asia and negotiating eco manufacturing contracts with other industries. From a stakeholder view, the new plant has benefited the community by eliminating wastes to air, land and water and has created positive relationships with other organizations such as research and teaching institutions.

Which system of democracy supports innovation of this kind and the diffusion amongst corporations of successful practices that are a win-win for all parties? It is significant that Fuji Xerox should be the company that has put the new policies in place. Its Japanese ownership is very conscious of Japanese legislation that now prohibits disposal of whitegoods and office equipment into landfill. The company has to meet these requirements in Japan and anticipates similar moves elsewhere in the world – already similar legislation is in place in some European countries. It has therefore determined to develop competitive advantage by innovating in sustainable products and production processes. We understand that the Australian plant is, however, the most advanced plant globally and there is no legislation in Australia requiring this level of sustainable operations. The reason for the leadership emerging in Australia appears to be the result of the personal enthusiasm for sustainability of two highly competent managers and the more generalist skill sets required in what is necessarily a smaller group of technical specialists in a plant serving a smaller market than say the US or Japan. This made it easier to rethink the production process in a holistic way. The strategy at the plant is very knowledge based. Each remanufacturing operation increases the technical understanding of the employees in the complex machine technologies.

However, the current economic liberal regime of the Australian federal government means that the government exhibits little interest in the important implications of what the plant has achieved. If these principles were systematically extended to other Australian manufacturing operations, foreign debt could be reduced as fewer imports of manufactured goods would be required and exports would be stimulated as remanufactured goods were exported. An economic liberal government regards this as a matter for the free market to sort out. So far, there appears to be little evidence of systematic diffusion of these initiatives to other companies.

We note this situation is symptomatic of a recurring pattern of failed innovation adoption and diffusion in Australia. Earlier works by Dunphy and Griffiths (1998) and Griffiths and Zammuto (2005) demonstrate that innovative approaches to work organization, technology adoption and innovation have not been supported by macro governance structures, rather the adoption of these innovations has been left to market forces. Under the system of governance Griffiths and Zammuto (2005) have classified as market governance, innovation capabilities are left to individual firms to develop, as is the case of Fuji Xerox. Choices over innovation and technology upgrades are left to corporate managers and managerial hierarchies. Such innovation systems are vulnerable to variations in individual firm performance and may not provide sustainable competitive outcomes and certainly impact on the ability of corporations to attain widespread 'total responsibility management'.

We conclude then that Fuji Xerox Eco Manufacturing Centre is an example of an individual success story, its innovations reflecting the drive of committed individuals inside the organization. We do not see 'compliance plus' in evidence in this case. As we noted in the Landcare case study, more active participation by Fuji Xerox employees in the Landcare networks, which could have assisted in embedding sustainability values across the Fuji Xerox organization, was thwarted by the segmentation of Landcare into two discourse arenas. This limited interaction between corporate and local elements of Landcare.

DISCUSSION

Each of the studies discussed above highlights the deficiencies of the prevailing paradigms of economic liberalism and social democracy. The three cases we present illustrate the theoretically identified deficiencies of each of these systems and reinforce our arguments that each lacks the capacity to support corporate total responsibility management. Our view is that the outworn political themes of traditional forms of social democracy and economic liberalism are not confronting the public with the need to decide what sort of society and natural environment is needed to support a sustainable world. The current form of pluralist representative democracy does not challenge corporations to move into the 'compliance plus' phase of our model. The economic liberal tradition is limited by its individualist ideology and the sanctity given to the market in decision-making processes; likewise the social democratic tradition is limited by a tendency to bureaucratization and commitment to top-down planning. Both create conditions that make it difficult to achieve the widespread acceptance and development of 'total responsibility management' governance systems.

The stalemate in decision-making and the discursive struggle characterizing respectively the Orica and Landcare case studies point to trust as a critical element in the development of multiple-stakeholder arrangements that encourage corporations to move to 'compliance plus' and thus to the implementation of the internal governance system of 'total responsibility management'. The cases also reflect the lack of public trust facing both systems of pluralist representative democracy as each political system reveals itself to be programmatically limited by its ideological origins. As well, each is limited by the pluralist tendency to treat unequal interest groups as equals. We have introduced the concept of deliberative dialogue as an alternative method of decision-making that could assist in building trust between interest and stakeholder groups in this context.

Our cases highlight that a particular issue for social democratic governments is the 'revolving door' relationship which fosters exchange of experts between industry and government; it is the experts, after all, who bear the responsibility for assessing highly uncertain risks and developing appropriate systems of compliance. The events of the Orica case show that the exchange compromises the likelihood of independent and objective appraisal of risks (Adams 2001) and marginalizes other stakeholders. While highlighting the importance of organizations like Greenpeace in drawing public critique into environmental disputes, the Orica case also points to the need for NGOs to contextualize their response. In this case, Greenpeace was acting in its global role and thus took its established position of opposition to transporting waste generated in one place to another for disposal. The community representatives could therefore be readily branded as NIMBY ('Not In My Backyard').

The Landcare case reveals the tendency for multiple-stakeholder arrangements to segment into opposing discourse arenas as a result of pressures emanating from the wider political system. With this case, there are clearly very different modes of discourse adopted by the various stakeholders. These different forms of discourse reflect the operations of Landcare as a segmented organizational domain consisting of two communicative arenas, concerning the interpretation of sustainability in relation to natural resource management. One arena is very tightly structured, the other very decentralized. Each needs the other but the fundamentally different discourses in each arena reflect different rationalities and make communication difficult.

A major source of tension is the emerging challenge to the local knowledge and capacity that has developed in association with the bottom-up process of community-based decision-making and face-to-face consensus negotiation in decentralized networks. This is currently threatened by top-down concerns over accountability and ecological irrationality, and challenged by bureaucratic understandings of the whole of catchment planning, involving centralized decision-making and funding. It seems both our political systems are failing Landcare: the one, demanding more rational planning and accountability; the other, giving little onground support. We see the effects in the disappointing relationship between Fuji Xerox and Landcare. We raise the question whether, without the broader stakeholder pressures of 'compliance plus', Fuji Xerox's committed managers will be able to implement and maintain the organization-wide values-based changes required for 'total responsibility management' and corporate sustainability.

All three cases reflect the sustainability challenges for government. In order to assess and manage the social and environmental risk associated with continued corporate activity, governments of all types now find themselves in public access forums and a variety of multiple stakeholder arrangements, constructed around ideas of participative democracy, individualized responsibility and active citizenship. The cases raise questions concerning the efficacy of such multiple stakeholder or inter-organizational arrangements in achieving effective decisions and in providing learning opportunities around sustainability. Do they have an inherent tendency to stalemate as in the Orica case, partly due to a perceived lack of equal access to expert knowledge and other resources, or is their functionality limited by conflict between different discursive understandings, as with Landcare? Would more emphasis on deliberative decision-making and consultation between stakeholders alleviate conflicts and resolve stalemates?

The Fuji Xerox case highlights another issue which relates to the lack of a more structured interorganizational domain within which the corporation could share its understandings of the culture of innovation. It highlights the programmatic incompatibility between economic liberal regimes and any system which might intervene to support technological diffusion for more sustainable business. It is hard to see how such policies of non-intervention could support the corporate–NGO relationships, the communities of practice or the introduction of the reflexive regulation necessary to institutionalize sustainability concerns into the everyday decision-making of business (Orts 1995).

This study also points to the relevance of recent work by Griffiths and Zammuto (2005) in understanding governance systems that may lead to corporate sustainability. These researchers argue that a focus on institutional governance systems could expand our understanding of innovation diffusion and adoption mechanisms by focusing on the intersection of state and industry activities to coordinate decision-making and economic activity. Their work distinguishes between market governance and state governance systems, which roughly equate to what we have called the economic liberal and social democratic approaches. Griffiths and Zammuto have shown that each of these political systems has a different set of capabilities and abilities to adapt responsively to changes in the vital factors for economic competitiveness in their markets. They show how the use of market forces by governance institutions to effect change discourages parties from coming together to negotiate outcomes or set industry priorities and directions. It also follows that innovation capabilities are either determined by interest group strength or are left to individual firms to develop for themselves. As we noted above, such a system may not only retard future economic growth performance (Griffiths and Zammuto 2005) but limit the application of 'total responsibility management' by corporations.

Finally, democratic systems must foster the decision-making conditions of 'compliance plus' and align them with the demands of a new arena of society where sustainability will be the focus of critical debate and action. It is in this self-determining, multiple-stakeholder and collaborative arena that corporations can develop the flexible relationships necessary for building, sharing and diffusing the tacit knowledge that can be transferred into innovative solutions for sustainability. The new discourse of 'active citizenship' or 'community' is seen to be vividly expressed in the Australian context by the local discourse coalition of the Landcare movement, representing a synthesizing of the ideas of individualist political theory and communitarianism, a rethinking of the relationship between the state, the corporation and the civil sector. The challenges in developing this new arena as a viable and ongoing decision-making forum is evident in both Landcare and Orica studies.

The pluralist assumption is that democracy is enabled because groups with more interest in the outcomes from a decision should have more influence in the decision-making process. However, this is not appropriate in the ad hoc, decentralized, multiple-stakeholder relationships now characterizing the corporate interface with society. The expanding role of science in environmental decision-making (Orts 2002) is clearly evident in all three of the cases discussed here. With Landcare and Orica, the issue becomes local access to this expertise. Currently pluralist systems cannot deliver this access and thus enable the vibrant civil sector essential for the development of the reflexive inter-organizational domain.

CONCLUSION

The case studies specifically indicate that the dominant political systems of democracy are incompatible with the reflexive management of corporations. We argue for the establishment of new structures providing for systems of corporate governance in order to encompass the widening group of organizational stakeholders at the 'sub-political' level. For a total responsibility management system of management to emerge, forms of reflexive regulation (Orts 2002; Matten and Crane 2005), are required. Their effect is the development of negotiation and communication across multiple stakeholders. This process of development will foster the self-critique necessary for an organization to be 'totally responsible' and hence sustainable.

We conclude that the different forms of democracy need to be constructed to support the redesign of corporations around sustainability. However we still lack a clear understanding of the connecting links that must be built between governments, corporations and the community if we are to create a sustainable world.

NOTE

1 Hajer describes discourse coalitions as groups of actors who take up a similar interpretation of a multi-interpretable concept. Development of a 'story line' by this coalition requires a certain loss of meaning as other interpretations of the concept are discarded in the process of language interaction. The discourse becomes hegemonic when it is translated into policies (Hajer 1995).

REFERENCES

Adams, W.M. (2001) *Green Development*, 2nd edn, London: Routledge.

Bauman, Z. (1993) *Postmodern Ethics*, Oxford: Basil Blackwell.

Beck, U. (1992) (trans. Mark Ritter) *The Risk Society*, London: Sage.

Beetham, D. (1993) 'Liberal democracy and the limits of democratisation', in D. Held (ed.) *Prospects for Democracy*, 9th edn, Cambridge: Polity Press, pp. 55–73.

Bellamy, R. (1999) 'Liberalism', in R. Eatwell and A. Wright (eds) *Contemporary Political Ideologies*, London: Pinter, pp. 23–50.

Benn, S. (2002) Interview with Graham Cavanagh-Downs, Australian Director Production and Supply, Fuji Xerox, Sydney, May 2002.

Benn, S. (2004) 'Managing toxic chemicals in Australia: a regional analysis of the risk society', *Journal of Risk Research*, 7(4): 399–412.

Benn, S. and Dunphy, D. (2004) 'A case of strategic sustainability: the Fuji Xerox Eco Manufacturing Centre', Special issue, Corporate Sustainability and Innovation: Governance, Development, Strategy and Method, *International Journal for Innovation Research, Policy Analysis and Best Practice*, 6(2): 258–68.

Benn, S. and Onyx, J. (2005) 'Negotiating interorganizational domains: the politics of social, natural and symbolic capital', in A. Dale and J. Onyx (eds) *Social Capital and Sustainability in Local Communities – What is the link?* Vancouver: UBC Press, pp. 87–104.

Brown, P. (1999) 'Our affair with hexachorbenzene: a case study in Australian chemicals management' , paper presented at The Environment: Risks and Opportunities, Third Annual International Public Policy and Social Science Conference, St Catherine's College, Oxford, 28–30 June 1999.

Brown, P. (2006) 'Toxic waste in our midst', draft paper, under review for Special issue, Toxic Risk and Governance, *Journal of Environmental Management*.

Carson, L. (2001) 'Innovative consultation processes and the changing role of activism', *Third Sector Review*, 7(1): 7–22.

Cary, J. and Webb, T. (2000) *Landcare, the National Landcare Program and the Landcare Movement: The Social Dimensions of Landcare*, Canberra: Bureau of Rural Sciences, Agriculture, Forestry and Fisheries.

Dunphy, D. and Griffiths, A. (1998) *The Sustainable Corporation*, Sydney: Allen and Unwin.

Dunphy, D., Griffiths, A. and Benn, S. (2003) *Organizational Change for Corporate Sustainability*, London: Routledge.

Eckersley, R. (1992) *Environmentalism and Political Theory*, Albany: State University of New York Press.

Frew, W. (2005) 'Toxic waste plant is up for grabs', *Sydney Morning Herald*, 25 October, p. 4.

Giddens, A. (1998) *The Third Way*, Cambridge: Polity Press.

Goodin, R. (1992) *Green Political Theory*, Cambridge: Polity Press.

Griffiths, A. and Zammuto, R. (2005) 'Institutional governance systems and variations in national competitive advantage', *Academy of Management Review*, 30(4): 823–42.

Habermas, J. (1996) *Between Facts and Norms: Contributions to a Discourse Theory of Law and Democracy*, Cambridge, MA: MIT Press.

Hajer, M. (1995) *The Politics of Environmental Discourse: Ecological Discourse and the Policy Process*, Oxford: Oxford University Press.

Jensen-Lee, C. (2003) 'Orica, HCB and geomelt: The Commission of Inquiry for Environment and Planning into Orica's proposal to build a HCB waste destruction facility at Botany using geomelt technology', Working Paper, School of Social Science and Policy, UNSW, Sydney.

Jermier, J., Forbes, L., Benn, S. and Orsato, R. (2006) 'Beyond the new corporate environmentalism' in S. Clegg, C. Hardy, W. Nord and T. Lawrence (eds) *Handbook of Organization Studies*, London: Sage.

Lloyd-Smith, M. (2001) 'HCB community information system'. Online. Available at: http://www.oztoxics.org/ (accessed 5 January 2002).

Lockie, S. (1999) 'Community movements and corporate images: "Landcare" in Australia', *Rural Sociology*, 64(2): 219–33.

Luskin, R and Fishkin, J. (2004) 'Deliberation and better citizens', Centre for Deliberative Democracy, Stanford University. Online. Available at: http://cdd.stanford.edu/research/index.html (accessed 4 October 2004).

McDonell, G. (1997) 'Scientific and everyday knowledge: trust and the politics of everyday initiatives', *Social Studies of Science*, 27: 819–63.

McIntosh, M. (2002) *Living Corporate Citizenship: Strategic Routes to Socially Responsible Business*, Harlow: Financial Times, Prentice Hall.

Matten, D. and Crane, A. (2005) 'Corporate citizenship: toward an extended theoretical conceptualization' *Academy of Management Review*, 30(1): 166–80.

Mol, A. and Sonnenfeld, D. (eds) (2000) *Ecological Modernisation Around the World: Perspectives and Critical Debates*, London: Frank Cass.

Orts, E. (1995) 'Reflexive environmental law', *Northwestern University Law Review*, 89: 1227–340.

Orts, E. (2002) 'Environmental law with Chinese characteristics', *William and Mary Bill of Rights Journal*, 11: 545–68.

Pierson, C. (1993) 'Democracy, markets and capital: are there necessary economic limits to democracy?' in D. Held (ed.), *Prospects for Democracy*, Cambridge: Polity Press, pp. 179–99.

Roome, N. (1992) 'Developing environmental management strategies', *Business Strategy and the Environment*, 1: 11–24.

Sobels, J., Curtis, A. and Lockie, S. (2001) 'The role of Landcare group networks in rural Australia: exploring the contribution of social capital', *Journal of Rural Studies*, 17: 265–78.

Stanfield, J. and Carroll, M. (2004) 'Governance and the legitimacy of corporate power: a path for convergence of heterodox economics?', *Journal of Economic Issues*; 38(2): 363–71.

Sternberg, E. (2000) 'How the strategic framework for UK company law reform undermines corporate governance' *Hume Papers on Public Policy*, 8: 54–73.

Stewart, J. and Jones, G. (2003) *Renegotiating the Environment*, Annandale, Sydney: The Federation Press.

Sundaramurthy, C. and Lewis, M. (2003) 'Control and collaboration: paradoxes of governance', *Academy of Management Review*, 28(3): 397–416.

Waddock, S., Bodwell, C. and Graves, S. (2002) *Academy of Management Executive*, 16(2): 132–49.

Wright, A. (1999) 'Social democracy and democratic socialism' in R. Eatwell and A. Wright (eds), *Contemporary Political Ideologies*, London: Pinter, pp. 80–103.

Yearley, S. (1996) *Sociology, Environmentalism and Globalization*, London: Sage.

Chapter 5

Towards a model of governance for sustainability

Networks, shared values and new knowledge

Andrew Martin, Suzanne Benn, Dexter Dunphy

INTRODUCTION

There are problems with adapting established models of governance to create a useful model of sustainable governance. In this chapter we suggest most models of governance are unsuitable for adaptation to governance for sustainability because of their failure to accommodate elements of change that lead to the generation of new knowledge. We suggest standard models of governance cannot accommodate this key dimension because they either focus too narrowly on organizational longevity; or they demonstrate a normative bias, advocating 'governance' as opposed to 'government' as an end in itself; or they are not readily susceptible to application in a range of organizational contexts.[1]

An appropriate starting point in our exploration of these criticisms is a broad model of 'governance' developed by Bressers and Kuks (2003), which anticipates the dynamics of change relevant to sustainability. The broad model has the advantage of facilitating comparisons of coordination and control mechanisms for sustainable practice across disciplines and organizational contexts.

The chapter reports on our field-based research which explores this model. In order to understand how and why factors were selected for study, and the relevance of the conclusions, it is necessary to examine the dynamics of change for sustainability discussed above.

GOVERNANCE FOR SUSTAINABILITY AS A MODEL OF CHANGE

Fostering sustainability necessarily involves fundamental changes in practices and resource use. What we did in the past has not worked, and given what little we know about the future, it is possible that the human species is rapidly approaching, or has already exceeded, the notional limits of its capacity to survive (see, generally, Flannery 2005). Exactly what we should do in the future to correct, and prevent continuation or repetition of our errors is highly debatable, but clearly patterns of governance must change to cope with continuing uncertainty and complexity. Sustainability is, in the words of Stephen Dovers, a 'messy, contested process' which involves a 'suite of issues' – resource depletion and degradation; pollution; ecological life support services; society and the human condition (Dovers 2005: 8–9) and its construction and interpretation is highly politicized (Irwin 2001). Despite that 'messiness', it must be accepted that environmental problems are fundamentally social problems which at times take on a moral or ethical character. However, measures to implement social changes required to address these problems have potentially significant economic effects. The intersection of this 'suite' of moral, social, economic and environmental issues in an area where the science is uncertain almost inevitably means key decision-making will be based on essentially political considerations (Dovers 2005: 26, 33) and will require government intervention unless institutions are adapted or developed that provide for 'productive open dialogue' among stakeholders in policy (Rosenbaum and Bressers 2000: 668).

In short, models of governance for sustainability need to concentrate more on change than stability, meaning that existing rules, customs, practices and rights are seen more as the subject matter of governance to be influenced, than as the main business of governance (Bressers and Kuks 2003: 69). Equally, models of governance for sustainability must recognize the limitations of the 'overburdened state' and the consequent need to take advantage of existing social institutions and structures that promote sustainability without heavy handed intervention – it being implicit that social change of this nature cannot simply be legislated.

The challenges of governance for sustainability lie in three broad areas of change and knowledge generation:

1 Innovation: creating innovative perspectives among geographic entities, government institutions and publics incorporated in new interorganizational, cross-scale arrangements.
2 Reconciliation: reconciling existing multilevel governance structures to arrangements based on sustainability principles.
3 Creativity and adaptability: creating scientific, regulatory and economic infrastructures supportive of these governance arrangements (adapted from Bressers and Rosenbaum 2003: 7).

In this chapter we argue that such 'new interorganizational, cross-scale arrangements' that foster innovative perspectives and encourage the creation of new, adaptive infrastructure resonate with Beck's (1995) description of the 'sub-political' arena of decision-making: decision-making operating outside the accepted sphere of representative politics. This chapter explores notions of governance for sustainability in this context.

CATEGORIES OF 'GOVERNANCE' MODELS

Any examination of the literature that uses the word 'governance' reveals a conceptual diversity of definition, use and context – a virtual taxonomy of governance models – that necessitates choices being made to suit any given purpose. Colebatch and Larmour suggest a three-fold categorization of 'governance' definitions – bureaucratic, market and community models (1993). Certainly the categories described by Colebatch and Larmour have at times been advanced as capable of promoting a sustainable future (Dryzek 1997; Livingston *et al.* 2005) and such a general categorization provides a convenient format for illustrating our three general criticisms, which, we argue, militate against the challenges of 'innovation', 'reconciliation' and 'creativity and adaptability' referred to above.[2]

It is not part of our argument that all models are subject to one, or other, or all of these criticisms. Nor do we argue that there are no lessons to be learnt from studies not specifically focused on sustainability. As our case study approach demonstrates, subject to providing an *appropriate* framework for comparison between models (which is at the heart of the problem), studies of inter-organizational cooperation and collaboration in one context may inform on sustainability practice in others. Indeed, that there is a danger of different disciplines re-inventing the wheel if an attempt is not made to develop such interdisciplinary guidelines for sustainable practice.

ORGANIZATIONAL LONGEVITY MODELS

In the social sciences and legal and policy studies, governance models can tend to be simplified 'ideal types', rather than descriptive models of reality (Livingston *et al.* 2005: 34). While these can provide a framework for comparison, such models often describe 'systems' of social institutions that are 'operatively closed' and relatively impervious to change, such as legal or bureaucratic institutions (Teubner 1993: 7, 11, 62; Hernes and Bakken 2003: 1516; Luhmann 2004). Governance for sustainability requires a model that is both cognitively and operatively open.

The inadequacy of the bureaucratic 'command and control' or 'command and implement' model of environmental regulation has been at the forefront of debate over appropriate models for sustainable development at least since the 1960s (Weale 1992). Bureaucratic regimes can work efficiently to preserve environmental balance, but typically they maintain control centrally and operate formally as 'regulators', positioned between 'the people' and their political masters – acting as de facto arbiters for the application of interpretation of norms (such as 'sustainable practice') to particular factual situations, subject only to the threat of review by the courts.[3] The availability of such review is inhibited when those who are aggrieved are deprived of informational resources (often a virtual monopoly of the bureaucracy in regard to environmental assets) or of an appropriate forum for review. Formality, centralization, and the perception of bureaucracies as regulators, not the players they really are, are widely recognized as counter-productive attributes in the complex and uncertain arena of environmental regulation. Equally, the 'pipes and dams' and media-specific or fragmented approaches of command and control regimes do not recognize the need for integration, adaptation and new decentralized forms of public management (Beck 1992; Orts 1995a: 1236; Stewart 1997: 259–60; Cole 2002: 43).

It is not surprising in those circumstances that reform efforts in regard to environmental governance have focused on the legal system, because of its role in supervision of the bureaucracy. Reform legislation frameworks typically delineate objects of the legislation that include sustainability principles, stipulate objects and functions of regulatory authorities, provide for the creation of instruments of management or control, identify relevant criteria for decision-making, and impose duties on statutory authorities. Provisions for enforcement are coupled with investigative and licensing powers of independent or quasi-independent regulatory agencies, subject to the overall supervision of the courts, sometimes under innovative procedures for review (Bates 2000:4). But how does the law apply these principles?

If there is one area where it is possible to generalize about governance models with some impunity, it is the law. Assuming we are discussing stabilized law in a democratic regime, all legal models of governance rest on assumptions that the 'system' is independent, impartial, even-handed and can maintain its own legitimacy. In order to preserve the attribute of disinterested independence, however, law operates by a process described by Luhmann (2004) as 'autopoiesis', the main features of which are self-production of all the components of the system, self-maintenance of the self-producing cycles and self-description (Teubner 1993: 24). In effect law, while 'cognitively open' to suggestions for change, is 'operatively closed' to pressure for change from social forces external to itself (Luhmann 2004). While legislation may force changes to the law, expectations of other social structures must be reinterpreted in terms of legal practice and art. Law may operate reflexively, but the reflexive reaction operates at glacial pace, and maintains its organizational longevity by paying careful regard to preserving its primacy, authority, legitimacy and centrality. New legislation is applied by regulatory agencies, and reviewed in lower courts, all of which insulate superior courts, which make final decisions on application of new norms to factual situations only when they arise on a case-by-case basis. In doing so, superior courts look not to the intent of the legislature, but to the 'legal' meaning of the legislation.

Thus in law, 'sustainability' as an object of legislation or as a criterion for decision-making, becomes an ideal state or aspirational goal like 'justice' – approached and defined through autopoietic stages of chance (conflict), trial-and-error (case law) and reflection (appeals). As Bates says: 'The law is media specific, jurisdiction based, and often lacks appropriate procedures for integration of decision-making . . .' (2000: 33). In the competition for resources, law will tend to ignore primacy (e.g. the choice between the environment and the rights of a private owner) in favour of the familiar legal concept of who bears the cost (Cole 2002: 176–7).

Appreciating the inherent difficulties of applying reformed environmental law, scholars world wide have advocated making the law more adaptable by introducing measures such as negotiated rulemaking, regulation by information, staged implementation, and other measures that fit within the broad category of 'reflexive regulation' (Ayres and Braithwaite 1992; Orts 1995a; Gunningham and Grabovsky 1998; Kleindorfer and Orts 1998; Fiorino 1999, Dryzek 2000; Lyster 2001; Coglianese and Nash 2002; Cole 2002; Farrier *et al.* 2002; Gallagher 2003; Matten 2004). While it is hard to fault the broad thrust of these arguments, it must be recognized that truly reflexive law is in fact yet another 'ideal state' (Teubner 1983, 1993; Orts 1995a, 1995b). Such recommendations provide useful information on how to implement the legal aspects of a system for sustainability, but not how to govern it.

Promotion of organizational longevity is not the sole province of law. The same characteristic can be seen in some models of corporate governance. Corporate models of governance are of course subject to the legal model – corporations do not exist without the law. The artificiality and ineffectiveness of the traditional corporate model of 'transparency, accountability and distribution of responsibility' arises because these terms are, like 'justice' and 'sustainability', open, contestable and readily politicized. The governance structures of Enron would probably have passed all such tests as then interpreted. In part, the fundamental vagueness of this governance terminology stems from a narrow focus on organizational longevity at the expense of consideration of externalities. While arguments might continue about how the duties of directors and managers should be best understood, there can be little doubt that the first reaction of any interested party in a corporation is likely to be to act so as to preserve and prolong the life of the company. In the process, it is possible to observe somewhat perverse 're-translations' of sustainability principles.

Avery (2005: 61), for example, quotes Dr Harald Bergsteiner describing a law that 'governs' organizational sustainability as:

> an enterprise that produces positive outcomes for voluntary stakeholders . . . but negative outcomes for non-contracting parties . . . is only sustainable (a) if no-one holds the enterprise accountable for negative outcomes and (b) until all the negative outcomes of similar firms eventually combine to undermine the entire industry.

Bergsteiner probably intended this law to be qualified by others that he enunciates, but taken literally, it would mean that the person who cut down the second last tree on Easter Island was acting sustainably! Nor is this a totally fabulous example. Holding a corporation 'accountable' (in law, 'liable') for negative outcomes is a function of the courts. Courts will hold a corporation liable only if a causative connection can be established between the acts of the corporation and the negative outcomes. The ability to establish causation, however, can change over time (largely a product of correcting informational deficits). This, of course, was the experience of tobacco companies, asbestos companies, and manufacturers of products such as DDT and CFCs. Belittling, failing to take into account, in reality postponing consideration of externalities in these instances involved in most cases failing to consider implications of the scale and the range of affected parties; a failure to consider the nature of the likely problems; a failure to develop strategies to cope; and ultimately, for some, a failure of adequate resources (capital) to cope with subsequent established liability. The nature of these failures helps to inform on elements for the broad model for change.

NORMATIVE MODELS

Although based to some degree on empirical observation, social science, policy studies and market models tend to reflect a normative view which almost always implies that a limited role for government promotes better governance (Bressers and Kuks 2003: 69). This is a criticism that is often directed at market models. Menell, for example, says of free-market environmentalists that their '[s]anguine view of markets and legal institutions contrasts sharply with their deeply cynical perception of public institutions' (1992).

Governance for sustainability we suggest, does not assume that 'governance without government' (Peters and Pierre 1998) is an end in itself. Rather it assumes that existing practices and use of resources must change if the human species is to survive (Bressers and Kuks 2003: 69; Dovers 2005:3) and must do so in circumstances where continuing uncertainty is inevitable, and continuing learning and innovation is essential (Rosenbaum and Bressers 2000: 668).

Criticisms of the normative nature of market models often arise in the debate that stemmed from the publication of one of the most cited scientific journal articles of recent times – Hardin's paper on the 'Tragedy of the Commons' (1968).[4] The debate aroused by Hardin's allegory stimulated much discussion of privatization as a solution to environmental degradation as opposed to regulation or (unthinkable to Hardin) socialist forms of collective ownership. It was only through privatization, it was argued, that appropriate valuation would be assigned to environmental assets.

Cole (2002) points out that there are many more forms of ownership and management of common pool resources than those considered by Hardin. An ownership regime is important only insofar as it impacts on externalities and transaction costs (Coase 1960). It is not good enough to specify a particular property regime for environmental goods – one must specify what rights and duties the regime entails (Ostrom1990: 22, quoted in Cole 2002: 12). Mixed property/regulatory regimes can be quite adequate for environmental protection: 'In a real sense, all existing property regimes are mixed. *Pure* public and *pure* private property exist only in the imaginations of economists, legal scholars, and political theorists' (Cole 2002: 45 – emphasis in the original).

Cole presents the argument that:

> the quest for optimal solutions in the real world is futile. There is no optimal level of environmental protection in the real world, only a demanded level, reflecting what decision-makers – whether private property owners, groups of resource users,

> stakeholders, voters, elected officials, or government bureaucrats – are willing to pay to achieve it [and:]
>
> that property regime is best which, in the circumstances, would achieve exogenously set societal goals at the lowest total cost, where total cost is the sum of compliance, administrative, and residual pollution or consumption costs.
>
> (Cole 2002: 17, 133)

Cole finds support in Ostrom's seven 'design principles' of 'robust' common property regimes: clearly defined boundaries; rules appropriate to local ecology, economy and institutional conditions; participation of the managed in rule making; monitoring of resource use; a graduated system of sanctions; low-cost systems for resolving conflict; and a common ownership regime recognized and respected by external government (Ostrom 1990, quoted in Cole 2002: 122).

Market models also encounter a more general problem of appropriate evaluation of environmental assets and sustainability. The problem is not simply one of measurement, but of identification and timing. What is being measured, when, and over what period of time? Common pool assets are often valued at nil until their utility is 'discovered' by the market – oil was not valued until the Industrial Revolution for example. The normative expectation of free-market environmentalists appears to be that the market will appropriately value environmental assets when their contribution to *sustainability* is identified. Since Coase (1960), however, it has been appreciated that the difficulty with specifying value for environmental goods and services is the cost of doing so. The reality is that markets have difficulty in defining, let alone deriving concepts of value from sustainability (see the example of defining sustainability as corporate longevity described by Avery above). As Costanza and Patten note, it is possible to separate the problem of defining sustainability from three other, more basic questions:

> 1 What system or subsystems or characteristics of systems persist?
> 2 For how long?
> 3 When do we assess whether the system or subsystem has persisted?
>
> (Costanza and Patten 1995)

Setting aside for the moment the second and third question, their proposed answer to the first of these questions helps to inform on what we should look for in the broad change model:

> A nested hierarchy of systems over a range of time and space scales must be considered (the metasystem). Within the socioeconomic subsystem, a social consensus on desired characteristics which are consistent with the relationship of these subsystems with other subsystems in the hierarchy (notably ecosystems) must be arrived at. These characteristics also function as predictors of what kind of system will actually be sustainable'.
>
> (Costanza and Patten 1995:196)[5]

THE PROBLEM OF ADAPTABILITY OF MODELS

There is a tendency for all governance models to fail to consider characteristics of flexibility, inclusiveness, persistence, purposefulness, and information-sharing, well recognized as providing 'commonality and comparison' in relation to cross-disciplinary analysis of environmental management (Bressers and Rosenbaum 2000, 2003; Haas 2000; Dovers 2003: 5–6[6], 2005: 37; Dunphy *et al.* 2003; Clarke 2004). This is a criticism of models that are historically based, and of the 'ideal types' referred to above, but it can equally apply to community models and indeed to the results of case studies in a range of disciplines. Stakeholder models, for example, are often advanced as a modification of the corporate model that promotes sustainability. These are discussed in more depth in Chapter 1 of this volume by Benn and Dunphy, but for our purposes it is useful to add Orts and Strudler's description of what they perceive as one of the principal limitations of the 'broad model' of stakeholder theory – '"the maddening variety" of who (and what) may count as a legitimate "stakeholder"' (2002: 227).

Integration is well recognized as a particular problem of the cross-disciplinary area of sustainability studies. Models that reflect characteristics of the 'real world' – in the form of existing social institutions and structures identified in studies within a range of disciplines as militating towards cooperation in common resource management, including community models – are not necessarily susceptible, or are perceived as not being susceptible to easy translation into other social or organizational settings. The broad change model, we suggest, offers a means of addressing this issue.

ELEMENTS OF GOVERNANCE

Bearing in mind the challenges of 'innovation', 'reconciliation' and 'creativity and adaptability' described above, Bressers and Kuks (2003: 65–88) set out the principal elements of governance structure as:

1 Level and scale – because governance assumes the *multilevel* character of policy implementation.
2 Actors in the policy network – because governance assumes the *multi-actor* character of implementation.
3 Policy perception and objectives – because it assumes the *multifaceted* character of the problems and objectives of policy implementation.
4 Strategy and instruments – because governance assumes the multi-instrumental character of policy strategies.
5 Responsibilities and resources – because governance assumes a complex *multi-resource base* for implementation.

This can of course be simplified as an approach that specifies in any given situation the answers to the questions 'Where?', 'Who?', 'What?', 'How?', and 'With what?' (Bressers and Kuks 2003: 71, 73–4).

Bressers and Kuks emphasize that interaction between these elements of change is important. Expressed simply: level and scale dictate the range of actor networks; networks provide logical sequence and continuity to problem perception and objectives; multilateral strategies can lead to corporatism; and resources can become the motive for cooperation (Bressers and Kuks 2003: 75). It is through these interactions that a model of sustainable governance can demonstrate characteristics of flexibility, inclusiveness, persistence, purposefulness, and information-sharing (Dovers 2003 and others above).

Bressers and Kuks argue that although change in governance patterns can be explained by internal interaction between the elements of the model (mutual adjustment), external shocks, interaction between actors, confrontation, or synthesis of visions (and perhaps other things) can bring about change. In whatever manner change occurs, however, most theoreticians, they say, share a 'joint basic conception of more or less vulnerable equilibrium' in such a system (Bressers and Kuks 2003: 75). They suggest three mechanisms – the constant values of actors, their constant reference frames and mutual dependence on resources – provide this stability, so that any such model is characterized by features of 'punctuated equilibrium' (Romanelli and Tushman 1994) rather than by transformational or incremental change (Bressers and Kuks 2003: 83).

JUSTIFYING THE FIVE ELEMENTS

The five elements offer structure to what Dovers calls the 'messiness' of sustainability which can be seen to stem from the multilevel, multi-actor, multifaceted, multi-instrumental, multi-resource based nature of governance for sustainability. Not only does this accord with Costanza and Patten's description of a metasystem (above), it also explains why stakeholder theory, addressing only the question of 'Who?' are the appropriate actors, presents a 'maddening variety' of answers – it does not address the questions 'Where?, What?, How? and With what?' Further, the five elements accord strongly with Costanza and Patten's answers to their second and third basic questions of 'How long?' and 'When?': 'a particular relationship between the longevity of component subsystems and their time and space scales may be necessary', and an assessment of persistence 'can only be done after the fact, so the emphasis shifts to methods to enable us to predict better what configurations will persist, and to policies and instruments to deal with the remaining uncertainty' (Costanza and Patten, 1995: 196).

The five elements also provide a useful model for integration research, facilitating comparison between studies from different disciplines regardless of differences in approach and terminology (see Bammer *et al.* 2005). Often, natural resource management is seen as divorced, for example, from the subject matter of organization or general management studies, so that new research on organizational arrangements does not feed into our understanding of natural resource management. A key aspect of our case study was to examine if organizational studies would provide a fertile basis for understanding sustainability. The five elements of this broad model supply a framework for this purpose.

FRAMING THE CASE STUDY

We can summarize the purpose of the study as twofold:

1. to explore whether aspects of governance concerning multi-actor collaboration for sustainable natural resource management would hold in regard to governance for multi-actor collaboration for sustainability in other contexts;
2. to ascertain implications for a model for governance for sustainability that ensures change through development of new knowledge.

Our initial starting point was an examination of 'sub-politics' in collaborations that involved natural resource management issues. Beck suggests that 'decentralized centres of sub-politics', as networks comprising individual actors, not for profits, community groups, government and corporate bodies and other forms of organizations, are challenging the authority of traditional institutions of industrial society (1995: 73). They take the form of citizens' committees, task forces, and include a wide range of collaborative arrangements for decision-making between corporations, local and regional bodies and communities. The theorized reflexivity of the 'sub-political' arena of politics comes back to this: a renewal of political subjectivity and a perceived need of the individual to engage in ecological decision-making. Beyond that, Beck offers no elaboration on how 'sub-political' arrangements might operate, and this was one area we sought to explore.

In doing so we were conscious that multiple stakeholder arrangements including community or not-for-profits and corporates can be strongly influenced by power relations (Gray 2000; Benn and Onyx 2005) and that collaborative relationships can be analysed according to a collaborative spectrum, ranging from philanthropic, through transactional to integrative (Austin 2000).

The role of community groups suggested other potentially relevant bodies of theory, concerning the cognitive dimension of bridging social capital (Adler and Kwon 2002), developed through shared understandings, and dependent upon shared narratives and language (Nahapiet and Ghoshal 1998). But one cannot read far into the literature on interorganizational collaboration without encountering two linked concepts – the role of networks and the role of new knowledge and knowledge sharing (Nonaka 1994; Tyre and Orlikowski 1994; Wilms 1994; Rothberg 2003). Rosenau (2000:5) describes governance for sustainability as 'multilevel governance' where authority is voluntary and legally dispersed among levels of the community where the problems are located and local needs require attention, and also as a process of 'shifting the balance between hierarchical and network forms of organization, between vertical flows of authority and horizontal flows', citing Rhodes (2000: 60): '[n]etworks are the analytical heart of the notion of governance in the Study of Public Administration'. Networks need to blend public and private resources and use multiple instruments (Peters and Pierre 1998: 226–7) and are essential for learning processes (Gray 1985; Knoepfel and Kissing-Näf 1998; Tsoukas and Mylonopoulos 2004). Such literature clearly influenced Bressers and Kuks in the formulation of their broad model (2003: 70–1, 83n.4).[7] Such a focus also features in writing concerning 'sub-politics'. In the sense that 'knowledge forces decisions and opens up contexts for action' (Beck 1999: 110) knowledge creation is seen by Beck as a factor underpinning reflexive management. If governance is to go beyond the stalemate that more central and formalized decision-making systems commonly face in dealing with managing our natural resources (Beck 1992, 1995, 1999), there is the need to establish processes which inform and adjust themselves in an ongoing cycle of trial, error and correction.

The work of Hardy *et al.* (2003) commended itself as a useful basis for the study because of their findings on interorganizational relations leading to new knowledge. They describe the value of networks as: 'the more collaborative ties the organization has, and the greater the diversity of its partners, the more successful it will be at generating new knowledge'. Their research indicates that collaborations associated with both high levels of embeddedness (interactions with third parties, representation and multidirectional information flows) and involvement (deep interactions, partnerships and bi-directional information flows) are associated with knowledge creation, thus suggesting like Gray, Knoepfel and Kissing-Näf, and Tsoukas and Mylonopoulos (above), a strong link between networks and new knowledge creation. Although involving a setting of great complexity and uncertainty, the work of Hardy *et al.* was not directed at collaborations concerned with environmental issues.

Setting and subjects

Rural and regional areas often suffer much environmental damage from development, yet have limited resources to restore the damage. Areas on the 'rural fringe' are among those most likely to experience pressure for increased development, and environmental stress. Knowledge about the means of prevention and rehabilitation is often uncertain – what works in one terrain or in one social location may fail in another. As a result, transforming the way we manage our land water, mineral and energy resources can seldom be the responsibility of a single stakeholder; it may involve multiple stakeholders with different rationalities, different understandings of sustainability and different management and governance expectations (Land and Water Audit Advisory Council 2001; Environment Australia and Agriculture, Fisheries, Forestry – Australia 2002). Therefore rural settings, particularly those situated in the urban/rural interface were appropriate for our study.

Since corporate involvement in collaborations was to be considered, we chose to examine companies that were both privately and state owned, and a range of corporate collaborations that were either voluntary or not, which provided some basis for comparison or contrast. The corporations represent three sectors associated with considerable environmental impact – three engaged in mining (M1, M2, M3), two state-owned water supply companies (W1, W2), and a privately owned chemical company (C).

Because of the significance of networks, we chose the Australian community-based network organization, Landcare, as a research subject. Landcare was chosen firstly because its purpose, structure and funding arrangements make it an exemplary sub-political interorganizational form. It is a networked, community-based organization, committed to sustainable development and community awareness raising about the need for changed practices of natural resource management. Considerable research had already been conducted on Landcare (e.g. Lockie 1997; Buchy and Race 2001; Byron and Curtis 2001; Sobels *et al.* 2002; Benn and Onyx 2005) which provided an overall organizational picture, and some idea of its power relations, limitations and achievements in terms of sustainability outcomes. To our knowledge Landcare had not been studied as an example of corporate citizenship in action or of the usefulness of multiple stakeholder relationships for knowledge creation. The third reason for the choice of Landcare was access. The authors were engaged in Landcare activities at a grass-roots level and could thus undertake participant observation research. Information on Landcare was also readily available from websites such as that of the Hunter Region Landcare Network (http://www.landcarensw.org/Hunter.htm) and national and state websites (http://www.landcareaustralia.com.au/; http://www.landcarensw.org/).[8] Our research, in two states of Australia, involved collaborations with groups in rural areas, particularly groups in areas that could be described as on the urban fringe.

A preliminary overview of the subject corporations reveals interesting aspects of commonality and contrast. Two of the mining companies (M1 and M2) were involved in Community Consultation Committees (CCCs) mandated under conditions of their statutory operating licences. One of these companies conducted two such CCCs relating to mine sites not far removed from one another – one of which had Landcare representatives (M1.1) – the other did not (M1.2). The second mining company conducted a CCC that did not feature Landcare membership (M2) and the third was voluntarily engaged with Landcare on a specific environmental project (M3). The collaborations of M1 and M2 operated at the local, or 'micro' level, while that of M3 was a regional project at what we would describe as the 'meso' level. Both water supply corporations were engaged with Landcare at a number of ('micro' and 'meso') levels. An interesting aspect of one of the water companies was that it conducted a community forum that had similar purpose and function to the mining CCCs, yet was not mandatory (W1.1). In the course of research it was decided to separately assess relationships established under this forum from those arising from what we described as W1's 'on-ground works' (W1.2). The chemical company was desirous of engagement with Landcare, but had no statutory obligation to engage with the community and no formal or informal links with Landcare.

The viability of the model

The case study involves testing a model from organizational studies, while considering the results of other case-based studies. The question that emerges is whether or not it is appropriate and viable to test a model based on that disclosed by the work of Hardy *et al.* (2003) in a sustainability context.

In considering the conclusions of Hardy *et al.*, one subject required particular attention. In the literature and in case studies of collaboration, a great deal of attention is focused on the concept of shared values of participants. Rondinelli and London (2003) argue that trust and willingness to share knowledge require mutually agreed governance mechanisms and shared values; similarly, Jänicke and Jörgens suggest that long-term policy perspectives (presumably dependent on shared values) are a prerequisite for institutions that facilitate essential learning (2000). In case study material significant to this research, Ostrom (1990: 211) argues that a shared common perception (that it is best to cooperate rather than not) is a first priority for successful cooperation; Bressers and Kuks say that a perception of a joint problem and a perception of joint gains from coherence are factors that militate in favour of cooperative management for sustainability (Bressers and Kuks 1999: 70–2); and Stewart and Jones say that environmental governance acknowledges the importance of values in structuring debate and promotes consensus as a criterion of success (Stewart and Jones 2003: 12). Hardy *et al.*, however (while it might be implicit in their assessment), make no particular mention of the concept of 'shared values', except to refer to 'collaborative ties'.

The work of these researchers is selected for comparison because of the diversity of the subject matter and levels of collaboration examined by each. Stewart and Jones study collaborations for natural resource management at a range of levels in Australia; Ostrom's studies are based on land management (mostly at the 'micro' level) in regions and societies as diverse as the last remaining example of the open field system in England, commonfield agriculture in the Andean mountains of Peru and Bolivia and as employed by Japanese *Iriachi* and Turkish fisheries; Bressers and Kuks' study covers water management, mostly at the 'micro' and 'meso' levels, in Belgium, France, Italy, the Netherlands, Spain and Switzerland, Rondinelli and London examine 50 corporations involved at various levels in collaborations with not-for-profit organizations, mostly at the 'macro' level, and Jänicke and Jörgens examine 'green plans' at the 'macro' level in the Netherlands, Denmark, Sweden, Canada, Austria, Japan and South Korea. Hardy *et al.*, on the other hand, examine collaborations at the 'micro' level involved in women's health issues in Palestine. If it is possible for these studies to inform on governance for sustainability, how do we compare them? Through the lens of Bressers and Kuks' five elements, we suggest, factors of commonality and comparison between this body of interdisciplinary research into interorganizational collaboration can be demonstrated.

In Table 5.1 we represent in summary the key factors identified by these researchers, cross-referenced with Bressers and Kuks' model of elements of governance. The table indicates the degree of commonality and comparison between them. It also, however, illustrates the lack of emphasis on shared values in the study by Hardy *et al.*

Table 5.1 *Factors of commonality and comparison*

Elements	*Stewart and Jones*	*Ostrom*	*Bressers and Kuks*	*Rondellini and London*	*Jänicke and Jörgens*	*Hardy* et al.
Where	A range of levels – most effective at the 'meso' level	'Micro' level, small, stable group, *norms of reciprocity and trust*	'Micro' and 'meso' levels – a tradition of cooperation in management	Mostly 'macro' level, cross-sector collaborations with *trusting, intensive levels of interaction*	'Macro' level	'Micro' level – large numbers of collaborative ties
Who	Between interests, across organizational boundaries	Groups similarly affected by rules or changes	Groups *sharing perception* of a joint problem	Collaborations between companies and not-for-profits	Targeted polluters, plans oriented to government, environment groups, societal actors	Diversity of partners
What	Based on dialogue, negotiation, and agreement-making	Employment of low discount rates	Through well-functioning institutional interfaces	Acquisition of new skills or tacit knowledge	Diagnostic capacities, capacity to communicate new knowledge base	Knowledge creation
How	Acknowledged *values*; implemented through networked management	*Shared perception* of cooperation	Perception of *joint gains* from coherence	*Mutually developed* collaborative procedures, information sharing, move from 'arm's length' to highly intensive alliances	Broad policy dialogue between stakeholders on priorities and necessities in environmental policy	High levels of involvement
With what	Leadership, management skills, consensus	Low transaction costs	Force of change agents	Availability of key internal resources, absorptive capacity	*Long-term orientation*, calculable conditions, intensified communication	High levels of embeddedness

The assignment of particular key factors identified in the case studies to the 'Where?, Who?, What?, How? and With what?' elements in Table 5.1 might be perceived as somewhat arbitrary. To use Ostrom's study as an example, a 'small, stable group', possessing 'norms of reciprocity and trust' might just as easily describe aspects of strategy and instruments (the 'How' element) and a 'shared perception of cooperation' could equally be placed under Actors in the Policy Network (the 'Who' element) and vice versa. This, we say, merely reflects the inter-relationship of the elements. As Cole says, commenting on Ostrom's work, a small, stable group will, 'all other things being equal, be relatively homogeneous, and social norms of reciprocity and trust tend to be significant *because* they reduce transaction costs' (Cole 2002: 124–5 – emphasis in the original). What is significantly demonstrated in this table is that each of these studies touch on all five interrelated elements of levels, networks, problem perception, strategies and distribution of responsibility and resources, thus suggesting that a model derived from the work of Hardy *et al.*, despite the fact that it does not make a specific reference to shared values, was a viable one for testing.

In framing our research question, then, we proposed a model for testing that brought together the five elements. Our overall proposition was that testing for these five elements is testing governance for sustainability. Our specific proposition was:

> The key qualities of multiple stakeholder relationships which enable the generation of change leading to new knowledge (policy perception) for environmental restoration at a range of levels are:
>
> 1 embeddedness – measured in Hardy *et al.*'s terms of interactions with third parties, representation and multidirectional information flows (responsibilities and resources);
> 2 involvement – measured in Hardy *et al.*'s terms by depth of interaction and bi-directional information flows (strategies); and
> 3 a shared sense of relevance and purpose (actors in the policy network).

It is implicit, then, that we argue that multiple stakeholder relationships which enable the generation of change leading to new knowledge for environmental restoration provide good models of governance for sustainability.

In effect, we were testing the conclusions of Hardy *et al.*'s research, yet challenging their lack of emphasis on the role that a shared sense of purpose played in generation of new knowledge.

Methodology

The concept of the study was to conduct an empirical exploration of interorganizational arrangements designed to increase sustainable land use in specific areas of Australia using the model described. In each case, in-depth semi-structured interviews were carried out with corporate representatives and with community group members, Landcare group members, local activists, local government representatives and other stakeholders in the arrangements. Each interview focused on the multiple stakeholder arrangement that the interviewee organization had entered, though interviews were also made outside the parameters of direct involvement in the six specific collaborations. Questions focused on the knowledge outcomes of the relationships, embeddedness, involvement, new knowledge and a shared sense of purpose. Interviews were taped, transcribed and then analysed.

The researchers also collected data by the 'participant as observer' method, as described by Babbie (1995: 284). Researchers attended community consultation meetings and workshops between corporations and community and Landcare representatives across two states. The researchers kept diaries of attendance at all meetings. The content analysis, interview and observer data were interpreted for evidence relating to the above propositions.

At an early stage it became apparent that the initially selected themes did not fully account for material in some sections of the data. Data in the cases then examined were organized independently by each of the researchers into categories of type of collaboration: core business and primary motivation of the corporate stakeholders; details on selection and representative capacity of other stakeholders; identification of the purposes of these other stakeholders; depth of involvement; embeddedness; overall outcomes; evidence of new knowledge; and perceived barriers to generation of new knowledge. The 'left-over' sections of the data were then examined to develop common themes, differences in views, and patterns in subjects, terms and phrases, thus widening the range of themes coded (Glaser and Strauss 1967; Miles and Huberman 1994: 9).

Then the tables were cross-checked across the research team for accuracy. Any differences in the assessments were followed up by further examination of the data and reclassification until consensus was reached between the researchers.

In regard to the initially selected themes it was apparent that new knowledge was easily detected – in some cases enthusiastically described by interviewees. But while depth of involvement and embeddedness could be fairly readily identified objectively, subjective perceptions of bi-directional and multi-directional information flows differed in some cases. Diversity of the stakeholder group (as suggested by Hardy *et al.*, but not specifically addressed in our model) was often perceived as significant to the generation of new knowledge. Opinions on relative persistence of the collaboration varied considerably and were closely related to subjective perceptions of success. One interesting observation was that levels and scales of engagement and differing strategies and resources of collaborations (particularly human resources of skill and experience) were considered significant by many interviewees – the researchers by this time being aware of Bressers and Kuks' work. This was, in many instances said to be 'evidenced' by involvement or non-involvement of government employees, though interestingly, staff from the state-owned corporations were not viewed in the same light as staff from government departments or agencies in each state.

Clearly no one case study was adequate to provide meaningful interpretation. A number of observations on the themes could be made at an early stage however:

1 Determination of 'success' was an important, but a subjective, and variable indicator.
2 Relative persistence of a collaboration could, however, be quantified by reference to the diversity of stakeholders and levels of engagement (e.g. government staff, Landcare, third parties).
3 Depth of involvement and embeddedness could be quantified in that interactions with third parties, representation, depth of interaction, bi-directional and multi-directional information flows could be separately assessed; further, this tended to reflect levels of interaction.
4 New knowledge could be readily detected, and its significance to a range of stakeholders ascertained and quantified; stakeholders from different backgrounds might share or not share views on its significance; in some instances, publishing of information gave an indication of perceptions of significance, and in other cases, procedures were in place for improving or developing it over time (e.g. adaptive management processes of monitoring, evaluation and re-planning).
5 The issue of whether or not the stakeholders had a shared sense of purpose was clear in some cases, but in others contrary views were evident; differences in discourse relating to 'us' and 'them' could, however, be described and to a degree 'quantified'.

Our methodology assumed that attitudes towards success or failure of interorganizational cooperation and perceptions of the commitment or values of partners in such a co-operation are individually subjective, as is the case with all opinions that have a potential political character (Dryzek and Berejikian 1993) and that such 'subjectivity' would not invalidate our findings.

The observations arising from reassessment of the data informed later research and ultimately provided researchers with a means of deducing factors of significance by comparison of the case studies. It was important in that regard to develop a comparative approach that was modest in its aims and based as far as possible on objective, quantifiable elements outlined above. Such analysis, as suggested above, could not emerge from a single case study, but derives its value from the comparison (Yin 2003). The researchers concluded that it was possible to identify whether a particular element (embeddedness, involvement, new knowledge, or a shared sense of purpose) was present or not, and whether there was firm, strong, inconsequential or no evidence of that element in the data. Thus, for example, observed interactions with third parties, diversity of representation and multidirectional information flows provided strong evidence of embeddedness, and evidence of new knowledge that was published could be described as firm evidence, but use of that knowledge for a persistent, adaptive management purpose would constitute strong evidence of the presence of the element. That comparative analysis complete, the results could be set out in a simplified table (Table 5.2).

Table 5.2 *Summary of field research*

Knowledge creation elements	*M1.1*	*M1.2*	*M2*	*M3*	*C*	*W1.1 Forum*	*W1.2 on-ground*	*W2*
Embeddedness								
■ Landcare	+++	~	+	+++	++	++	+++	+++
■ government	~	—	~	++	~		++	++
Depth of involvement	+	+	~	~	+	++	+++	+++
Shared sense of purpose	++	—	—	~	~	+	+++	+++
Practices showing new knowledge	++	—	~	+++	~	—	+++	+++

Evidence that element is present	+
Firm evidence	++
Strong evidence	+++
Inconsequential or irrelevant	~
No evidence (or negative)	—

RESULTS – ANALYSING THE RELATIONSHIPS

M1.1 and M1.2

The most striking differences in terms of knowledge creation were evident between the two mandatory CCCs involving mining company M1. The committees related to two mines operated by the same company with the same Group Environmental Manager, yet the outcomes, particularly for knowledge creation, were remarkably different. The key differentiating factor was the degree of embeddedness – M1.1 was interlinked with connections enabled through Landcare, while M1.2 had no links to Landcare and low embeddedness.

We hesitate on the basis of this study alone to conclude that lack of connectivity was the only reason that M1.2 was in stalemate – there may have been (e.g.) some differences in environmental effects from the two mines that were also influencing the outcomes. But the comparison between the two mines and their 'sub-political' arrangements highlights the importance of the community-based networks in facilitating multi-directional information flows. The Landcare network's involvement in M1.1 encouraged the translation of corporate knowledge of occupational health and safety into local understandings specific to natural resource management. It also allowed for the creation of site-specific new knowledge, developed through combining the mine environmental officer's knowledge of environmental impacts on waterways and the landcarers' local natural resource management knowledge. It enabled this new holistic knowledge to flow out to enrich other information flows in government departments, improving sustainable practice and developing reputational and social capital for all stakeholders, despite occasional scepticism from all sides as to the motives of others.

By contrast, M1.2 was an example of the 'congestion' that can result from such arrangements: according to Beck the only source of power for the individual or activist organization is congestion (Beck 1997: 107). The data here supports Beck's (1997) general contention that 'sub-political' arrangements reflect a loss of enforcement power – the stalemate and high inactivity at the government level result from persistent and ongoing local activism. There was little (or no) engagement with Landcare or other supportive community-based organizations.

M2

The Consultative Committee called M2 shows that while individuals may theoretically be 'empowered' by such sub-political forms, the reverse can happen in practice. This committee was not delivering new knowledge. There was sponsorship for Landcare, but the information flow was unidirectional. A top-down corporate-driven approach hindered community engagement and sharing of local knowledge. The individual community members on the committee did not have the relevant expertise to contribute to the construction of new understandings concerning appropriate land rehabilitation – their participation was mainly cosmetic.

M3

This collaboration took the form of a relatively persistent project for monitoring of environmental health. It shows generation of new knowledge can occur without a shared sense of purpose. The relationship was intended by the corporate stakeholder to be only temporary – as with the other resource-based companies – the embeddedness was short term. Compared to M1.1, the knowledge of local Landcarers was not incorporated into the multidirectional flows unless it accorded with the corporation's scientific understanding of sustainability. The level of involvement of corporation staff was only medium–low, and the relationship maintained many aspects of a transactional rather than an integrative relationship (Austin 2000). Yet the manifest new practices which emerged from the relationship seemed to deny this low involvement and overcame the limitation of a difference in rationality. The community-based network structure of Landcare appeared to be the means by which a shared working understanding of sustainability was obtained. This shared understanding broke down some barriers between expert and local knowledge and facilitated the connection of other stakeholders into the relationship which continued even after the founding corporate had left the arrangement. An interesting facet of M3 is that Landcare facilitated the involvement of the local water authorities in the 'sub-political' decision-making.

W1.1, W1.2 and W2

Water companies are government-owned corporations which usually are subject to laws requiring application of principles of sustainability. W1 and W2 both incorporated collaborative practices in their decision-making, reflecting attempts to establish an integrative relationship (Austin 2000) and shared sense of purpose with Landcare. A high level of embeddedness was facilitated with numerous connections with other organizations; a high level of new knowledge practice was the result in each case.

We observed a striking difference between the operations of W1's Consultative Forum (W1.1) and the relationships developed outside the forum with Landcare and other social groups (W1.2 – which for convenience we describe as 'on-ground'). It took considerable effort on the part of the corporation to generate a collection of individuals who were able to contribute to new knowledge making in the Forum context, and even that was not regarded as legitimate by those outside due to accusations of corporate capture. The 'sub-political' arena supported by Landcare showed a very different result.

The observations in regard to W2 were significant in that they revealed strong evidence of knowledge creation despite a much smaller resource base than was the case with W1.2. It is worth noting a subtle difference between the two corporations. Both evidenced high levels of embeddedness and involvement, but in the case of W1, engagement of staff in Landcare, or related activities, was largely done voluntarily outside working hours, whereas W2 accepted that engagement of staff in Landcare-related activities fitted with staff job descriptions and could be carried out in work hours.

The Chemical Company

This company displayed the sense of an isolated organization, which despite strong ideological convictions of its founders, remained remote from any shared discourse of sustainability. It suffered the 'taboo' (Dovers 2003) associated with a chemicals company despite its development of environmentally friendly products. It experienced difficulty in developing more legitimacy at the local level. Little real benefits have resulted to the corporation or to knowledge generation for sustainability from its relationship with Landcare. To generate new knowledge, it is not sufficient to sponsor community-based organizations – what is important is the degree of connection with the multi-directional information flows of the network. Sharing an ideological commitment to sustainability will only produce results if the multiple stakeholder relationship is a genuine 'sub-political' arrangement; where the multiple stakeholders are involved in actual decision-making rather than simply used as an avenue for discussion of information.

DISCUSSION – RETHINKING KNOWLEDGE CREATION FACTORS FOR SUSTAINABILITY

A number of further generalizations can be made. Community-based network structures, which focus on local on-ground work and education rather than advocacy, enable the development of a shared grass roots understanding of sustainability and are less constrained by ideology in developing and maintaining relationships, and can therefore benefit from increased interconnections with third parties. This shared understanding can be built on to develop new knowledge and practice. It provides a structure for the dissemination of knowledge, with multiple intersecting points where new knowledge can be created in the process. It encourages high involvement (Hardy *et al.* 2003) and provides structures which enable managers and coordinators at different levels to engage with community relations issues.

Another key reason that Landcare seems to work well on the whole is that it offers an understanding of sustainability which is limited to sustainable natural resource management. Sustainability discourse is a challenge for the creation of new knowledge because of its interdisciplinary nature and Landcare gives focus to this broad, contestable and interdisciplinary area.

Evidence from comparative analysis of Landcare in the two very different consultative committees of M1.1 and M1.2, in particular, indicate the negative impacts of confrontational relationships and the current lack of capacity of government to address such issues. In a situation where government services are increasingly reduced, the structure of a national community-based network is of great importance to the development of new practice. In such networks as formed by Landcare, which involve government and corporations, we are seeing the development of new forms of governance – social forms of governance at the 'sub-political' level – that can lead to both knowledge and action.

CONCLUSION

A mere confirmation of the research of Hardy *et al.* or of the relevance of Bressers and Kuks' model would perhaps be of little interest. The value of this series of studies, we suggest, lies in four broad areas:

1 It confirms Bressers and Kuks' elements of governance can be used as a basis to assess and compare models from different disciplines, indicating a useful direction for integration research, and confirms the viability of using organization studies to inform on sustainability issues.
2 It suggests mechanisms that describe the operation of 'sub-political' forms of organization in the broader scheme of governance.
3 It confirms the importance of decentralization, diversity of representation and adaptability for facilitating new knowledge, but suggests that not all forms and contexts of decentralization and flexibility produce genuine dialogue, such as bi-directional or multidirectional exchanges (Arentsen *et al.* 2000). It confirms that trust is an essential ingredient for productive open dialogue among stakeholders – hence the importance of embeddedness and involvement – and supports findings that though stakeholders may speak different 'languages' in discussing policy, this need not prevent constructive dialogue (Brown 2000; Halfacre *et al.* 2000).
4 The research results challenge the proposition that 'shared values' such as may be required for early determination of long-term policy perspectives are a 'prerequisite' for institutions that facilitate new knowledge (Jänicke and Jörgens 2000). Shared values do appear to be highly significant in maintaining persistent collaboration, but it might be that long-term perspectives can develop from the sharing of information and development of knowledge even when the parties have divergent views on sustainability.

The research demonstrates the value of community-based networks as a form of social governance in that they facilitate the creation of new knowledge in 'sub-political' arrangements. It shows that these networks, connected in various forms with corporations, can deliver the embeddedness, involvement, conflict resolution capacity and shared sense of relevance and purpose to enable the generation of new knowledge for sustainability.

It has also led us to question the efficacy of 'sub-politics' in terms of the construction of new knowledge that might come 'from below', enabling the development of governance institutions that foster sustainability. Our results to date lead us to challenge Beck's assertion that these sub-political arenas will necessarily empower individuals and democratize decision-making through giving individuals a voice in new policies and knowledge (Beck 1995). Rather, our research indicates the futility of multiple stakeholder arrangements, which offer inclusiveness through the participation of individuals, but little opportunity for intersections between multiple sources of information. As

Beck himself has pointed out, the individualization processes of the post-industrial era can be equated to 'solitary-confinement', where individuals, through such sub-political arrangements as consultative committees, are held responsible for decision-making on all sorts of issues, including the natural environment (Beck 1995: 40). Our results show that without the support of the community-based network, individual activists may indeed be in 'solitary confinement' in terms of any contribution to reflexive management practices. The individual does not have that same legitimacy that can be gained through association with an organization with reputational capital such as Landcare.

IMPLICATIONS FOR SUSTAINABLE GOVERNANCE

Corporations do not have grandchildren, a fact that suggests that incentives or regulation rather than development of shared moral assessments may be required to foster an ethic of corporate sustainability. Our research, still continuing in this field, suggests already that there are other mechanisms by which such changes can be wrought to improve 'governance without government'.

At the social level, even the modest results of our case studies, which need to be followed up with further more detailed research, indicate that some structures of 'sub-politics' demonstrate the capacity to deliver collaborative arrangements that encourage governance for sustainability. If the dysfunctional aspects of 'congestion' can be avoided, networked organizations of social groups with shared perceptions of environmental problems demonstrate this capacity because of a range of features:

1. They have the ability to promote values or problem perception at local or regional ('micro' or 'meso') levels.
2. They tend to be less confrontational than (e.g.) advocacy groups.
3. They seem to demonstrate a 'boundary spanning' capacity, perhaps because they possess local knowledge valued at the 'micro' level and diversity of knowledge bases demonstrated at the 'meso' level.
4. These qualities allow for development of new knowledge which seems to operate as a medium which neutralizes power differentials and by which perceptions of lack of commonality or conflict of opinion on sustainability and governance issues can be moderated or eliminated.
5. New knowledge is therefore both an element and an outcome of this suggested model of governance.

From a policy perspective, encouragement and support for such networked collaborations that include corporations as the key economic unit of society should perhaps be considered as a priority. It may be appropriate to consider whether such networked organizations, even at the 'macro' level, may be more effective at negotiating rule making than existing government structures and institutions.

NOTES

1 It should be noted that we are discussing 'models', which describe operational characteristics of a system, rather than 'definitions', which describe social functions of a system.

2 Rhodes lists six categories of publications discussing the topic – corporate governance, 'good' governance, minimal state, new public management, socio-cybernetic systems theory, and self-regulating networks (1996). To this list could be added 'international governance', a term used to describe relations between international organizations and authorities (see e.g. Marks *et al.* 1996; Bressers and Kuks 2003: 83n1). It is acknowledged that most situations will allow or even mandate hybrid models, many of which are described in the last four categories of literature referred to by Rhodes.

3 We include acts done under ministerial or executive discretion as part of bureaucratic behaviour.

4 Hardin's paper is, we suggest, too often cited in shortened form. It is often overlooked that he was discussing the population issue, and an 'extension of morality' required to address it.

5 This formulation also addresses the failures arising from underestimation of the significance of externalities discussed above in relation to tobacco, asbestos, DDT and CFCs.

6 This conceptual framework is adopted by all contributing authors to this collection.

7 The case studies were commenced before publication of Bressers and Kuks' work on the broad model described above, though the researchers were aware of their earlier research (1999) and became aware of an early draft of their work (Bressers and Kuks 2001) during the course of research.

8 See further detail on Landcare structure and politics in Chapter 4 this volume.

REFERENCES

Adler, P. and Kwon, S. (2002) 'Social capital: prospects for a new concept, *Academy of Management Review*, 27(1):17–40.

Arentsen, M.J., Bressers, H.T.A. and O'Toole, L.J. (2000) 'Institutional and policy responses to uncertainty in environmental policy: a comparison of Dutch and U.S. styles', *Policy Studies Journal*, 28(3): 597–611.

Austin, J. (2000) *The Collaboration Challenge: How Nonprofits and Businesses Succeed Through Strategic Alliances*, San Francisco, CA: Jossey-Bass.

Avery, G.C. (2005) *Leadership for Sustainable Futures: Achieving Success in a Competitive World*, Cheltenham: Edward Elgar.

Ayres, I. and Braithwaite, J. (1992) *Responsive Regulation. Transcending the Deregulation Debate*, Oxford: Oxford University Press.

Babbie, E. (1995) *The Practice of Social Research*, Belmont: Wadsworth Publishing Co.

Bammer, G., O'Connell, D., Roughley, A. and Syme, G. (2005) 'Integration research for natural resource management in Australia: an introduction to new challenges for research practice', *Journal of Research Practice*, 1(2): Article E1 [Editorial]. Online. Available at: http://jrp.icaap.org/content/v1.2/editorial.html (accessed 1 November 2005).

Bates, G. (2000) 'Environmental law: past and present', paper presented at National Environmental Law Association Conference, Perth, September 2000.

Beck, U. (1992) *The Risk Society*, London: Sage.

Beck, U. (1995) *Ecological Enlightenment – Essays on the Politics of the Risk Society*, trans. M. Ritter, New Jersey: Humanities Press.

Beck, U. (1997) *The Reinvention of Politics*, trans. M. Ritter, Cambridge: Polity Press.

Beck, U. (1999) *World Risk Society*, Cambridge: Polity Press.

Benn, S. and Onyx, J. (2005) 'Negotiating interorganizational domains: the politics of social, natural and symbolic capital', in A. Dale and J. Onyx (eds) *Social Capital and Sustainability in Local Communities – What is the link?*, Vancouver: University of British Columbia Press, pp. 87–104.

Bressers, H.T.A. and Kuks, S.M.M. (1999) 'Integrated water management regimes and more sustainable water resources in Europe – a case study comparison', in *EUWARENESS, European Water Regimes and the Notion of a Sustainable Status*, Enschede: University of Twente, 1–92.

Bressers, H.T.A. and Kuks, S.M.M. (2001), *What does Governance Mean? From Conception to Elaboration*. Online. Available at: http://www.utwente.nl/cstm/research/articles/Multiscale-Governance.pdf (accessed 19 May 2002).

Bressers, H.T.A. and Kuks, S.M.M. (2003) 'What does "governance" mean? From conception to elaboration', in H.T.A. Bressers and W.A. Rosenbaum (eds) *Achieving Sustainable Development. The Challenge of Governance Across Social Scales*, Westport, London: Praeger, 65–88.

Bressers, H.T.A. and Rosenbaum, W.A. (2000) 'Innovation, learning, and environmental policy: overcoming "a plague of uncertainties"', *Policy Studies Journal*, 28(3): 523–39.

Bressers, H.T.A. and Rosenbaum, W.A. (2003) 'Social scales, sustainability, and governance: an introduction', in H.T.A. Bressers and W.A. Rosenbaum (eds) *Achieving Sustainable Development. The Challenge Across Social Scales*, Westport, London: Praeger, 3–23.

Brown, M.L. (2000) 'Scientific uncertainty and learning in European Union environmental policymaking', *Policy Studies Journal*, 28(3): 576–96.

Buchy, M. and Race, D. (2001) 'The twists and turns of community participation in natural resources management: what is missing?', *Journal of Environmental Planning and Management*, 44: 293–308.

Byron, I. and Curtis, A. (2001) 'Landcare in Australia: burned out and browned off', *Local Environment*, 6: 311–25.

Clarke, T. (2004) 'Sustainable and responsible investment: creating knowledgeable action', paper presented at Academy of Management Conference, New Orleans, August 2004.

Coase, R.H. (1960) 'The problem of social cost', *Journal of Law and Economics*, 2: 1–44.

Coglianese, C. and Nash, J. (2002) 'Policy options for improving environmental management in the private sector', *Environment*, 44(9): 10–23.

Cole, D.H. (2002) *Pollution and Property: Comparing Ownership Institutions for Environmental Protection*, Cambridge: Cambridge University Press.

Colebatch, H.K. and Larmour, P. (1993) *Market, Bureaucracy and Community*, London: Pluto Press.

Costanza, R. and Patten, B.C. (1995) 'Commentary – defining and predicting sustainability', *Ecological Economics*, 5: 193–6.

Dovers, S. (2003) 'Processes and institutions for resource and environmental management: why and how to analyse?', in S. Dovers and S. Wild River (eds) *Managing Australia's Environment*, Leichhardt: Federation Press, pp. 3–12.

Dovers, S. (2005) *Environment and Sustainability Policy. Creation, Implementation, Evaluation*, Leichhardt: Federation Press.

Dryzek, J.S. (1997) *The Politics of the Earth – Environmental Discourses*, Oxford: Oxford University Press.

Dryzek, J.S. (2000) *Deliberative Democracy and Beyond. Liberals, Critics, Contestations*, Oxford: Oxford University Press.

Dryzek, J.S. and Berejikian, J. (1993) 'Reconstructive democratic theory', *American Political Science Review*, 87(1): 48–60.

Dunphy, D., Griffiths, A. and Benn, S. (2003) *Organisational Change for Corporate Sustainability*, London: Routledge.

Environment Australia and Agriculture, Fisheries and Forestry – Australia (2002) *The Future of Facilitation and Coordination Networks under Natural Resource Management Planning and Implementation*, Environment Australia and Agriculture, Fisheries and Forestry. Online. Available at: http://www.nht.gov.au/publications/nrm/ (accessed 3 January 2006).

Farrier, D., Whelan, R. and Brown, C. (2002) 'Addressing scientific uncertainty in local government decision-making processes', *Environmental and Planning Law Journal*, 19: 429–44.

Fiorino, D.J. (1999) 'Rethinking environmental regulation: perspectives on law and governance', *Harvard Environmental Law Review*, 23: 441–69.

Flannery, T. (2005) *The Weather Makers. The History and Future Impact of Climate Change*, Melbourne: Text Publishing Company.

Gallagher, D.R. (2003) 'Reflexive law: a framework for improving business–government–stakeholder relationships', unpublished thesis, Nicholas School of the Environment and Earth Sciences, Washington, August 2003.

Glaser, B and Straus, A. (1967) *The Discovery of Grounded Theory: Strategies for Qualitative Research*, Chicago: Aldine.

Gray, B. (1985) 'Conditions facilitating interorganizational collaboration', *Human Relations*, 38: 911–36.

Gray, B (2000) 'Assessing inter-organizational collaboration: multiple conceptions and multiple methods', in D.O. Faulkner and M. DeRond (eds) *Cooperative Strategy: Economic, Business, and Organizational Issues*, New York: Oxford University Press, 243–60.

Gunningham, N. and Grabosky, P. (eds) (1998) *Smart Regulation: Designing Environmental Policy*, Oxford: Oxford University Press.

Haas, P.M. (2000) 'International institutions and social learning in the management of global environmental risks', *Policy Studies Journal*, 28(3): 558–77.

Halfacre, A.C., Matheny, A.R. and Rosenbaum, W.A. (2000) 'Regulating contested local hazards: is constructive dialogue possible among participants in community risk management', *Policy Studies Journal*, 28(3): 648–67.

Hardin, G. (1968) 'The Tragedy of the Commons. The population problem has no technical solution; it requires a fundamental extension in morality', *Science*, 162(859): 1243–8.

Hardy, C., Phillips, N. and Lawrence, T. (2003) 'Resources, knowledge and influence: the organizational effects of interorganizational collaboration', *Journal of Management Studies*, 40: 321–47.

Hernes, T. and Bakken, T. (2003) 'Implications of self-reference: Niklas Luhmann's autopoiesis and organization theory', *Organization Studies*, 24: 1511–35.

Irwin, A. (2001) *Sociology and the Environment*, Cambridge: Polity Press.

Jänicke, M. and Jörgens, H. (2000) 'Strategic environmental planning and uncertainty: a cross-national comparison of green plans in industrialized countries', *Policy Studies Journal*, 28(3): 612–32.
Kleindorfer, P.R. and Orts, E.W. (1998) 'Informational regulation of environmental risks', *Risk Analysis*, 18: 155–201.
Knoepfel, P. and Kissing-Näf, I. (1998) 'Social learning in policy networks', *Policy and Politics*, 26(3): 343–67.
Land and Water Audit Advisory Council (2001) 'Australian agricultural assessment 2001', Canberra: National Land and Water Resources Audit. Online. Available at: http://audit.ea.gov.au/ANRA/agriculture/docs/national/Agriculture_Partnership.html (accessed 4 May 2004).
Livingston, D.J., Stenekes, N., Colebatch, H.K., Waite, D.T.D. and Ashbolt, N.J. (2005) 'Governance of water assets: a reframing for sustainability', *Water, Journal of the Australian Water Association*, August: 34–38.
Lockie, S. (1997) 'Beyond a good thing: political interests and the meaning of landcare', in S. Lockie and F. Vanclay (eds) *Critical Landcare*, Wagga Wagga: Centre for Rural Social Research, Charles Sturt University, 29–44.
Luhmann, N. (2004) *Law as a Social System*, Oxford: Oxford University Press.
Lyster, R. (2001) '(De)regulating the rural environment', *Environmental Planning and Law Journal*, 18: 445.
Marks, G., Scharpf, F.W., Schmitter, P.C. and Streck, W. (1996) *Governance in the European Union*, London: Sage.
Matten, D. (2004) 'The impact of the risk society thesis on environmental politics and management in a globalizing economy – principles, proficiency, perspectives', *Journal of Risk Research*, 7(4): 377–98.
Menell, P.S. (1992) 'Institutional fantasylands: from scientific management to free market environmentalism', *Harvard Journal of Law and Public Policy*, 15: 489–510.
Miles, M.B. and Huberman, A.M. (1994) *Qualitative Data Analysis: An Expanded Source Book*, Thousand Oaks, CA: Sage.
Nahapiet, J. and Ghoshal, S. (1998) 'Social capital, intellectual capital, and the organizational advantage', *Academy of Management Review*, 23(2): 242–66.
Nonaka, I. (1994) 'A dynamic theory of organizational knowledge creation', *Organization Science*, 5(1): 14–36.
Orts, E.W. (1995a) 'Reflexive environmental law', *Northwestern University Law Review*, 89: 1227–340.
Orts, E.W. (1995b) 'A reflexive model of environmental regulation', *Business Ethics Quarterly*, 5(4): 779–94.
Orts, E.W. and Strudler, A. (2002) 'The ethical and environmental limits of stakeholder theory', *Business Ethics Quarterly*, 12(2): 215–33.
Ostrom, E. (1990) *Governing the Commons: the Evolution of Institutions for Collective Action*, Cambridge: Cambridge University Press.
Peters, B.G. and Pierre, J. (1998) 'Governance without government? Rethinking public administration', *Journal of Public Administration and Theory*, 18: 223–43.
Rhodes, R.A.W. (1996) 'The new governance: governing without government', *Political Studies*, 44: 652–67.
Rhodes, R.A.W. (2000) 'Governance and public administration', in J. Pierre (ed.) *Debating Governance: Authority, Steering and Democracy*, Oxford: Oxford University Press, pp. 54–91.

Romanelli, E. and Tushman, M. (1994) 'Organizational transformation as punctuated equilibrium: an empirical test', *Academy of Management Journal*, 37: 1141–66.

Rondinelli, D. and London, T. (2003) 'How corporations and environmental groups cooperate: assessing cross-sector alliances and collaborations', *Academy of Management Executive*, 17, 61–76.

Rosenau, J.N. (2000) 'The governance of fragmentation: neither a world republic nor a global interstate system', paper presented at International Political Science Association Conference, Quebec, August 2000.

Rosenbaum, W.A. and Bressers, H.T.A. (2000) 'Uncertainty as environmental education', *Policy Studies Journal*, 28: 668–71.

Rothberg, S. (2003) 'Knowledge content and worker participation in environmental management at NUMMI', *Journal of Management Studies*, 40: 1783–802.

Sobels, J., Curtis, A. and Lockie, S. (2002) 'The role of landcare group networks in rural Australia: exploring the contribution of social capital', *Journal of Rural Studies*, 17: 265–78.

Stewart, J. (1997) 'Australian water management – towards the ecological bureaucracy?', *Environmental Planning and Law Journal*, 14: 259–68.

Stewart, J. and Jones, G. (2003) *Renegotiating the Environment*, Leichhardt: Federation Press.

Teubner, G. (1983) 'Substantive and reflexive law elements in modern law', *Law and Society Review*, 17: 239–85.

Teubner, G. (1993) *Law as an Autopoietic System*, Oxford: Blackwell.

Tsoukas, H. and Mylonopoulos, N. (2004) 'Introduction: knowledge construction and creation in organizations', *British Journal of Management*, 15: S1–S8.

Tyre, M.J. and Orlikowski, W.J. (1994) 'Windows of opportunity: temporal patterns of technological adaptation in organizations', *Organization Science*, 5(1): 98–118.

Weale, A. (1992) *The New Politics of Pollution*, Manchester: Manchester University Press.

Wilms, W.W., Hardcastle, A.J. and Zell, D.M. (1994) 'Cultural transformation at NUUMI', *Sloan Management Review*, 36(1): 99–113.

Yin, R.K. (2003) *Applications of Case Study Research*, 2nd edn, Thousand Oaks CA: Sage.

Chapter 6

Financing environmental sustainability

A new role for the law

Benjamin J. Richardson

THE CONNECTIONS BETWEEN FINANCIAL MARKETS AND THE ENVIRONMENT

The environmental performance of corporations should improve if their financial sponsors care more about the environment (Delphi International 1997; Jeucken 2001; Richardson 2002a). A seminal insight of the ethical investment and ecological economics literature is the environmental impact of financial markets (Daly 1992; Kinder *et al.* 1992; Sparkes 1995, 2002; Costanza *et al.* 1997a; Haigh and Hazelton 2004). Private financial institutions – such as banks, pension plans and mutual funds – control a huge share of development capital in the world. The biggest environmental impact of financiers is not their own ecological footprint, but the consequences of their allocating capital to other businesses (Rada and Trisoglio 1992; Thomas 2001). Because the financial sector sponsors and profits from economic growth, it should share responsibility for ensuring such development meets society's environmental goals and standards. Thus, if financiers were more sensitive to sustainable development, then probably so would be their borrowers and other financial beneficiaries.

Financial markets are environmentally significant because they transform money by scale, time and location into an instrument of development. The sector holds a strategic place in the economy, because it is where 'wholesale' decisions regarding future development arise. The choices made by financiers have a tremendous downstream effect on the prospects for sustainability in the economy. Commercial financiers also gain influence through their ownership stakes in companies and seats on company boards, particularly in the bank-based corporate governance systems of Japan and continental Europe. Some studies show a correlation between corporate environmental and social performance and share value (Lanoie *et al.* 1998; Foerster and Asmundson 2001). Financial markets can indirectly punish polluters by reducing prices for their company shares (Cormier *et al.* 1993; Lanoie *et al.* 1998).

But most financiers seem to disregard the environmental consequences of their loans and investments. There occasionally arise discrete situations where they scrutinize corporate environmental activities, such as projects that pose acute pollution risks and expose a borrower to crippling regulatory penalties. However, more often than not, loans and investments proceed with just superficial and perfunctory regard to long-term sustainability. Myriad legal, institutional, informational and market factors impede the careful consideration of environmental factors in financial decision-making.

Encouragingly, however, environmental awareness is emerging among some institutions in this sector. There are increasing calls for more government supervision of capital markets (Delphi International 1997; French 1998; Panayotou 1998; Bouma *et al.* 2001; Jeucken 2001; Labatt and White 2002; Hunt 2004). Already, for several decades, the public development finance sector has implemented environmental procedures and standards for project lending (World Bank 1995). While the World Bank has been the target of most pressure for reform, the European Bank of Reconstruction and Development has made the greatest strides and is the only multilateral development bank (MDB) to have a specific legal mandate to promote sustainable development.[1] In the 1990s, an emerging catalyst to boost the profile of environmental issues in global financial markets was the United Nations Environment Programme's (UNEP) Finance Initiative. Under this mechanism, banks and other financial entities could pledge themselves to specified sustainable development principles.[2] In 2003, a new set of soft law environmental standards known as the 'Equator Principles' emerged.[3] Drafted under the auspices of the World Bank's International Finance Corporation, the Equator Principles had been ratified by 41 banks by July 2006.[4] This voluntary code provides a framework that commits interested banks to develop individual policies, procedures and practices to ensure that projects are assessed and carried out according to specific social and environmental considerations. And, most recently, in March 2006 the UNEP released its 'Principles of Responsible Investment' to guide investors to best practices on social and environmental criteria.[5]

But voluntary standards and self-regulation alone are unlikely to induce fundamental change in the financial sector. In other environmental policy contexts, corporate codes of conduct and other voluntary performance undertakings have mostly failed to generate systematic change (Maitland 1995; Wood 2003). As commercial entities, banks and institutional investors desire profitable operations and will normally not pursue ethically laudable practices for their own sake. They are not in the business of subsidizing good environmental practices per se. Certainly, a few financiers boast socially and environmentally responsible policies, but they cater to a small, niche market. Specialist environmental banks of this type include UmweltBank in Germany, the Triodos Bank in the Netherlands, and Britain's Co-operative Bank. Similarly, several hundred ethical mutual funds in Europe and North America have arisen (Sustainable Development Research International Group 2002). Some stock markets have also introduced indices to track ethical investments, notably the Dow Jones Sustainability Group Index and the United Kingdom (UK) Financial Times Stock Exchange Ethical Index.

Investors and lenders have crafted several methods for socially and environmentally responsible financing. Primarily, they rely on positive and negative screens (Kinder *et al.* 1992; Sparkes 1995). A negative screen excludes companies involved in pre-identified activities (e.g. nuclear power and pesticides manufacture) while a positive screen selects firms engaged in perceived desirable practices (e.g. renewable energy). Alternatively, 'best of sector' approaches entail investments in companies that perform best in their sector as measured against specified indicators. An 'index-based' method constructs investment portfolios using established indices of environmentally and socially responsible companies. Another methodology is corporate 'engagement', where the fund actively communicates with companies and/or uses its share voting rights and other sources of influence to exert pressure on the company to improve its environmental performance (Vogel 1983; Prevost and Rao 2000).

Yet, the total size of the ethically responsible financing sector as a proportion of the capital market remains miniscule. For example, in Western Europe ethical investment in recent years has hovered between 2 and 4 per cent share of the capital investment market (European Social Investment Forum 2003). But the EU ethical investment mutual fund market is growing rapidly, and by June 2004 there were estimated to be some 350 ethical funds in operation, compared to a mere 50 such funds in the early 1990s (Avanzi SRI Research 2004). The United States (US), with the largest share, has about 11 per cent of its funds explicitly dedicated to social and environmental causes (Social Investment Forum 2003).

Thus, the ethical fund sector currently appears too small to promote sustainable development simply by generating a meaningful share price differential between companies based on their environmental performance. Financial market economists explain that stock markets tend to function according to a 'horizontal demand' curve, rather than the traditional 'demand and supply' relationships of markets (Krugman and Wells 2005). Consequently, if one segment of the market comprising ethical investors refuses to buy shares of certain sin companies, this should have little or no broader consequence as there would remain other non-ethical investors prepared to buy those shares.

Where screening is ineffectual, ethical investors must rely on shareholder activist and engagement strategies. But the picture is not too promising here either. For instance, social and environmental policy shareholder resolutions are uncommon. In the 1998 shareholder proposal season in the US, for example, only 289 ethical policy shareholder resolutions were filed at 116 companies (Becker and McVeigh 2001: 64). In Canada, the number of shareholder proposals increased from less than three in each year from 1982 to 1996, to 63 and 40 in 2000 and 2001 respectively. But only two of the 40 filed in 2001 addressed ethical concerns, and none won a majority of shareholder votes (Richardson 2004: 183). These figures though do not reflect additional, behind-the-scenes diplomacy, such as investors meeting privately with management.

Presently, there are too many legal, institutional, informational and market barriers to more extensive environmental financing. The ecological economics literature emphasizes the structural weaknesses of markets to address environmental concerns. These include markets' under-valuation of ecosystem functions (Common 1996), excessive risk taking (von Amsberg 1995) myopia (Costanza *et al.* 1997b) and markets' addiction to growth (Daly 1992). Capital market institutions also tend to resist investing ethically when it reduces the diversity of their investment portfolios: market theorists correlate lower diversity with higher financial risks (Lee 1987). Money managers lack awareness of environmental issues and equity prices do not sufficiently reflect social and environmental performance (UNEP Finance Initiative 2004). Money managers also tend to hold widely defined investment powers delegated from fund principals, thereby creating agency and accountability problems (Mathieu 2000). Relevant informational barriers include financiers' lack of access to accurate information about corporate environmental performance and its relationship to financial performance. Legal obstacles include fund managers' fiduciary duties interpreted to require maximization of financial returns (Ellison 1991; Ali and Yano 2004: 128–40), and company law barriers to shareholder activism (Guercio and Hawkins 1999).

THE FRAMEWORK FOR ENVIRONMENTAL REGULATION OF FINANCIERS

To harness the financial sector as a means for sustainable development will surely depend on astute policy intervention and regulation. This would involve largely new territory for environmental law systems worldwide. Environmental law targets the companies that extract, consume and pollute, but rarely their financial sponsors. But policy change is necessary given that land use planning, environmental impact assessment (EIA), pollution licensing and other elements of environmental law have hardly realigned our economies towards sustainable development (Richardson and Wood 2006). On the other hand, extending the reach of environmental law to financial markets sits uncomfortably with the present growth of transnational, deregulated financial markets. Technological advances and market deregulation have greatly accelerated the geographical mobility of capital in its search for the most lucrative investments (Walter 1993: 202–4). The globalization of banking and investment services reduces the power of states individually to regulate financial institutions (Braithwaite and Drahos 2000: 7–8).

Direct environmental regulation of financiers is presently doubtful for many reasons. Governmental regulation of capital markets has principally responded to market failures of information asymmetry, externalities and monopolistic practices (Frankel and Kirsch 1999). Market failures to protect the environment have not ordinarily been seen as part of this picture. Western governments have not sought to usurp market-based capital allocation, but merely to improve its efficiency and liquidity. Too much state intervention risks provoking capital flight, fragmentation of capital markets and other inefficiencies (Shaw 1975; Yago 1993).

There have however arisen some cautious, ad hoc reforms for social and environmental responsibility in the financial services sector. In the 1970s and 1980s, some legislatures and courts introduced 'defensive' measures to remove a few of the obstacles to more responsible financing. Principally, the reforms were lender liability for borrowers' pollution, especially in the context of the US Superfund legislation (James 1988; Tietenberg 1989; Pitchford 1995), and the removal of some obstacles to shareholder activism in corporate governance (Parkinson 1995; MacIntosh 1996; Guercio and Hawkins 1999). But only in relation to international development financiers, such as the World Bank, did reformers consider policies to actually *encourage* green financing (Muldoon 1987). Development banks were expected to assess the environmental consequences of their borrowers' projects before lending.

Lately, governments have adopted a new suite of mechanisms for sustainable financing. They have emphasized financial and informational policy instruments (Richardson 2002a). Among the reforms, legislation requiring pension funds to disclose their policies on environmental, social and ethical considerations has arisen in Australia, Austria, Belgium, France, Germany, Spain and the UK since 2000 (Richardson 2002b). Also, the European Commission has amended its Eco-Label Regulation (2000) and Eco-Management and Audit Scheme (2001) to extend them to financial services (Richardson 2002c). Corporate environmental reporting requirements, of which the US has the most developed precedents, have also been revamped in many jurisdictions (KPMG 1999; von Ahsen *et al*. 2004;). Further, economic incentives (e.g. Dutch Green Investment Directive) in some countries are providing tax concessions for environmental investment funds (Scholtens 2001; Duff 2003).

These reforms reflect a broader shift in preferred styles of regulation towards less intrusive, cooperative partnerships with the private sector (Donahue 1989; Rein 1989). A combination of ideological influences and pragmatic considerations has engendered the retreat from heavy bureaucratic regulation. Because of the perceived advantages of the private sector's managerial skills, cost efficiencies and client knowledge, in many Western countries private institutions are being enlisted to help implement public policy. The harnessing of financiers as a means of public policy is however not unprecedented; for instance, the contractual relationship between banks, institutions and their customers has long been regulated to meet public policy objectives and standards concerning consumer protection and fraud control (Cranston 1997: 153). Thus, many regulatory theorists speak of contemporary governance as a process of 'negotiated relationships' (Freeman 2000) or shared 'regulatory spaces' (Hancher and Moran 1989) between public and private sector partners.

In this regulatory milieu, reformers favour informational and financial incentive policy mechanisms. The well-documented failings of command-and-control regulation suggest that the financial sector would reject strict rules such as mandatory financing of ethical causes or adoption of complex environmental performance standards (Ackerman and Stewart 1985). Such substantive regulation has been ceding ground to a type of law referred to by commentators as 'reflexive law'. In contrast to the heavy hand of command regulation, which aims to control behaviour directly, it provokes reflection and self-correction by regulated actors in line with regulators' goals (Teubner 1983: 254–6).

According to one definition, a governance system based on reflexive law

> attempts to create incentives and procedures that induce entities to act in certain ways and to engage in internal reflection about what form that behaviour should take . . . the state sets goals, but shares more of the responsibility for achieving them with regulated entities'.
>
> (Fiorino 1999)

Corporate environmental reporting illustrates a reflexive law method. Economic instruments such as pollution taxes and tradeable emission allowances also have reflexive properties, as they can convey in the language of the market the price of engaging in environmentally inappropriate activities (Orts 1995). These informational and incentive mechanisms can help make corporate environmental performance more relevant to financial institutions' evaluation of corporate *economic* performance.

Financial markets may contribute directly to reflexive environmental regulation. Financial organizations can be viewed as decision-making communities, potentially providing spaces for reflection, learning and experimentation with environmental management norms and practices. Banks for instance can provide institutional settings for assessing and pricing environmental risks and advising clients on risk management. Financiers can also be vehicles for communication of legal information, transmitting norms about appropriate corporate environmental behaviour (e.g. a lender's expectation that a borrower will comply with applicable pollution control regulations as a condition of finance). Jessop (1990: 329) argues that organizations straddling the boundaries of different 'subsystems' of society – the market, civil society, public sector – are potentially well placed to 'enhance mutual understanding' and 'play a role in linking sub-systems'. Financiers hold such strategic, intermediate positions between the state and market for channelling environmental norms to industry.

But, what exactly should we expect of financial institutions as they join the matrix of environmental governance? Financial service providers lack the expertise and management systems to undertake many of the specialist functions of modern environmental agencies in government. More realistically, we should expect financiers to incorporate pollution risks and other environmental harms into their financial evaluations. Developments or businesses posing unacceptable risks might thus not receive finance. Correspondingly, environmentally sound companies should receive preferential access to finance. The value of the financial services sector therefore lies in its strategic market position, which may be manipulated by government rules, information and monetary incentives to enable environmentally sound companies to flourish at the expense of polluters and resource degraders.

The prospects for these changes, however, vary somewhat around the world. Different regulatory styles and market structures among countries affect the direction and pace of reform. For example, institutional investors can usually only act as an effective lever for corporate environmental responsibility in those jurisdictions with mature equity markets open to influence from pension funds and other large institutional investors. In the European Union (EU), these conditions exist extensively only in the UK, the Netherlands and Switzerland (Blommestein 1998). In some jurisdictions, notably France, Germany and Japan, banks have traditionally controlled corporate financing (Frank and Mayer 1990). However, in recent years extensive reforms to corporate governance and securities market laws in these jurisdictions have expanded capital markets and thereby scope for equity investments (Morin, 2000; Omar 2001). Occupational pension plans are spreading rapidly in continental Europe as a solution to the demographic problem of an ever-climbing ratio of retirees to the employed that can no longer be fully supported by state pensions (Rhodes and van Apeldoorn 1998).

Another relevant variable is the presence of lobby groups for ethical investment. These exist in several countries, such as Australia's Ethical Investment Association and the US's Social Investment Forum. Other, more general, factors that affect the prospects for regulatory reform include the extent of financial market deregulation, public environmental concern and the political salience of environmental policy.

The increasing transnational character of financial markets will also shape reform. Finance capital is much more mobile than governments, making it difficult for authorities in even the largest individual economies to control the direction and nature of international investment (Walter 1993: 202–4). Domestic regulation that threatens economic interests can prompt the migration of financial resources to jurisdictions perceived as offering a more benign legal milieu. National regulators may also face capacity and information deficits when supervising enterprises engaged in complex trans-border commerce. International agreements and institutions are thus necessary to prevent environmentally enlightened financial service providers from suffering competitive disadvantages in their transnational business. While this chapter does not explore the global regulation of financial bodies, it can be noted that, apart from in the EU, the existing international regulatory mechanisms in this sector are underdeveloped (European Commission 2000).

INSTITUTIONAL AND LEGAL CHARACTERISTICS OF FINANCIERS

Policy reformers must understand how differences in the specific legal and institutional characteristics of financial organizations affect their receptivity to environmental issues. The financial services sector is heterogeneous. Despite some convergence and assimilation of financial services in recent years, financial organizations retain distinctive institutional characteristics shaped by their legal structure and obligations, and their market functions. Consequently, financiers such as pension trusts and mutual funds may respond differently to the same environmental reforms.

Occupational pension funds, which pay benefits from accumulated investments upon the retirement of their members, are possibly constrained by fiduciary obligations from taking into account non-financial criteria when investing (Hutchinson and Cole 1980;

Hayton 1999). In the UK, fiduciary responsibility standards were interpreted in Cowan v. Scargill,[6] Martin v. City of Edinburgh District Council[7] and Bishop of Oxford v. Church Commissioners for England[8] as constraining pension fund trustees from implementing an ethical investment policy. This is because the best interests of trust beneficiaries have generally been considered to be their *financial* interests (Hudson 1999). From the US case law, in Board of Trustees of Employee Retirement System of the City of Baltimore v. Mayor and City Councillors of Baltimore,[9] a court found that a city ordinance requiring a local government pension fund to disinvest from companies engaged in business in South Africa did not cause trustees to violate their prudential investment duties so long as the cost of investing according to social responsibility precepts was *de minimis*, as was considered in this case. Thus, pension funds wishing to invest ethically should have a mandate in their governing plan to mitigate such legal obstacles in these common law jurisdictions.

Alternatively, legislatures could direct pension funds to consider the environmental effects of their investments, or at least to report publicly on their policies (if any) in this respect. In the 1980s and 1990s, the governments of Manitoba and Ontario legislated to improve the prospects for ethical investment in their provinces. Manitoba's Trustee Act was amended in 1995 to permit trustees to consider non-financial criteria in their investment policies (Manitoba Law Reform Commission 1993: 32). Ontario's South African Trust Investments Act 1988 allowed trustees to divest or reject investments in companies doing business in apartheid South Africa without breach of their fiduciary duties. More recently, in 1999, the UK was the first country to require occupational pension fund trustees to disclose their policies on socially responsible investment and the exercise of shareholder rights.[10] Similar reforms emerged in several European countries (e.g. France,[11] Germany,[12] and Belgium[13]) (Richardson 2002b). The French law allows environmental and social issues to be taken into account in selecting investment.[14] Australia's Financial Services Reform Act 2001[15] applied an ethical disclosure obligation to a wider range of investment products than the European laws, covering pensions, managed investment products and investment life insurance products. But, like the UK initiative, none of these laws define comprehensively 'ethical investment' or similar concepts, and none adequately consider how compliance will be monitored and enforced. Only in Australia has the regulator sought to provide investors with compliance guidelines (Australian Securities and Investments Commission 2003).

Surveys of the effect of the UK pension reforms suggest that while there has been a significant increase in the adoption of ethical investment policies by pension funds, the quality and implementation of such policies has been quite variable (Coles and Green 2002: 1). A 2004 study of the Australian reform disappointedly found that: 'most mainstream investment managers state either that they do not take into account ethical considerations, or claim that they are taken into account to the extent they financially affect the value of underlying investment' (Berger 2004).

Mutual funds, by contrast, can more easily adapt to a variety of investment goals. Of course, a mutual fund must still, consistently with its contractual and fiduciary responsibilities, carefully seek the optimal financial returns within the parameters of its stated policy. Dedicated ethical investment funds usually require more than mere compliance with environmental law as a criterion for inclusion of a company in an investment portfolio. For example, Canada's Ethical Funds demand that businesses adopt 'an effective environmental management system', and demonstrate 'a level of commitment to disclosure of environmental practices including compliance record'.[16] Presently, no jurisdiction's mutual fund regulations distinguish between ethical and conventional mutual funds. Some commentators have suggested that investment regulation should make such a distinction because the distinct investment agenda of ethical funds gives rise to specific expectations from investors (Djurasovic 1997).

Although mutual funds may seem a superior vehicle for ethical financing, the mutual fund sector generally is not a natural ally of sustainable finance. Pension fund investment is probably more compatible with sustainability. Pension funds tend, on average, to hold shares for longer periods than mutual funds because of their longer-term financial liabilities. Since their portfolio turnover ratios are also lower compared to other institutional investors, pension fund managers also have more opportunity to pursue shareholder activism. Mutual fund managers typically vote according to the recommendations in the proxy circular, and tend to passively support corporate management (MacIntosh 1996: 160; Harmes 2001). Furthermore, unlike the mutual fund industry, pension funds are not competitive. Their performance is measured by ensuring returns adequate to meet anticipated liabilities, not to attract investors. Mutual funds compete fervently to attract investors, and this competition leads to pursuit of profitability and market share, rather than long-term returns. However, the distinction between mutual and pension fund investment styles can blur given that pension funds sometimes invest through mutual funds rather than devise their own investment portfolios (World Bank 1997: 129).

Another material distinction arises between equity financiers and banks. Banks face some unique challenges and opportunities for addressing environmental concerns. Banks focus on debt finance, catering particularly to small, unlisted companies unable to raise money from the equity markets. Thus, the banking sector has most potential to influence the environmental activities of small firms. Unlike pension or mutual funds, which rely on publicly reported information to assess the environmental performance of companies, banks have the advantage that they can obtain additional information about environmental risks through contractual techniques in the loan process.

Another difference between investors and lenders stems from corporate liability rules. Whereas investment shareholders are largely protected by the rules of limited corporate liability from the environmental liabilities of their investee companies, lenders face creditor liability risks if they become too closely involved in their borrower's business or take possession of loan security (Lyons 1986; Pitchford 1995). The US litigation has demonstrated the sobering effect that lender liability for cleanup of a borrower's pollution can have on a bank's environmental policies (Alexander 1991). Even if a lender is shielded from direct environmental liability, its borrower's financial difficulties might still cause concern. The bank's borrower might default, and insolvency law in some jurisdictions gives priority to the claims of other creditors in the division of a bankrupt firm's assets (Baker 1993).

Although, therefore, the heterogeneity of financial service providers requires various institution-specific reforms, some common regulatory themes persist. Liability rules, economic incentives, fiduciary responsibilities and informational policy instruments, while all requiring adaptation to specific financial institutional contexts, should apply throughout financial markets. They can create a stronger foundation for sustainable investment. These policy instruments can support a reflexive style of environmental governance that works with, rather than against, the protocols and norms of financial markets.

POSSIBLE POLICY TOOLS FOR PROMOTING ENVIRONMENTALLY SUSTAINABLE FINANCE

Because shareholder activism and engagement are primary means of ethical investment, corporate governance should be overhauled where it hinders shareholders from participating in corporate policy-making. Most ethical mutual funds and pension trusts rely merely on a screening approach, rather than direct engagement with corporate management. But many companies ignore ethical pressures derived simply from buying or selling their shares (Miller 1991: 7). Ethical fund screening practices tend to reward 'good' businesses, but may do little to change the behaviour of 'bad' ones. A more activist approach is thus justified in some circumstances.

A protracted theme in the corporate governance literature is shareholder rights and the democratization of company policy-making. Commentators have offered various explanations for the low levels of shareholder activism in the Anglo-American corporate governance systems, noting the difficulty of coordinating and communicating among shareholders, agency costs, and free rider problems (McCall and Wilson 1993). MacIntosh (1996) contends that institutional investors' ability to monitor investee companies is hampered by their large portfolios, limited staff and insufficient expertise (see also Parkinson 1995). He also suggests that investors' desire to maintain liquid portfolios can result in the acquisition of small shareholding stakes without significant voting clout. Fund managers also tend to side with company management for fear of losing collateral business such as banking and insurance services (Pound 1988).

But the main barrier is arguably an antagonistic legislative framework. Proxy contest and shareholder communication rules are some of these legal impediments to ethically minded shareholders (Sommer Jr 1990: 371–2). Consider the case of the Canada Business Corporations Act 1975 (CBCA). Previously, section 137 of the Act allowed shareholders to file proposals provided that they were not submitted for 'promoting general economic, political, racial, religious, social or similar causes'. The exclusion clause had been exploited to justify refusals to circulate shareholder proposals, such as in 1987 when the

Ontario Court of Appeal upheld Varity Corporation's refusal to circulate a proposal on disinvestments in South Africa.[17] The since amended CBCA requires, by section 137(5), that management circulate all shareholder proposals unless they fail to deal substantially with the business affairs of the corporation. Concomitantly, the word count for proposals was increased from 200 to 500 words (section 137(3)), and the definition of 'solicitation' clarified to allow shareholders to communicate more freely with each other before a vote (section 147). Similarly, the regulatory trend in other jurisdictions such as Australia and the US has been for securities watchdogs to progressively liberalize rules restricting shareholder proposals from management's proxy statement (Richardson 2004: 186).

Significant reforms to the corporate governance regimes in continental Europe have also emerged in recent years. The traditionally bank-based corporate governance systems of France, Germany and other states are changing to accommodate more liquid and open equity markets. For instance, France's Economic Regulations Act of 2001 permits proxy voting by non-resident shareholders, who are typically institutional investors investing on behalf of people not resident in France (Omar 2001). The 'stakeholder' model of corporate governance in the region, epitomized most strongly by Germany's model of trade union representation on company supervisory boards, continues to provide leverage for the articulation of socially responsible investment policies (Prigge 1998).

Commentators have suggested other corporate governance reforms that could further empower institutional investors. Scholars of Anglo-American company law have debated at length how the power of CEOs – perceived as the main stumbling block – can be made more accountable to boards of directors and shareholders (e.g. Donaldson and Davis 1994; Muth and Donaldson 1998). Among the proposals, Gilson and Kraakman (1991: 870) favour appointment of minority independent directors to corporate boards, nominated by institutional investor groups rather than enterprise management. Investment institutions could be obliged to register their share votes, and thereby encouraged to formulate and express a view on all issues voted on at shareholder meetings (Department of Work and Pensions 2002: 8). The US has made reforms in this area: in August 2003, the Securities Exchange Commission amended regulations under the Investment Advisers Act to require all domestic mutual fund companies and investment advisors to disclose to the public their proxy votes and voting policies, and actual voting record.

Financial institutions also need more information about corporate environmental activities. In many jurisdictions, businesses do not have to report to financial regulators on their environmental activities and impacts. Traditional corporate reporting methods do not adequately capture all the financial consequences of a company's environmental management (Owen 1992). Such information can only be gleaned indirectly from miscellaneous sources such as public pollution databases and EIA reports commissioned for ad hoc projects. Such data are usually not presented in a format that can translate easily into financial terms. There is no obvious formula to explain the relationship between the stated pollution risk and the implied financial risk. Only banks, through contractual techniques as part of the loan process, can readily demand environmental information. Institutional investors lack an equivalent contractual nexus and therefore rely on information in the public domain.

Consequently, governments should require major companies to report publicly on their environmental activities, and to present their environmental information in financially relevant terms. Reliable information is crucial to the proper functioning of capital markets; it helps to price securities accurately and enable the market to allocate capital efficiently (Baskin and Miranti Jr. 1997: 322). Disclosure of environmental information can help inform money managers, investor shareholders and consumers about a firm's resource use, emissions and other environmental impacts.

Certainly, there is a move worldwide towards greater corporate environmental performance disclosure, including through emerging voluntary standards such as the CERES Principles and the Global Reporting Initiative, and formal reporting regulations. Among EU states, mandatory environmental reporting has been instituted in France, the Netherlands, Sweden and Denmark (Emtairah 2002). The US also has environmental reporting requirements, which are appropriately integrated into mainstream company law through regulations of the Securities and Exchange Commission (Monsma and Buckley 2004). Environmental reporting is most useful when it captures an enterprise's entire operations, including subsidiaries and franchisees that may otherwise be manipulated by their parent company to disguise its environmental impacts.

Financiers arguably also need more concrete economic incentives to heed the environmental consequences of their loans and investments. By taxing resource consumption and pollution emission, authorities can convey the cost and benefits of corporate environmental activities in a more financially relevant manner. Environmental liability rules can also price harm to the environment. Indeed, environmental liability can be imposed not only on front-line polluters, but also on their financial sponsors. Evidence from the US suggests that the targeting of lenders caused banks to alter quite dramatically their financing practices in response to the Superfund legislation for remediation of contaminated land (Harper and Adams 1996: 107).

Apart from financial incentives and reporting requirements, the internal governance of financial organizations warrants reform. People who contribute to investment funds arguably should be consulted in investment policy-making. Elements of the labour movement have struggled for years to strengthen worker control of their pension plans to ensure that they invest in industries and companies known to treat workers well. In 1976, Drucker prematurely claimed in his book, *Unseen Revolution: How Pension Fund Socialism Came to America*, that the US was the world's first socialist country because workers, through their pension funds, had acquired a significant stake of the equity capital of American businesses. But Drucker overlooked that the pension plan beneficiaries did not control or direct the corporations in which their pension monies were invested, and he ignored that corporate management typically appointed the trustees who oversee occupational pension plans (Rifkin and Barber 1978). Trade union, university and civil service pension plans offer the best prospects for democratizing pension administration because they are less closely tied to market pressures and corporate management influences.

Crucially, the prudential controls governing financial organizations should incorporate environmental risk factors. Financial regulators could introduce some environmental standards as conditions of financial institutions' statutory licensing. For instance, authorities could oblige lenders and investment institutions to report on the environmental profiles and risks. Further, they could oblige financiers *to take into account* the social and environmental effects related to companies or projects they finance. This would amount to a system of environmental appraisal, working in conjunction with existing government EIA regulations. Already, the insurance sector undertakes a similar surrogate regulatory role concerning assessment of pollution liability risks (Richardson 2002d). Regulators would need to provide financiers with clear environmental assessment guidelines and establish verification and auditing mechanisms. Various bodies including ethical advisory and research bodies already offer standardized EIA criteria (Ethical Investment Research Service 1999). Reform of financial regulation may also require giving lenders incentives to offer borrowers differential interest rates (and hence the cost of capital) to reflect the environmental risks assessed for different types of development. For example, the Netherlands in 1995 introduced a Green Investment Directive to provide tax deductions for interest and dividend payments from approved environmental investment funds (Jeucken 2001: 92–4).

To ensure that financial regulators would implement and monitor compliance with such environmental provisions, some core environmental duties would need to be superimposed on the applicable financial legislation. No precedents for such a reform exist. Relevantly, however, during the drafting of the UK's Financial Services and Market Act 2000, the UK Social Investment Forum (1999) unsuccessfully proposed to the House of Commons Environmental Audit Committee that the Act impose a duty on the Financial Service Authority to promote environmental investment and environmental lending products. Ultimately, sustainable development must be legislated as a core mandate of financial regulators to ensure that the environment is not trivialized as a marginal concern.

CONCLUSIONS: FUTURE RESEARCH DIRECTIONS

Many questions about the direction of financial sector reforms and practices need answering. As a priority, we require more empirical research about not only changes in the nature and extent of environmentally responsible financing in light of relevant legal and policy reforms, but also the eventual impact of ethical financing on the environmental behaviour of companies. The informational- and incentive-based policy reforms adopted resonate a style of 'reflexive' regulation. Regulation, suggest some theorists, is more likely to succeed when it uses methods congruent with the codes and norms of the market; therefore informational, incentive and other procedural (rather than substantive) policy tools that facilitate rather than dictate behavioural changes are preferred (Teubner 1983, 1994; Orts 1995). Whether such strategies will work in the context of financial markets requires investigation. Can the commercial aims of banks and investors align with societal demands for more ethical financing through the current menu of policy instruments?

One troubling uncertainty is the lack of agreement on what qualifies as ethical, socially or environmentally responsible finance. Current legal reforms, such as the ethical investment disclosure obligations on pension funds do not define such pivotal terms. 'Ethical investment' tends to be a self-awarded title; the institutions set their own ethical criteria. The absence of any objective basis for determining what qualifies as 'ethical' or 'environmentally responsible' may impede the expansion of the ethical fund market (Mackenzie 1998; Knoll 2002). Furthermore, passively contributing to ethical investment funds arguably cannot substitute for proper ethical deliberation about questions of social and environmental responsibility in the market. Deliberation is an important facet of shareholder activism styles of ethical investment (Ramshaw 1998: 134). The integrity of ethical financing can improve where independent, ethical investment think tanks and research services formulate relevant criteria and methodologies (e.g. Investor Responsibility Research Center 1992).

Another research question of an empirical kind is to assess how variations in the nature of environmental problems affect the response of financiers. In other words, why does ethical investment seem more likely for some causes but not others? Do differences in the character of environmental issues, such as climate change, farming or deforestation, elicit different responses from financiers? So far, climate change has emerged as one of the most significant environmental issues on the radar of financial institutions (Forsyth 1999). It is a key focus of UNEP's Finance Initiative (UNEP 2004). Dealing with climate change requires massive financial support, such as renewable energy supplies and energy efficient technologies. Are specialist policy instruments required for each type of ecological challenge, and does the complexity of climate change imply some ecological concerns need more state intervention?

Given the limitations of financial markets, should the public sector assert a more direct role in capital allocation to foster sustainable development? It would be politically problematic for the state to direct where private financial institutions allocate capital in order to defend social and environmental causes. Further, economic inefficiencies may occur given that regulators typically lack the requisite information and expertise. Already, national pension schemes allow governments to some extent to shape capital allocation (Unger 1998). And, at an international level, governments can get involved in capital allocation for sustainability through mechanisms such as multilateral development banks and export credit agencies (Staniskis and Stasiskiene 2003).

Already, the national pension funds of Sweden and New Zealand are governed by legislative directions to take social, ethical and environmental factors into account when selecting investments (Myles and Pierson 2001: 305). Since January 2001, the five largest state-controlled pension funds in Sweden must include environmental and ethical concerns in their investment policy and report to the government annually on how they fulfil this policy (Tredje AP-fonden 2002: 6). New Zealand's Superannuation and Retirement Act 2001 specifies that a 'statement of investment policies, standards, and procedures must cover (but is not limited to) . . . ethical investment, including policies, standards, or procedures for avoiding prejudice to New Zealand's reputation as a responsible member of the world community' (section 61(d)).

Whatever approach is favoured, government regulation and policy must ultimately make corporate environmental performance relevant to financial institutions' evaluation of corporate *economic* performance. Without such a synergy, financial organizations will likely reject demands for their involvement in environmental governance as extraneous to their core market functions. Numerous options for legal and policy reforms are available. But we need further research before definitive conclusions can be made about which methods will work.

NOTES

1 Article 21(vii) requires the Bank to 'promote in the full range of its activities environmentally sound and sustainable development': *Agreement establishing the European Bank for Reconstruction and Development*, 1990 OJ L 372, 31/12/1990.
2 See www.unepfi.org.
3 The text of the principles is available at www.equator-principles.com.
4 For analysis of implementation of the principles, see Freshfields Bruckhaus Deringer, *Banking on Responsibility* (Freshfields Bruckhaus Deringer, July 2005).
5 See www.unepfi.org/work_programme/investment/principles/index.html.
6 [1985] 1 Ch 270; [1984] 2 All ER 750.
7 [1988] SLT 329.
8 [1992] 1 WLR 1241; [1993] 2 All ER 300.
9 562 A.2d 720 (Court of Appeals of Maryland, 1989).
10 Enacted pursuant to Pensions Act 1995, s. 35(3)(f): Occupational Pension Schemes (Investment, and Assignment, Forfeiture, Bankruptcy etc.), Amendment Regulations 1999, cl. 2(4).
11 Projet de loi sur l'épargne salariale, 7 February 2001. No. 2001–152, article 2; Projet de loi portant diverses dispositions d'ordre social, éducatif et culturel. 28 June 2001, Chapitre Vbis, article L.135–8.
12 Betriebliche Altersvorsorge: article 10, Änderung des Versicherungsaufsichtsgesetzes.
13 Projet de loi relative aux pensions complémentaires, article 42.
14 Projet de loi portant diverses dispositions d'ordre social, educatif et culturel. 28 June 2001, Chapitre Vbis, article L.135–8.
15 Now embodied in s. 1013D of the Corporations Act 2001.
16 Ethical funds, at www.ethicalfunds.com/do_the_right_thing/sri/ethical_principles_criteria/environmental.asp.
17 *Varity Corporation c. Jesuit Fathers of Upper Canada* (1987) 60 O.R. (2d) 640, 41 D.L.R. 284 (C.A.).

REFERENCES

Ackerman, B.A. and Stewart, R.B. (1985) 'Reforming environmental law', *Stanford Law Review*, 37: 1333–65.

Alexander, S.R. (1991) 'CERCLA's web of liability ensnares secured lenders; the scope and application of CERCLA's security interest exemption', *Indiana Law Review*, 25: 165–210.

Ali, P. and Yano, K. (2004) *Eco-Finance*, The Hague: Kluwer.

Australian Securities and Investments Commission (ASIC) (2003) *Section 1013DA Disclosure Guidelines*, Canberra: ASIE.

Avanzi SRI Research (2004) *Green, Social and Ethical Funds in Europe 2004*, Milan: SIRI Group.

Baker, D.L. (1993) 'Bankruptcy – the last environmental loophole?', *South Texas Law Review*, 34(3): 379–428.

Baskin, J.B. and Miranti, P.J., Jr. (1997) *A History of Corporate Finance*, Cambridge: Cambridge University Press.

Becker, E. and McVeigh P. (2001) 'Social funds in the United States: their history, financial performance, and social impacts', in A. Fung, T. Hebb and J. Rogers (eds) *Working Capital: The Power of Labor's Pensions*, Ithaca: Cornell University Press, pp. 44–67.

Berger, C. (2004) *Disclosure of Ethical Considerations in Investment Product Disclosure Statements: A Review of Current Practice in Australia*, Melbourne: Australian Conservation Foundation.

Blommestein, H. (1998) 'Impact of institutional investors on financial markets', in Organisation for Economic Co-operation and Development (OECD), *Institutional Investors in the New Financial Landscape*, Paris: OECD, pp. 46–67.

Bouma, J.J., Jeucken, M.H.A. and Klinkers, L. (eds) (2001) *Sustainable Banking: The Greening of Finance*, Sheffield: Greenleaf Publishing.

Braithwaite, J. and Drahos, P. (2000) *Global Business Regulation*, Cambridge: Cambridge University Press.

Coles, D. and Green, D. (2002) *Do UK Pension Funds Invest Responsibly?*, London: JustPensions.

Common, M. (1996) *Environmental and Resource Economics*, Harlow: Longman.

Cormier, D., Magnan, M. and Morard, B. (1993) 'The impact of corporate pollution on market valuation: some empirical evidence', *Ecological Economics*, 8(2): 135–55.

Costanza, R., Cumberland, J., Daly, H., Goodland, R., Norgaard, R. *et al.* (1997a) *An Introduction to Ecological Economics*, Florida: St. Lucie Press.

Costanza, R., d'Arge, R., de Groot, R., Farber, S., Grasso, M., Hannon, B., Limburg, K., Nacem, S., O'Neill, R.V., Paruelo, J., Raslim, R.G., Sutton, P. and van den Belt, A. (1997b) 'The value of the world's ecosystem services and national capital', *Nature*, 387: 253–60.

Cranston, R. (1997) *Principles of Banking Law*, Oxford: Clarendon Press.

Daly, H. (1992) 'Allocation, distribution and scale: towards an economics that is efficient, just and sustainable', *Ecological Economics*, 6: 185–93.

Delphi International and Ecological GMBH (1997) *The Role of Financial Institutions in Achieving Sustainable Development*, London: Delphi International.

Department of Work and Pensions (DWP) (2002) *Encouraging Shareholder Activism: A Consultation Document*, London: DWP.

Djurasovic, G. (1997) 'The regulation of socially responsible mutual funds', *Journal of Corporation Law*, 22: 257–95.

Donahue, J.D. (1989) *The Privatization Decision: Public Ends, Private Means*, New York: Basic Books.

Donaldson, L. and Davis, J.H. (1994) 'Boards and company performance – research challenges the conventional wisdom', *Corporate Governance: An International Review*, 2(3): 151–60.

Drucker, P. (1976) *Unseen Revolution: How Pension Fund Socialism Came to America*, New York: Harper and Row.

Duff, D. (2003) 'Tax policy and global warming', *Canadian Tax Journal*, 51(6): 2063–118.

Ellison, R. (1991) 'The golden fleece? Ethical investment and fiduciary law', *Trust Law International*, 5(4): 157–62.

Emtairah T. (2002) *Corporate Environmental Reporting: Review of Policy Action in Europe*, Lund: International Institute for Industrial Environmental Economics.

Ethical Investment Research Service (EIRIS) (1999) *Company Environmental Management, Policy and Reporting*, London: EIRIS.

European Commission (2000) *Institutional Arrangements for the Regulation and Supervision of the Financial Sector*, Brussels: EC Internal Market Directorate General.

European Social Investment Forum (Eurosif) (2003) *Socially Responsible Investment Among European Institutional Investors: 2003 Report*, Paris: Eurosif.

Fiorino, D.J. (1999) 'Rethinking environmental regulation: perspectives on law and governance', *Harvard Environmental Law Review*, 23: 441–69.

Foerster, S. and Asmundson, P. (2001) 'Socially responsible investing: better for your soul or your bottom line?', *Canadian Investment Review*, 14(4): 26–34.

Forsyth, T. (1999) *International Investment and Climate Change*, London: Earthscan.

Frank, J. and Mayer C. (1990) 'Capital markets and corporate control: a study of France, Germany and the U.K', *Economic Policy*, 10: 191–231.

Frankel, T. and Kirsch, C.E. (1999) *Investment Management Regulation*, Durham: Carolina Academic Press.

Freeman, J. (2000) 'The private role in public governance', *New York University Law Review*, 75: 543–675.

French, H. (1998) *Investing in the Future: Harnessing Private Capital Flows for Environmentally Sustainable Development*, Washington DC: Worldwatch Institute.

Freshfields Bruckhaus Deringer (2005) *Banking on Responsibility*, London: Freshfields Bruckhaus Deringer.

Geltman, E.G. (1992) 'Disclosure of contingent environmental liabilities by public companies under the federal securities laws', *Harvard Environmental Law Review*, 16: 129–73.

Geltman, E.G. and Skroback, A.E. (1997) 'Environmental activism and the ethical investor', *Journal of Corporation Law*, 22(3): 465–504.

Gilson, R.J. and Kraakman, R. (1991) 'Reinventing the outside director: an agenda for institutional investors', *Stanford Law Review*, 43: 863–906.

Guercio, D.D. and Hawkins, I. (1999) 'The motivation and impact of pension fund activism', *Journal of Financial Economics*, 52: 293–340.

Haigh, M. and Hazelton, J. (2004) 'Financial markets: a tool for social responsibility?', *Journal of Business Ethics*, 52(1): 59–71.

Hancher, L. and Moran, M. (1989) 'Organizing regulatory space', in L. Hancher and M. Moran (eds) *Capitalism, Culture and Economic Regulation*, Oxford: Clarendon Press, pp. 271–99.

Harmes, A. (2001) *Unseen Power: How Mutual Funds Threaten the Political and Economic Wealth of Nations*, Toronto: Stoddart.

Harper R.K. and Adams, S.C. (1996) 'CERCLA and deep pockets: market response to the superfund program', *Contemporary Economic Policy*, 14(1): 107–16.

Hayton, D. (1999) 'English fiduciary standards and trust law', *Vanderbilt Journal of Transnational Law*, 32: 555–609.

Hudson, A. (1999) *Principles of Equity and Trusts*, London: Cavendish Publishing.

Hunt, P.C. (ed.) (2004) *Values to Value: A Global Dialogue on Sustainable Finance*, Nairobi: United Nations Environment Programme Finance Initiative.

Hutchinson J.D. and Cole, C.G. (1980) 'Legal standards governing investment of pension assets for social and political goals', *University of Pennsylvania Law Review*, 128(4): 1340–88.

Investor Responsibility Research Center (IRRC) (1992) *Institutional Investor Needs for Corporate Environmental Information*, New York: IRRC.

James, W.D. (1988) 'Financial institutions and hazardous waste litigation: limiting the exposure to superfund liability', *Natural Resources Journal*, 28: 329–55.

Jessop, B. (1990) *State Theory: Putting the Capitalist State in its Place*, Cambridge: Polity Press.

Jeucken, M. (2001) *Sustainable Finance and Banking: The Financial Sector and the Future of the Planet*, London: Earthscan.

Kinder, P., Lydenberg, S. and Domini, A. (1992) *The Social Investment Almanac*, New York: Henry Holt.

Knoll, M.S. (2002) 'Ethical screening in modern financial markets: the conflicting claims underlying socially responsible investment', *Business Lawyer*, 57: 681–710.

KPMG Environmental Consulting (1999) *International Survey of Environmental Reporting*, London: KPMG.

Krugman, P. and Wells, R. (2005) *Microeconomics*, New York: Worth Publishers.

Labatt S. and White, R.R. (2002) *Environmental Finance: A Guide to Environmental Risk Assessment and Financial Products*, New York: John Wiley & Sons.

Lanoie, P., Laplante, B. and Roy, M. (1998) 'Can capital markets create incentives for pollution control?', *Ecological Economics*, 26: 31–41.

Lee, W.A. (1987) 'Modern portfolio theory and the investment of pension funds', in P.D. Finn (ed.) *Equity and Commercial Relationships*, Sydney: Law Book Co., pp. 284–91.

Lyons, J.J. (1986) 'Deep pockets and CERCLA: should superfund liability be abolished?' *Stanford Environmental Law Journal*, 6: 198–344.

McCall, C. and Wilson, R. (1993) 'Shareholder proposals: why not in Canada?' *Corporate Governance Review*, 5(1): 12–15.

MacIntosh, J.G. (1993) 'The role of institutional and retail shareholders in Canadian capital markets', *Osgoode Hall Law Journal*, 32: 371–472.

MacIntosh, J.G. (1996) 'Institutional shareholders and corporate governance in Canada', *Canadian Business Law Journal*, 26: 145–88.

Mackenzie, B. (1998) 'The choice of criteria in ethical investment', *Business Ethics*, 7(2): 81–6.

Maitland, I. (1995) 'The limits of business self-regulation', *California Management Review*, 27(3): 132–47.

Manitoba Law Reform Commission, (1993) *Ethical Investment by Trustees*, Winnipeg: Manitoba Law Reform Commission.

Mathieu, E. (2000) 'Response of UK pension funds to the SRI disclosure regulation', in

UKSIF *Response of UK Pension Funds to the SRI Disclosure Regulation*, London: UKSIF.

Miller, A. (1991) *Socially Responsible Investment: The Financial Impact of Screened Investment in the 1990s*, London: Financial Times Business Information.

Monsma, D. Esq. and Buckley, J. (2004) 'Non-financial corporate performance: the material edges of social and environmental disclosure', *University of Baltimore Journal of Environmental Law*, 11: 151–203.

Morin, F. (2000) 'A transformation in the French model of shareholding and management', *Economy and Society*, 29(1): 36–53.

Muldoon, R. (1987) 'The international law of ecodevelopment: emerging norms for development assistance agencies', *Texas International Law Journal*, 22(1): 1–40.

Muth, M. and Donaldson, L. (1998) 'Stewardship theory and board structure: a contingency approach', *Corporate Governance: An International Review*, 6(1): 5–28.

Omar, P.J. (2001) 'Company law reform in France: the economic imperative', *European Business Law Review*, March–April: 76–8.

Orts, E.W. (1995) 'Reflexive environmental law', *Northwestern University Law Review*, 89(4): 1227–340.

Owen, D. (ed.) (1992) *Green Reporting: Accountancy and the Challenge of the Nineties*, London: Chapman and Hall.

Panayotou, T. (1998) *Instruments of Change: Motivating and Financing Sustainable Development*, London: Earthscan.

Parkinson, J.E. (1995) *Corporate Power and Responsibility: Issues in the Theory of Company Law*, Oxford: Clarendon Press.

Pitchford, R. (1995) 'How liable should a lender be? The case of judgement-proof firms and environmental risk', *American Economic Review*, 85: 1171–86.

Pound, J. (1988) 'Proxy contests and the efficiency of shareholder oversight', *Journal of Financial Economics*, 20: 237–65.

Prevost, A.K. and Rao, R.P. (2000) 'Of what value are shareholder proposals sponsored by public pension funds?', *Journal of Business*, 73(2): 177–204.

Prigge, S. (1998) 'A survey of German corporate governance', in K.J. Hopt *et al.* (eds) *Comparative Corporate Governance*, Oxford: Clarendon Press, pp. 943–1043.

Rada, J. and Trisoglio, A. (1992) 'Capital markets and sustainable development', *Columbia Journal of World Business*, 27(3/4): 42–9.

Ramshaw, P.F. (1998) 'Ethical investment: retail ethics and participatory democracy', *Cambrian Law Review*, 29: 105–38.

Rein, M. (1989) 'The social structure of institutions: neither public nor private', in S.B. Kamerman and A.J. Kahn (eds) *Privatization and the Welfare State*, New Jersey: Princeton University Press, pp. 67–98.

Rhodes, M. and van Apeldoorn, B. (1998) 'Capital unbound? The transformation of European corporate governance', *Journal of European Public Policy*, 5(3): 406–27.

Richardson, B.J. (2002a) *Environmental Regulation through Financial Organisations*, The Hague: Kluwer.

Richardson, B.J. (2002b) 'Pensions law reform and environmental policy: a new role for institutional investors?', *Journal of International Financial Markets: Law and Regulation*, 3(5): 159–69.

Richardson, B.J. (2002c) 'Implications of recent changes to the EMAS and eco-label regulations for the financial services sector', *Environmental Law and Management*, 14(2): 131–5.

Richardson, B.J. (2002d) 'Mandating environmental liability insurance', *Duke Environmental Law and Policy Forum*, 12(2): 293–329.
Richardson, B.J. (2004) 'Financing environmental change: a new role for Canadian environmental law', *McGill Law Journal*, 49(1): 145–202.
Richardson, B.J. and Wood, S. (eds) (2006) *Environmental Law for Sustainability: A Reader*, Oxford: Hart Publishing.
Rifkin, J. and Barber, R. (1978) *The North Will Rise Again: Pensions, Politics and Power in the 1980s*, New York: Beacon Press.
Scholtens, L.J.R. (2001) *Greenlining: Economic and Environmental Effects of Government Facilitated Lending to Sustainable Economic Activities in the Netherlands*, Groningen: University of Groningen.
Securities Exchange Commission (SEC) (2003) *Proxy Voting by Investment Advisers*, Washington DC: SEC.
Shaw, E.S. (1975) *Financial Deepening in Economic Development*, Oxford: Oxford University Press.
Social Investment Forum (SIO) (2003) *2003 Report on Socially Responsible Investing Trends in the United States*, New York: SIO.
Sommer, A.A. Jr. (1990) 'Corporate governance in the nineties: managers vs. institutions', *University of Cincinnati Law Review*, 59: 357–83.
Sparkes, R. (1995) *The Ethical Investor*, London: HarperCollins.
Sparkes, R. (2002) *Socially Responsible Investment: A Global Revolution*, New York: Wiley.
Staniskis J.K. and Stasiskiene, Z. (2003) 'Promotion of cleaner production investments: international experience', *Journal of Cleaner Production*, 11(6): 619–28.
Sustainable Development Research International Group (SDRIG), (2002) *Green, Social and Ethical Funds in Europe in 2001*, London: SDRIG.
Teubner, G. (1983) 'Substantive and reflexive elements in modern law', *Law and Society Review*, 17: 239–85.
Teubner, G. (1994) *Law as an Autopoetic System*, Oxford: Blackwell.
Thomas, W.L. (2001) 'The green nexus: financiers and sustainable development', *Georgetown International Environmental Law Review*, 13: 899–944.
Tietenberg, T.H. (1989) 'Indivisible toxic torts: the economics of joint and several liability', *Land Economics*, 65(4): 305–19.
Tredje AP-fonden, (2002) *Third Swedish National Pension Fund Annual Report 2002*, Stockholm: Tredje AP-fonden.
UK Social Investment Forum (UKSIF), (1999) *UK Social Investment Forum Tells MPs of Need to Include Environment in Framework for Financial Services Regulator*, Press Release, 19 April 1999, London: UKSIF.
Unger, R. (1998) *Democracy Realised: The Progressive Alternative*, London: Verso.
United Nations Environment Programme (UNEP) Finance Initiative (2004) *The Materiality of Social, Environmental and Corporate Governance Issues in Equity Pricing*, Nairobi: UNEP.
Vogel, D. (1983) 'Trends in Shareholder Activism: 1970–1982', *California Management Review*, 25: 68–85.
von Ahsen, A., Lange, C. and Pianowski, M. (2004) 'Corporate environmental reporting: survey and empirical evidence', *International Journal of Environment and Sustainable Development*, 3(1): 5–17.
von Amsberg, J. (1995) 'Excessive environmental risks: an intergenerational market failure', *European Economic Review*, 39: 1447–64.
Walter, A. (1993) *World Power and World Money*, New York: Harvester Wheatsheaf.

Wood, S. (2003) 'Green revolution or greenwash? Voluntary environmental standards, public law and private authority in Canada', in Law Commission of Canada (ed.) *New Perspectives on the Public-Private Divide*, Vancouver: University of British Columbia Press, pp. 123–65.

World Bank (1995) *Mainstreaming the Environment: The World Bank Group and the Environment*, Washington DC: World Bank.

World Bank (1997) *Private Capital Flows to Developing Countries: The Road to Financial Integration*, Oxford: Oxford University Press.

Yago, G. (1993) 'Financial repression and the capital crunch recession: political and regulatory barriers to growth economics', in B.S. Zycher and C. Lewis (eds) *Economic Policy, Financial Markets, and Economic Growth*, Boulder: Westview Press, pp. 81–105.

Part III

Redesigning governance for sustainability

Chapter 7

Sustainability in paradigms and practices at board level in Anglo-American plc

Tudor J. Maxwell[1]

INTRODUCTION

In a great neo-classical economic text written more than 100 years ago, Alfred Marshall made the point that social systems have inertia that enables them to carry flaws and imperfections along with them, to the detriment of the members of those social systems.

> Adam Smith was yet careful to indicate many points in which the system failed. . . . But many of his followers with less philosophical insight, and in some cases with less real knowledge of the world, argued boldly that whatever is, is right. . . . they did not see that the very strength of the system as a whole enabled it to carry along with it many incidents which were in themselves evil.
>
> (Marshall 1898: 325)

Marshall's comment on inertia in social systems is highly relevant to the topic of corporate governance and sustainability, and to paradigms that guide practices at board level, because changes in the natural environment are usually not synchronous with changes in the social environment. In most cases there is a delay between the time that societies cause damage to the natural environment and the time that those societies eliminate their destructive practices. For example, our awareness of the causes and impacts of global warming has grown rapidly over recent decades, and yet our initiatives to check the effect are still far from mature – partly because our dependence on fossil fuel has become entrenched over the course of a century.

To avoid extinction, social systems need to respond to changes in their natural environments. To avoid extinction, companies need to respond to changes in their social environments, and if they do so efficiently enough they could gain strategic advantage in the process. Since the responsibility for adapting corporate practices and processes rests most importantly with a company's top managers and board members, paradigms governing boards' decisions are a very powerful dimension of the inertia inherent in a company's environmental practices.

In this chapter, I present my understanding of how the Anglo American plc board has responded to sustainability challenges in recent years, with a view to highlighting ways in which the practice fits, or has gone beyond traditional corporate governance paradigms. I compiled the case study from public documentation, and from interviews with Anglo board members and senior managers conducted during 2005. The case study does not represent the company's opinion on this topic, nor is it intended to present an unequivocally right or wrong approach to sustainable development. Rather it is intended to demonstrate – from the perspective of an outsider – how a large mining company is grappling with the many challenges associated with sustainability, and how it is supported or hindered in this task by dominant corporate governance paradigms.

I begin with a brief discussion of what I understand to be dominant corporate governance paradigms. I then present a brief overview of Anglo American plc (Anglo) and its responses to sustainability-related challenges. In the final section, I comment on the impact of dominant and challenging paradigms in corporate governance.

DOMINANT PARADIGMS IN CORPORATE GOVERNANCE

No paradigm is more influential in shaping approaches to, and understandings of, business practice than neo-classical economic theory. According to Alfred Marshall,

> the first systematic attempt to form an economic science on a broad basis was made in France about the middle of the 18th century by a group of statesmen and philosophers [who] gave to economics its modern aim of seeking after such knowledge as may help to raise the quality of human life.
>
> (Marshall 1898: 55–6)

Economic theory was strongly influenced by the work of Adam Smith's *The Wealth of Nations*, as he was 'the first to make a careful and scientific enquiry into the manner in which value measures human motive, on the one side measuring the desire of purchasers to obtain wealth, and on the other the efforts and sacrifices undergone by its producers' (Marshall 1898: 58). The contributions of economists and social scientists such as Ricardo, Pareto, Keynes and Marshall, in the late nineteenth and early twentieth centuries have been classified as neo-classical economic theory, and while successive contributions added to the complexity of economic theories of the firm, it seems the underlying assumptions remained surprisingly stable.

Neo-classical economic theory seeks to maximize social welfare through the analysis of the costs and benefits of alternative models of action under carefully controlled circumstances. Such analysis has always required that the systems of interest are carefully delimited, by defining those variables that are 'external' to the problem of interest. So when a company's activities are deemed to have negligible impact on the natural environment, sustainability issues are externalized. Externalities are assumed to be the responsibility of the state, based on the argument that democratic systems of governance are the institutions best suited to determining the bounds within which business should operate. The argument suggests that businesses operating within those bounds can focus on the task of generating wealth for shareholders, through which they make an optimal contribution to society. Private strategic interests may cause firms to go beyond regulatory compliance, but to do so should not be necessary for environmental sustainability or social development. A particularly powerful argument in favour of the maximization of shareholder wealth under this neo-classical economic paradigm is the fact that the shareholders' return on investment is calculated after all other contractual stakeholders have received their interests. Thus, assuming all contracts are complete, optimally formulated and justly upheld, the interests of all contractual stakeholders are met by maximizing the benefit of the shareholders.

In 1976 Jensen and Meckling made a fundamental contribution to the extension of the economic paradigm to the realm of the firm, and hence of corporate governance, through their writings on agency theory. Their contribution was founded on the following statements:

> While the literature of economics is replete with references to the 'theory of the firm', the material generally subsumed under that heading is not a theory of the firm but actually a theory of markets in which firms are important actors. The firm is a 'black box' operated to meet the relevant marginal conditions with respect to inputs and outputs, thereby maximising profits, or more accurately, present value. Except for a few recent and tentative steps, however, we have no theory which explains how the conflicting objectives of the individual participants are brought into equilibrium.
>
> (Jensen and Meckling 1976: 307)

> The private corporation or firm is simply one form of legal fiction which serves as a nexus for contracting relationships and which is also characterised by the existence of divisible residual claims on the assets and cash flows of the organisation.
>
> (Jensen and Meckling 1976: 311)

The impact of this renewed exploration of the contractual relations within the firm was profound. It facilitated a focus on stakeholders contracting with the firm (though it has maintained a primary focus on the relationship between non-managing owners and non-owning managers). In this sense, agency theory can be classified as a stakeholder theory of the firm, but one in which only contractual stakeholders are considered. In agency theory, optimal firm operations depend on the minimization of costs associated with principal-agent contracts. Applying their theory to the issue of environmental or social sustainability, Jensen and Meckling (1976: 311) argued that a nexus of contracts – or a 'legal fiction' – cannot have a social conscience. They therefore endorsed the neo-classical economic approach to the natural environment, which proposes that its care be externalized from the realm of corporate governance.

Resource-dependence theory, presented in 1978 by Pfeffer and Salancik (2003), offered an alternative theory base of relevance to boards of directors. The theory focused attention on the fact that even efficient companies can fail if they are unable to gain access to scarce resources critical to their survival. Firms therefore need to co-opt the sources of constraints in their supply of critical resources in order to survive and thrive. This entails maintaining good relationships with powerful external stakeholders, such as regulators, powerful individuals in large companies in the supply chain, NGOs and so on. It therefore expands the frame of reference of corporate governance beyond contractual stakeholders, to include a selection of non-contractual stakeholders directly linked to the firm.

Together agency theory and resource-dependence theory have formed the dominant paradigm governing board practice in recent decades. Under this paradigm, boards have focused on controlling top managers through extensive auditing, and on maintaining important relationships with external stakeholders that could influence strategic success. Broader social and environmental issues are the responsibility of government.

A number of other theories have been developed to challenge the dominance of agency theory, usually by challenging the simplifying assumptions on which it has been developed. Examples are institutional theory and social network theory. In an early text contributing to institutional theory Selznick (1957: 12) noted that institutionalization is the process by which routine actions are infused 'with value beyond the technical requirements of the task at hand' (Selznick 1957: 17). Institutionalization enables large organizations to make routine decisions with a minimum of effort, to the point where, under steady conditions, they run themselves. According to Selznick, leaders are agents of institutionalization, establishing the frames of reference within which routine and critical decisions are made. Institutional theory suggests a role for boards of directors that extends beyond the control of senior managers or the securing of access to external resources, because the task of imbuing routine actions with meaning implies a deep integration of business with society. In institutional theory, it is possible to understand firms to be co-creators of the environments in which they operate, and systems of interpretation in those environments.

Social network theory offers a deeper understanding of how people make decisions, arguing against the rational, maximizing calculation assumed in the economic theories. In developing this line of thought, Callon (1998) proposed that people deal with complexity and uncertainty beyond their calculative capacity by replacing a calculative algorithm with a trusted point of reference. Points of reference could be the opinions of trusted individuals or institutions in the social system. Decisions are always made within the frames of reference constituted by social networks, and decision-making is facilitated by determining those relations that will and will not be considered relevant to the decision. This understanding of decision-making also endorses a deep integration of business and society, thereby challenging the neat externalization of responsibility for the natural and social environments.

Institutional and social network theories draw attention to the fact that companies are embedded in (or 'co-constitute') their social systems, and that they impact upon and are affected by a cross-section of stakeholders much broader than those people contractually or relationally linked to the firm. They suggest a role for boards in defining values and purpose in a company that resonate with their social systems and therefore support its access to markets and scarce resources. Consistent with these theories, though not specifically endorsing either of them, Charles Handy (2002: 51) defined a business as a 'community with a purpose'.

Figure 7.1 represents a multi-theoretic approach to corporate governance, by differentiating between the theories discussed above on the basis of the stakeholders that are internalized in the pursuit of firm survival, and on the extent to which the theories consider the external environment to be dynamic and created.

The representation of dominant paradigms in Figure 7.1 highlights two interesting features. First, it suggests that the theory bases can be treated as complementary rather than mutually exclusive. The dominant economic paradigm is very powerful under relatively stable conditions. Indeed, economic, material and contractual efficiency are

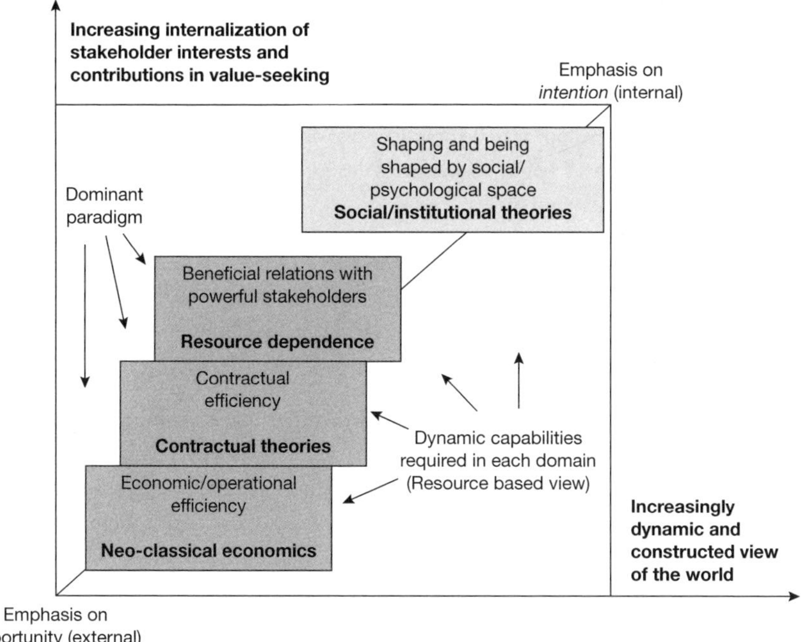

Figure 7.1 *Dominant and emerging paradigms in corporate governance (adapted from Maxwell 2004)*

highly desirable in most business contexts, and material efficiency is particularly desirable from a sustainability perspective. If all relevant environmental issues are dealt with through regulation, then the simple pursuit of profit can be consistent with the pursuit of sustainable development. (This does not imply that shareholder wealth maximization need then become the purpose of the firm: as Handy (2002: 51) notes, profit is to a company what food is to people – essential, but not the whole purpose of existence.) But the economic paradigm has limited application when conditions are very dynamic or when they are in the process of being defined by influential participants in the social system. Social and institutional theories place greater emphasis on the way in which companies and their leaders create market realities in accordance with their own intentions.

The second point of interest is that the dominant paradigm needs to be augmented by a focus on capabilities such as is offered explicitly by the resource-based view of the firm (presented by Barney in 1991) and the subsequent discussion of dynamic capabilities (see, for example, Eisenhardt and Martin 2000). Barney perceived a world in which the supply of capabilities required to pursue desired courses of action was not elastic in the short term, as a result of causal ambiguity, social complexity or path dependence. This being the case, he argued that companies are able to develop sustainable competitive advantage if they can develop rare capabilities that are not easy to imitate or substitute. This approach can easily be combined with each of the theories described above.

The Anglo case study described in the next part of this chapter presents an opportunity to assess the extent to which board practice in a large mining company conforms with or departs from the dominant corporate governance paradigms. It is made interesting by the fact that Anglo has a reputation as being a traditional, old-economy company, and yet there appear to be practices that depart from the traditional corporate governance paradigms. I begin with a brief description of Anglo and then discuss its sustainable development initiatives.

ANGLO AMERICAN PLC

Company profile and history

Anglo American plc (Anglo) is the world's third largest mining company when ranked by turnover – only BHP Billiton and Rio Tinto generate more revenues in that sector. Anglo has operations in 65 countries and employs over 200,000 people. In 2004, total profit for the year was US$2.9 billion (83 per cent higher than 2003). In the six months to June 2005, Anglo reported profits of US$1.838 billion, which can be compared with profit reported by BHP Billiton (US$6.4 billion) in the same period, and Rio Tinto (US$2.1 billion). Anglo is made up of eight operating units, with businesses in the areas of gold, platinum, diamonds, coal, ferrous metals and industries, base metals, paper and packaging, and industrial minerals. The geographical breakdown of headline earnings during the first reporting period in 2004 was as follows: Americas (41 per cent), South

Africa (29 per cent), Europe (15 per cent), and the rest of the world (15 per cent). Aside from the stake held by the founding Oppenheimer family (a little over 4 per cent of the company), the ownership of Anglo is widely dispersed among large institutions.

Anglo American Corporation (AAC) was formed in 1917 by Sir Ernest Oppenheimer, who had raised one million British pounds from UK and US sources for the purpose of exploiting gold resources in South Africa. In 1926, AAC became the largest single shareholder in De Beers (diamond mines), and in 1929, Ernest Oppenheimer became chairman of De Beers. Whereas Johannesburg Consolidated Investments (JCI) and Goldfields pioneered mining of the Hans Merensky platinum reef, AAC later bought a majority stake in JCI to gain exposure to its platinum and diamond investments, and to set it on course to become the world's biggest platinum producer. During 1961, AAC bought Hudson Bay Mining and Smelting Company in Canada as its first major international expansion. Later in the same decade, Anglo entered into the steel industry through an acquisition, and it founded a paper and packaging company (Mondi). The 1990s saw AAC undergoing major restructuring of its assets and focus. It acquired a number of international mining and minerals operations, including copper mines in Chile, a gold mine in Mali, coal assets in Latin America, nickel mines in Venezuela, and a zinc mine in Ireland. In 1996, AAC participated in an empowerment deal through the sale of major stakes in two South African companies to the National Empowerment Consortium, and the African Mining Group. In 1998, AAC eliminated many of the cross-holdings that were characteristic of corporations operating in apartheid-South Africa, and combined the assets of its Luxembourg-based Minorco with the Johannesburg-based AAC to form Anglo American plc (Anglo), with a primary listing in London, with effect from 24 May, 1999. Anglo moved its head office to London in the same year. Since then, Anglo has been through a process of refocusing its core assets through a number of large transactions. Anglo acquired aggregates company Tarmac plc in the UK, various businesses in the pulp and paper industry (Frantschach, Assi Domain and Syktyvkar Forest Enterprise), Shell's coal interests in Australia and Venezuela, a copper producer in Chile (Disputada) and a controlling stake in iron-ore company Kumba Resources Limited in South Africa. It also eliminated its cross-holding in De Beers, of which it now owns 45 per cent.

Anglo's environmental impact and sustainability initiatives

Anglo's operations have enormous impact on the natural environment. For example, Anglo uses one-thousandth of the world's energy annually, an amount equivalent to the annual energy consumption of Chile or the Czech Republic. The consumption of energy constitutes 7 per cent of Anglo's annual operating costs, making it a focal point for stakeholders both outside and within the company. Anglo is also a major coal producer. It has large forestry operations. It mines uranium as a by-product of its gold mining operations. It has recently invested in aggregates mining operations in China, and it has smelting operations historically associated with large scale emissions into the atmosphere.

Aside from possible unintended deviations on a micro-level, Anglo complies with social and environmental regulation in all the countries in which it has operations. In the majority of those countries, though, Anglo operates beyond compliance. Anglo's sustainable development efforts were recognized by a number of organizations during 2004. As noted by the CEO in the Report to Society (Anglo American plc 2004b: 3)

> Anglo American was recognized as the top mining company in the Basic Resources Sector of the World Index of the Dow Jones Sustainability Index 2004–2005 and the STOXX Index – the benchmark for European resource sustainability investment funds. Anglo American, Anglo Platinum, Kumba Resources and AngloGold Ashanti were also included in the Johannesburg Securities Exchange SRI index. Our 2003 Report to Society: Contributing to Sustainable Development received a commendation from the UK's Association of Chartered Certified Accountants for articulating the sustainable development challenges for the business. The president of the Philippines, for the third year in a row, has especially recognized our exploration division's work on biodiversity.

Anglo is also credited with a number of other sustainability-related achievements. For example, Anglo has achieved exemplary sustainability reporting standards. It was the first company to offer to pay for anti-retroviral treatment for all employees afflicted by AIDS in its South African operations (despite initial government resistance to the plan!), and Anglo is represented on a number of business organizations addressing sustainability, as indicated in Table 7.1.

Anglo's board-level responses to environmental challenges can be discussed under three broad (and overlapping) headings: strategic investment decisions, institutional and structural responses, and interventions at the level of organizational processes.

Table 7.1 *Anglo's participation in industry – and multilateral organizations*

Organization	*Role*
World Business Council on Sustainable Development	Member
International Council on Mining and Metals	Chairman
International Business Leaders Forum	Member
World Coal Institute	Chairman
Global Business Coalition on HIV/AIDS	Chairman
Extractive Industries Transparency Initiative	Participant
World Bank's Extractive Industries Review	Contributor
Global Reporting Initiative	Adherent
Global Compact	Signatory
United Nations Environment Program	Joint projects
World Conservation Union	Joint projects
International Finance Corporation 'safeguard policies'	Reviewer
WWF	Joint projects

Strategic investment decisions

Four examples of interventions in key investment decisions were described during an interview in 2005 with outgoing technical director, Mr Bill Nairn.

> We had a case in South America where they came along with a viable looking gold operation, and we rejected it because it was in the Amazon jungle. We looked at what they wanted to do. It was to fell trees, dig up areas and create dumps in an area that was pristine . . . so we decided not to do it.
>
> We are busy in China . . . we bought a quarry there . . . its name was 'snow white', because within a kilometre of the place everything was white dust. It was unbelievable. They had an average of three deaths every two months. We found out that the people would abseil down the rock-face, drill some holes, charge them up, whistle to someone below to say 'Clear Out', and then climb out! Then some explosions would occur, rocks would fly in every direction, and if someone didn't get out the way he was killed. When we bought the place, we said it was on condition that they close down the whole mine, redesign it, bring in modern machinery, retrain everyone, and then re-open it. Thereafter any fatal accident would count against management as it would anywhere else in the world. They did that – stopped it for 6 months. They have been running for a year now, and have not had one fatality. The Chinese love it, and the productivity is great. In fact it is higher than it was before the intervention.
>
> In the UK we had a paper operation where they wanted to bury the combustible waste. They did a financial exercise to say it didn't pay us to burn the waste – that it was better to bury it. We said 'You can't just decide on a [purely] financial basis what is right and wrong. What's right is to get energy from that material, and if it costs us a bit [extra], then factor that into your operation'. They did that. Actually, when the cost of power went up, the whole exercise became very viable.
>
> At Rustenburg [in a platinum smelter operation] . . . the SO_2 'capture' was at a level of about 55 per cent, amounting to emissions of about 300 tonnes of sulphur per day. We put in a new converter there. It cost over R1.5 billion [approximately US$230 million]. The converter has dropped the emissions to less than 20 tonnes of sulphur per day. You have to ask what the benefit was. There were no financial benefits. It cost a lot of money. We made more sulphuric acid . . . but you can't give sulphuric acid away! So a lot of decisions are made at board or exec level that doesn't have a payback. But there is a moral payback. There is a community payback. Since we have done it the community has changed its attitude towards the mine.

At the group level, another type of intervention in strategic investment decisions relates to group sustainability projects. In 2004 Anglo initiated an energy efficiency project. Under the initiative the board set energy reduction targets of 10 per cent over 10 years. The potential savings associated with the project could amount to US$400 million for the group, with relatively little cost in human resources, and almost no risk (which makes it remarkable that such a project was commissioned so recently).

The Anglo board also implemented a requirement that all new investments be subject to a socio-economic assessment, following a standard approach, and involving constructive engagement with affected communities and stakeholders. A Socio-Economic Assessment Toolkit (SEAT) has been designed for this purpose, requiring community engagement processes to be conducted for all major investments.

Institutional and structural responses

A primary institutional response to environmental challenges is made through the Safety and Sustainable Development (SSD) Committee of the board of Anglo American plc. The committee was formerly known as the Safety, Health and Environment Committee, but was renamed during 2004 in order to reflect the requirement to address sustainable development issues more generally. The committee is chaired by Mr Chris Fay, and is made up of a number of high-profile board members, including Sir Mark Moody-Stuart. The SSD committee meets regularly through the year, and initiates work, or reviews progress in critical areas.

A second set of institutional responses to environmental challenges is made in the form of high-level appointments to positions with direct responsibility for areas of specific environmental concern. For example, Mr Roger Wicks was appointed to a newly created position entitled 'Head of Energy' in response to the challenges associated with climate change and volatile energy prices.

A third, major institutional response to the emerging environmental challenges has taken the form of the creation of a sustainable development team reporting directly to the CEO, with responsibility for addressing sustainable development issues across the entire group. Although the team has only been in operation since 2003, it brings together other Safety, Health and Environment initiatives that had been in operation in the company prior to, or from the time of its move to London in 1999. Mr Dorian Emmett – formerly a Chief Operating Officer in the platinum division – was appointed to head the sustainable development team in 2003. He is based in the London head-office. The team has a lean structure, as the intention is that sustainable development activities will be enacted through line management in the operating divisions. To this end, three levels of engagement with line functions have been put in place. 'Communities of practice' involve managers at all levels across all the managed units, and focus on specific areas of improvement (such as energy efficiency, biodiversity and so on). A 'sustainable development forum' involves leaders or prime-movers from the managed units in an ongoing discourse on the topic of sustainable development. And a 'sustainable development council' involves CEOs of operating units and meets annually to assess progress towards sustainable development. The council reports directly to the Executive Board facilitating integration of sustainable development initiatives at the highest level.

The sustainable development team facilitates many of the activities carried out through the communities of practice and the sustainable development forum. The team's role is therefore one of initiation, implementation, information gathering, support and

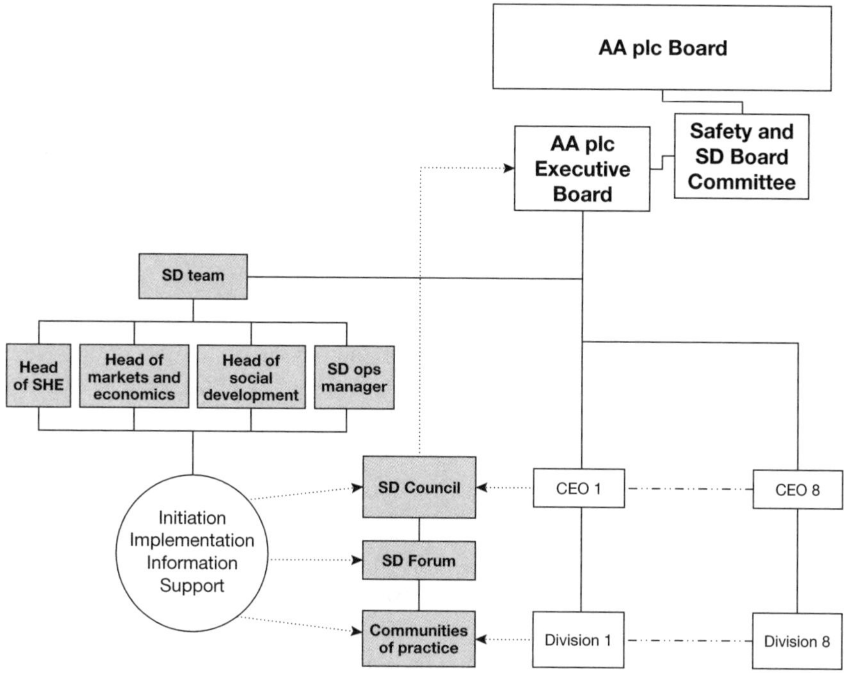

Figure 7.2 *Anglo's sustainable development team structure*

facilitation, depending on the nature of the issues being addressed at any point in time, as illustrated in Figure 7.2.

Interventions in organizational processes

With some adaptations from Chester Barnard's *Functions of the Executive* (first published in 1938), it can be said that there are five main processes that determine the nature of the daily operations of any organization: selection, visioning, interaction, motivation and learning. These processes are in constant operation in all organizations, so interventions on these levels can have a profound impact on an organization. Each of the processes is discussed below.

Selection: the selection of board members and top managers has the potential to influence greatly the orientation adopted by the board over time. For example, the appointment of Sir Mark Moody-Stuart as chairman of Anglo has undoubtedly strengthened Anglo's orientation towards sustainable development. Interestingly, though, he was not the first choice of replacement for Mr Ogilvie-Thompson. In fact Mr Göran Lindahl was the first choice for Chairman prior to 2002, but negative press associated with his leadership role in ABB caused the Anglo board to reconsider. Although an overt intention to select board members or top managers on the basis of their orientation towards or skills in addressing environmental sustainability was not apparent, a more subtle adaptation to the growing significance of the topic could be deduced from the appointment of Sir Mark as chairman.

Motivation: the motivation process is made up of the material and psychic rewards that are enjoyed by executive and non-executive directors directly associated with their involvement in Anglo. From the 2004 Annual Report it is evident that non-executive directors' remuneration is determined by the Chairperson and the executive directors, in accordance with four principles: the fees are intended to attract and retain non-executive directors of the highest, internationally-available capability; they are set in accordance with best practice in the industry; they are paid in cash (though the possibility exists for such payment to be made in the form of company shares); and they are increased when non-executive directors take on additional responsibilities, such as chairing committees. Non-executive directors do not participate in performance incentives of any sort. During 2004, the lowest remuneration received by a non-executive director was £55,000, and the highest pay received by a non-executive director other than the chairman, was £77,000. The chairman was paid £330,000. A formal evaluation of directors' performance is conducted each year, including a review of the chairman conducted in his absence. No direct link was evident between the remuneration of non-executive directors and environmental sustainability, but it is likely that members of the SSD committee would have their performance on that committee reviewed annually.

For executive directors, remuneration is intended to 'attract and retain high-calibre executives, and motivate them to develop and implement the Company's business strategy in order to optimize long-term shareholder value creation' (Annual Report 2004: 29). Remuneration comprises a fixed salary component, a performance-related annual bonus, and a performance-related long-term incentive plan. During 2004, the expected breakdown for the CEO was 33 per cent, 33 per cent and 34 per cent for each of the elements of total reward, respectively. The basic salary level is intended to be similar to the median salary for companies of comparable size, sector, level of internationalization and complexity. The annual bonus is calculated based on corporate performance (using 'stretching' earnings per share targets), business unit performance, and individual performance targets. Bonus parameters are tailored to each executive director, though it is usually the case that 70 per cent is awarded to company or business performance, and 30 per cent to the attainment of individual objectives. The overall bonus value is reduced if safety targets have not been met. The long-term incentive plan is based on share awards that are discretionary, made by a sub-committee of the board on the basis of performance over a three year period, calculated as: total shareholder return (measured relative to Anglo's main competitors), and the return on capital employed (measured relative to targets set for this indicator each year).

Thus it seems that the motivation process is strongly aligned to achieving superior returns for shareholders, and sustainability indicators have very little representation there. Only safety is singled out as an exceptional item considered in all executive-director rewards.

Interaction: the interaction process involves both the formal and informal communication that takes place within and between groups of stakeholders. The sustainable development team initiatives are designed to facilitate interaction on sustainability issues throughout the organization. As a result, it is unlikely that senior managers could avoid participation in sustainable development discussions, whereas at middle or lower levels of management it is possible that there is a tendency for people committed to the principles of sustainable development to participate, and other managers to avoid such involvement. This concern was raised by members of the sustainable development team. At board level it is impossible to determine the extent to which discussions of sustainability are represented in full board meetings, but since there is a committee dedicated to such issues, it must be assumed that there is time dedicated to the topic.

Visioning: visioning is the process by which company purpose is formulated, formed and expressed on an ongoing basis at all levels. It involves the annual strategy sessions held by the board, but is equally influenced by interaction on the topics of purpose, principles and projects that take place throughout the organisation throughout the year. At board level, the focus of the visioning process would be medium- and long-term plans, large-scale investments, and the core principles with which those decisions must accord.

Elements of the board's perspective, purpose and principles can be inferred from interviews with board members, and from speeches or public statements made by the CEO and the chairman in the company or public press, and are included in Table 7.2.

The comments attributed to the chairman describe his business case for sustainable development in terms of long-term licence to operate, a reduction in cost of capital, access to top-quality recruits, and enhancing the value of the corporate reputation. In the second comment, he delimits the company's responsibilities from the point of view of sustainable development, saying that it should not be a prime-mover in areas that are outside Anglo's immediate business activities.

The CEO, understandably, spends considerably more time commenting on Anglo's operating challenges and achievements in his speeches and reports. His orientation towards sustainability appears to be instrumental to achieving success in business operations, one indicator of which is steady growth in returns for shareholders.

The extract from company documentation is consistent with the perspective offered by the CEO. No explicit statement of vision or purpose appeared on the website prior to July 2005. Instead, as has been noted above, there is a statement of company strategy that appears, for example, in the Interim Report, and is repeated in a number of public Anglo documents:

> Anglo American's strategy is to achieve real growth and added value for its shareholders across the cycle through acquisitions, brownfields and greenfields projects and by continuously improving the operating efficiency of existing assets. We aim to achieve world class performance in all areas of our business, to provide a safe and healthy environment for employees and to demonstrate commitment to sustainable development.

Table 7.2 Excerpts from the chairman's and CEO's speeches and company reports

Sir Mark Moody-Stuart, Chairman
Sustainable development is absolutely central to the future acceptability of our business and to its ongoing success and profitability. Our businesses have high environmental and social impacts, many deplete a non-renewable . . . resource, and global concerns like climate change and HIV/AIDS are highly relevant to us. These issues reflect upon our licence to operate, our sustainability as an investment, our ability to attract the most talented recruits and our acceptability to governments and communities. Moreover, our ability to understand and address societal concerns is fundamental to our good name and the value of that reputation. (Anglo American plc 2004a: 2) Outside our immediate business activities, we cannot and should not be the prime movers in tackling corruption or human rights abuses; in countering HIV/AIDS, or in planning local economic development. (Anglo American plc 2004: i)
Mr Tony Trahar, CEO
Our business strategy is to achieve world class performance across all our businesses based on growth through acquisitions, developing new operations, innovation and efficiency and through leveraging our core competencies. Sustainable development principles are central to achieving our business strategy and challenge us to: improve the management of our social and environmental risks thereby securing continued access to natural resources and protecting our licence to operate; create social partnerships to tackle social problems like HIV/AIDS; improve efficiencies and minimize waste and pollution . . .; attract develop and retain talented staff, stimulate innovation and share knowledge . . .; ensure that our values and practices reflect international norms, community and societal expectations; and create value where we operate. This approach will assist us in reducing the cost of capital and operational management and position us as a business partner of choice (Anglo American plc 2003: 2)
Anglo public documentation
Our primary responsibility is to our investors. We will seek to maximize shareholder value over time. We believe that this is best achieved through an intelligent regard for the interests of other stakeholders including our employees, the communities associated with our operations, our customers and business partners. A reputation for integrity and responsible behaviour will underpin our commercial performance through motivating employees and building trust and goodwill in the wider world (Anglo American plc 2002: 2)

The impression obtained from both company documentation and interviews with senior managers was that Anglo has traditionally preferred to demonstrate its purpose through its actions, rather than through statements of purpose on company documentation or posted in company offices. However, an innovation in this approach is evident in the formal reports at least since 2004 (and on the website since July 2005), which carry subtitles that communicate corporate purpose in broad terms. For example, the annual report in 2004 and the interim report in 2005 are subtitled 'Meeting the World's Needs'. This by-line had not appeared in previous documentation, and appears to be intended to communicate the fact that the commodities Anglo produces are an essential part of modern life, and that Anglo intends to generate value in a sustainable way. The 2004 Annual Review begins with the following statements: 'Anglo American is a global leader in mining and natural resources. Our diversified products are essential parts of modern life. Anglo American is committed to operating in a profitable, sustainable and responsible way.'

Holistic vision incorporates also the principles by which the company intends to operate. During 2002, Anglo published a set of business principles that are to be applied in all business dealings throughout the group. The principles are described in a document entitled 'Good citizenship: our business principles', to which reference is made in the annual report. The principles can be accessed through the company web-page, though (at least until the end of 2005) reading the company principles involved downloading a separate document. It is not clear why Anglo has also been reluctant to state its principles in a more lucid format, which would facilitate their inclusion in annual reports and on the company website, and which would make it possible for employees to commit them to memory. It does, however, seem that the failure to represent the principles in more of the public documentation follows the separation of business and society common in neo-classical economic approaches described by Gladwin *et al.* (1995) as a 'fracture in corporate epistemology'. Further evidence of this separation comes from the Annual Reports in 2003 and 2004, in which each operating division presents a summary of the year's performance, including financial performance, events in the markets, operational performance and a future outlook. Not one of the summary reports makes direct reference to sustainable development issues. All sustainability reporting was separated out into the Report to Society published annually.

Relating to the natural environment specifically, the corporate principles document states:

> We recognize the need for environmental stewardship to minimise consumption of natural resources and waste generation and to minimise the impact of our operations on the environment. . . . We will work to keep health, safety and environmental matters at the forefront of workplace concerns and will report on the progress against our policies and objectives. . . . We are committed to the principles of sustainable development, by which we mean striking an optimal balance between economic, environmental and social development. We will strive to innovate and adopt best practice, wherever we operate, working in consultation with stakeholders.
>
> (Anglo American PLC 2002: 4)

Learning: the public documentation did not describe a formal approach to induction or ongoing learning at the board level, but there is evidence of an attempt to expose board members to operations in the Anglo group. So, for example,

> During 2004, non-executive directors visited the following operations: Richards Bay and SilvaCel paper mills, the Sishen iron ore mine and the Potgietersrust Platinum mine in South Africa and the Hippo Valley, Unki and Zimbabwe Alloys operations in Zimbabwe, as well as operations in Canada and China.
>
> (Anglo American plc 2004a: 24)

In summary, it is apparent that the board of Anglo recognizes the importance of sustainability for corporate performance. It has supported sustainability through advocacy on sustainability issues, through championing the process of engagement with stakeholders in society, through participation in external organizations, through interpreting trends in the natural and institutional environment and communicating the relevance of those trends in strategies and policies, through establishing organizational structures and routines supportive of sustainable operations, through statements about the value of sustainability to the organization, and through interventions in organizational processes. The board appears to understand the direct benefits of exemplary environmental performance to gain access to scarce resources (capital, talent and mining rights), and in some cases access to markets through enhanced company reputation.

As a large company, it is not surprising that the levels of commitment to sustainability are differentiated – both within the senior management of the company, and between senior and middle management of the many operations. Differentiation occurs in terms of the relative importance attributed to sustainability issues and the resources committed to those issues. The integration of sustainability objectives into core strategy obviously requires effort: whereas economic and operational aspects do not become any less important, indicators of social and environmental performance become more important. Despite exemplary work in the area of reporting, it appears from my perspective as an outsider that integration of sustainability issues has not yet been achieved in the annual report. Also from the perspective of an outsider, it appears that integration has been only partially achieved in statements of company purpose and in core organizational processes. Thus, while considerable progress has been made in the interaction process, less progress has been made with respect to the inclusion of sustainability indicators in senior executive remuneration.

UNDERSTANDING ANGLO'S RESPONSE TO ENVIRONMENTAL CHALLENGES

Whereas the dominant paradigm suggested by Anglo's statements of purpose, its board composition and motivation processes appear to be consistent with the neo-classical economic, contractual and resource dependence perspectives, other corporate literature and interviews with senior executives provide evidence of an emerging paradigm consistent with social and institutional theories. Some of Anglo's responses to environmental challenges go beyond compliance with regulation, and it seems useful to ask the question, why?

The most obvious answer, is that it is a response to pressures from stakeholders. Interviews with Anglo directors and employees support this conclusion. A number of stakeholders were cited as driving the sustainable development agenda, including Anglo's own board members, the CEO, shareholders, NGOs, employees (who in some cases generated creative responses to environmental challenges before the business case was fully developed), the market for potential employees, and a number of external institutions (including the governments of countries or groups of countries, regulatory bodies, research partners, and competitors).

Three interesting features accompany the conclusion that it is stakeholders that drive companies to act beyond compliance with environmental regulation.

First, the stakeholders mentioned were contractual and non-contractual, directly and indirectly related to the company. Pressures from shareholders and employees could be anticipated and dealt with through an agency theory approach to governance. Pressures from NGOs or research partners could be dealt with through resource-dependence theory. But pressure from the market for talented employees requires a more inclusive paradigm – one that recognizes the fact that all stakeholders are at least loosely linked through social networks, and affected by widely held norms and values in society. Supporting this opinion, Mr Bobby Godsell, non-executive director of Anglo, and CE of Anglo Gold Ashanti, said:

> I just know from moving around the company and looking at the 20 and 30 year olds we employ – they wouldn't feel proud if we were destroying the environment. So we have to work in a way that is consistent with modern social values. You can't make money out of lying and cheating, you can't have slave labour. You have to be modern in the way you approach the environment. I think that competitive edge lies in the way you do this. I mean, leaving a community better off is a tough challenge. It means you have to engage with communities. And I think that some companies engage with stakeholders better than others do. That could be a competitive advantage.

Second, the stakeholders referred to in the case study appear not to respect the strict separation of business and society that has become entrenched in some economic paradigms. Potential employees, for example, may be attracted by a company acting beyond compliance with respect to the natural environment, despite the fact that purists might say this is not socially or economically optimal.

And third, Anglo's experience of positive engagement with stakeholders suggests that it generates positive benefits for the company that outweigh, in many cases, the costs. Mr Dorian Emmett, Head of Sustainable Development in Anglo, said: 'In general . . . engagement is more productive than evasion. It challenges the business which is very healthy. Energy is released in the business.' And Mr Bill Nairn, outgoing technical director of Anglo, said: 'We don't believe that improving our handling of the environment has had a negative impact on productivity. Generally it is the opposite way around. Better energy consumption means better management; less use of brute force, and more intellect.'

Donaldson and Preston (1995) pointed out that stakeholder approaches could be descriptive (simply an expression of what it means to be in business), instrumental (intended to maximize benefit for shareholders through effective management of stakeholders), or normative (following a set of principles in interactions with stakeholders even when it is not clear that this would maximize shareholder wealth). In practice it is apparent that it is very difficult to distinguish between instrumental and normative approaches. Whereas it is evident in the extent to which companies incorporate the interests and contributions of its stakeholders in their efforts to survive and thrive, it is often the case that different members of the board and executive management demonstrate these approaches in varying degrees, and ultimately it is the net result that is important. Also, the interests of stakeholders are often not mutually exclusive. Senior executives have the challenging task of determining priorities for the application of their scarce resources, in the interest of the whole organization, and therefore of the bulk of its stakeholders. Mr Roger Wicks, Head of Energy in Anglo, commented:

> Short-term and long-term financial objectives go hand-in-hand. It is not that traditional measures of performance are reducing in importance, but that the profile enjoyed by sustainability issues has grown. The amount of comparison with our competitors is enormous, and the requirements for generating profits remain. There is often a huge work-stream that derives from the sustainable development issues, and they are not perceived to be revenue generating. People taking a narrow shareholder definition of the company perceive there to be conflicts of interest. It is important to represent the issues as contributing to performance: becoming more productive, building better relationships with the community.
>
> (Wicks 2005)

CONCLUSION

Returning to the discussion of dominant paradigms in corporate governance, the Anglo case study supports a multi-theoretic approach that allows for the pursuit of economic and contractual efficiency without precluding the possibilities of generating value through enhanced relations between a company and its social context. Such an approach supports the role of private companies in addressing the challenges of environmental sustainability which have traditionally been externalized from the problem of firm survival.

The internalization of environmental criteria in business decisions is highly relevant from a societal point of view. First it allows environmental best practice to spread across the range of countries in which a company such as Anglo conducts its business. And second, there is a flaw in the logic that suggests that national governments can manage environmental impact without the support of business. Whereas it is true that governments have the power to regulate against environmental atrocities, to offer incentives for outstanding performance, and to undertake some projects in the development of critical technology, it is private companies that contain the bulk of the potential to generate the social and technological innovations that are essential to sustainability. A partnership in which companies demonstrate the potential for more sustainable production and consumption through incremental or breakthrough innovation, and in which regulators support companies that are doing so and pressure companies that are not, appears to be an effective mechanism for addressing the social inertia that holds the world on its unsustainable course. A paradigm that recognizes the dynamic and constructed nature of the world, and that incorporates social and environmental values into economic practices through constructive engagement with stakeholders is therefore essential. It need not negate the enormous benefit of operational or contractual efficiency in business; it need only hold that pursuit in the context of a more holistic progression towards social and environmental sustainability. Since environmental challenges are unlikely ever to be static, it is unlikely that business will ever be able to settle into an operational steady state in which all necessary responses have been incorporated into regulation.

NOTE

1 The author wishes to gratefully acknowledge the support of Sir Mark Moody-Stuart and a number of other Anglo board members and senior managers in the research resulting in this case study.

REFERENCES

Anglo American plc (2002) *Good Citizenship: Our Business Principles*, London: Anglo American plc.

Anglo American plc (2003) *Report to Society*, London: Anglo American plc.

Anglo American plc (2004a) *Annual Report*, London: Anglo American plc.

Anglo American plc (2004b) *Report to Society*, London: Anglo American plc.

Anglo American plc (2005) *Interim Report*, London: Anglo American plc.

Barnard, C. (1938) *The Functions of the Executive*, Boston: Harvard University Press.

Barney, J.B. (1991) 'Firm resources and sustained competitive advantage', *Journal of Management*, 17(1): 99–120.

Callon, M. (1998) *The Laws of the Markets*, Oxford: Blackwell Publishers.

Donaldson, T. and Preston, L.E. (1995) 'The stakeholder theory of the corporation: concepts, evidence and implications', *Academy of Management Review*, 20(1): 65–91.

Eisenhardt, K.M. and Martin, J.A. (2000) 'Dynamic capabilities: what are they?', *Strategic Management Journal*, 21: 1105–121.

Emmett, D. (2004) Formal interview conducted by author at Anglo American plc Offices in London, December, 2004.

Gladwin, T.N., Kennelly, J.J. and Krause, T. (1995) 'Shifting paradigms for sustainable development: implications for management theory and research', *Academy of Management Review*, 20 (4): 874–907.

Godsell, R. (2005) Formal interview conducted by author at Anglo American plc Offices in Johannesburg, September, 2005.

Handy, C. (2002) 'What is a business for?', *Harvard Business Review*, 80(12): 49–55.

Jensen, M.C. and Meckling, W.H. (1976) 'Theory of the firm: managerial behaviour, agency costs and ownership structure', *Journal of Financial Economics* 3: 305–60.

Marshall, A. (1898) *Principles of Economics*, vol 1. London: Macmillan and Co. Ltd.

Maxwell, T.J. (2004) *Board Management for Competitive Advantage in a Changing Climate: An Intervention Research Design*, Brussels: Workshop on Corporate Governance, European Institute for Advanced Studies in Management.

Moody-Stuart, M. (2004) Formal interview conducted by author at Anglo American plc Offices in London, December, 2004.

Nairn, W. (2005) Formal interview conducted by author at Anglo American plc Offices in Johannesburg, September, 2005.

Pfeffer, J. and Salancik, G.R. (2003) *The External Control of Organisations*, California: Stanford University Press.

Selznick, P. (1957) *Leadership in Administration*, New York: Harper and Row.

Wicks, R. (2005) Formal interview conducted by author at Anglo American plc Offices in Johannesburg, September, 2005.

Chapter 8

Codes of conduct as a tool for sustainable governance in MNCs

Krista Bondy, Dirk Matten and Jeremy Moon

INTRODUCTION

This chapter discusses and analyses an increasingly popular tool that companies use to meet the goal of corporate sustainability. Codes of conduct (CoC), codes of ethics and codes of practice have become extremely popular over recent years and have been widely adopted across industries, countries and sectors (Leipziger 2003; Sethi 2003; Wood *et al*. 2004). While initially codes have tended to focus on corporate governance issues (Aguilera and Cuervo-Cazurra 2004), this has increasingly shifted towards broader societal issues. In particular multinational corporations (MNCs) have adopted CoCs in the context of growing public concern about working conditions in their overseas operations and the responsible use of their economic power more generally (e.g. Emmelhainz and Adams 1999; Kolk *et al*. 1999; Gordon and Miyake 2001; Pearson and Seyfang 2001; Kolk and van Tulder 2004; Kolk 2005).

Elsewhere in this volume the concept of sustainability has been discussed at length and we follow a similar path in this chapter by understanding sustainability as the simultaneous effort of balancing economic, social and environmental goals for a corporation, often epitomized in the popular concept of the 'triple bottom line'. As such, sustainability is another metaphor for describing corporate social responsibility, corporate citizenship or ethical business conduct and for the purpose of this chapter we will use sustainability as a synonym for these concepts.

The chapter begins by describing the context in which codes exist and the importance of self-regulation (codes more specifically) in governing corporate attitudes and behaviours, particularly when operating in a transboundary environment. Codes are then defined, described and characterized to ensure a thorough understanding of what codes are and how they can be used by organizations. Lastly, the chapter discusses the issue of codes, sustainability and governance, and where and how codes can be used most effectively to further societal objectives.

CODES OF CONDUCT AS REFLEXIVE REGULATION

CoCs are an approach of voluntary corporate self-regulation. As such they represent a clear contrast to governmental, mandatory regulation. To better understand the function, role and constraints of CoC for sustainable corporate governance, it is helpful to discuss the antecedents and characteristics of the social, political and economic factors that have encouraged this trend towards more self-regulation of industry. We would like to highlight three crucial developments.

First, the *institutional failure* of governmental institutions in most developed economies to maintain a consistently high level of regulation in the last quarter century or so. Some have argued there is a more fundamental failure of modern democracy in regulating societies towards sustainability (e.g. Beck 1994, 1996, 1997a; Giddens 1990). They suggest that while a highly regulated welfare state was a key element of the 'modernization' process of Western society over the last two centuries, we have entered a phase where governments are increasingly faced with the – mostly unintended – 'consequences of modernity' (Giddens 1990). While these governmental institutions have been able to implement the logic of wealth distribution, they are intrinsically unable to serve as institutions which 'manage' the side-effects of industrial modernity. As Beck argues, societies as a result are governed by a form of 'organized irresponsibility' which leaves in particular the ecological, economic and social risks of modern societies unaddressed. Consequently, at the heart of the new epoch of 'reflexive modernity' we witness the emergence of a political arena below the institutions of traditional political actors. In this sphere of 'subpolitics' (Beck 1997b) these 'consequences of modernity' are tackled by a plethora of actors, including civil society groups and – most notably – corporations which, due to resource and power differentials in relation to other civil society actors, take a dominant role in this process – a role which in many cases replaces or at least eclipses those of governments (Moon 2002). CoCs play a crucial element in this process, and as we will discuss later in this chapter, this often results from collaboration between multi-stakeholders from civil society.

A second reason for governmental retreat from direct regulation is of a more *political* and *ideological nature* (White 2003: 8–15). Partly informed by institutional failure of the classic welfare state but also as a phenomenon in its own right, there has been a significant shift in political thinking and practice since the 1980s in most liberal democracies. The more extreme view, on the right of the political spectrum, is highly suspicious of the idea of a government responsible for so many aspects of its citizens' life. At the core of this libertarian model is the key importance of private property, a free market economy and a limited state. Consequently, beginning with the Reagan and Thatcher governments, we witnessed a reduction of state involvement which leaves significant areas of former governmental functions delegated to private actors or simply abandoned.

The new centre-left governments in Europe in the late 1990s, most notably in the UK, have followed a similar approach. In principle, the state is still responsible for guaranteeing basic citizenship rights, but in practice it ensures access to the goods and services for its citizens by enabling their provision by private actors. The 'enabling state' (Gilbert and Gilbert 1989; Deakin and Walsh 1996) involves corporations increasingly delivering goods and services which in the initial liberal model were clearly a responsibility of governments. However, the more corporations deliver telecommunications, public transport or health services, the higher are the public demands that the companies involved adhere to certain standards and be accountable to the public about the quality and price of their services. CoCs are a tool enabling corporations to address these issues.

The third contributing factor to this shift in regulatory approaches is the increased internationalization of economic, social and political processes, often referred to as 'globalization' (Turner 2000). The central characteristic of globalization is the progressive *deterritorialization* of social, political and economic interaction (Scholte 2003), whereby a growing number of social activities are now taking place beyond the power and influence of the nation state. This development is closely linked to the rise of new libertarian political thinking which in particular encouraged liberalization of world trade, reduction of regulation for foreign direct investment and increased economic freedom for corporate actors. Theoretically the governments of nation states still have full sovereignty in their own territories. However, crucial changes effected by globalization place limitations on the exercise of that sovereignty because: (a) nation states are exposed to economic, social and political action beyond their own control; and (b) actors within their own territories encounter fewer constraints on relocating activities into territories beyond the control of their original government. While the first aspects put governments under pressure to provide more freedom to economic actors in order to secure employment and attract investment, the latter exposes government to the constant threat by corporations to exit if the government imposes unacceptable levels of regulation, taxation and control, sometimes referred to as the 'race to the bottom'. Thus globalization provides an incentive to governments to refrain from the often costly and controversial regulation of sustainability-related issues, such as environmental issues or protection of workers' rights. At the same time, corporations are increasingly exposed to public scrutiny of and outrage at many of their (perceived) shortfalls in achieving sustainability. As a consequence, in the absence of governmental regulation some corporations increasingly resort to self-regulation.

Governments also encourage corporate self-regulation as a way to meet societal objectives with alternatives (primarily CoCs) that sidestep the limitations associated with more traditional forms of legislation and regulation discussed above (e.g. Ruhnka and Boerstler 1998; International Council on Human Rights Policy 2002; Lenox and Nash 2003). These self-regulatory strategies involve participation from non-legal bodies in the development, monitoring and enforcement of desired social objectives (Wotruba 1997; Ruhnka and Boerstler 1998; Carroll and McGregor-Lowndes 2001; Martin 2003). Self-regulatory initiatives offer a means to control corporate behaviour across borders as they are not tied to any particular political system or territory, and therefore can be applied in a variety of locations within corporations, industries or sectors, depending on the scope of the initiative and the will of the corporation in implementation.

In the context of decreased governmental influence on regulatory processes CoCs are part of a wider trend in regulation which has been discussed under the label of 'reflexive regulation'. Reflexive regulation can be defined as 'a legal theory and a practical approach to regulation that seeks to encourage self-reflective and self-critical processes within social institutions concerning the effects they have on the natural environment' (Orts 1995b: 780; see also Orts 1995a). Reflexive regulation contrasts with the conventional models in sustainability-related regulation. Reflexive models of environmental politics are to be found in many forms and appearances (Gibson 1999; ten Brink 2002). Common to all is the fact that the corporations are no longer only the object of environmental regulation, but are also becoming active participants in the regulatory process also referred to as 'responsive' or 'enforced' self-regulation (Ayres and Braithwaite 1992). On the transnational level, voluntary codes of conduct adopted by MNCs have become the most common form of reflexive regulation of the last decades (Kaptein 2004).

BASIC TYPES OF CODES OF CONDUCT

There is no standard definition of CoC. Virtually every piece of literature on codes has its own definition, although the definitions are largely similar. Whether written by the corporation, or by a multi-stakeholder alliance for a wide range of corporations, CoCs can be defined as a voluntary set of commitments that either influence corporate attitudes and behaviours or are undertaken by the corporation to define their intentions and/or actions with regard to ethical and other issues, or towards a range of stakeholders from a market-based perspective (Alexander 1997; Forcese 1997; Dickerson and Hagan 1998; Diller 1999; Kolk *et al.* 1999; United States Council for International Business 2000; OECD 2001; Kaptein and Wempe 2002; ILO n.d.a; ILO n.d.b).

As with definitions, there are a variety of ways to understand the types of codes. Some are typified by the organization that created the code, some by the kind of content found in the codes, some by the intended function of the code and some by the progression of codes over time. Table 8.1 summarizes different ways in which codes have been categorized.

The literature on code types suggests two main debates: First, should codes be written by corporations, or should they be written by external bodies, and second, should code content be written as principles or rules, as both have different implications for understanding and implementing the code from various stakeholder perspectives? The next section discusses the debate within the literature on these questions.

Company vs multi-stakeholder codes

Company codes provide limited information on CSR (corporate social responsibility) and the kinds of initiatives expected of corporations operating in a global market due largely

Table 8.1 *Summary of code types*

Code types	*Example of criteria used*	*Real world example of codes*
Author/organization (e.g. Jenkins 2002; World Resources Institute 2003; Wotruba 1997)	■ Company	■ Nike Code of Conduct
	■ Industry association	■ Responsible Care (chemical industry)
	■ Model (acts as an example – created by variety of organizations)	■ International Code of Ethics for Canadian Business
	■ Inter-governmental	■ OECD Guidelines for Multinational Enterprises
	■ Multi-stakeholder (negotiated between numerous stakeholders)	■ CERES Principles
Content (e.g. Langlois and Schlegelmilch 1990; ILO n.d.a.; Rezaee *et al.* 2001)	■ Regulatory	■ Vodafone Code of Ethics
	■ Philosophical	■ Global Compact (quasi-code)
	■ Social responsibilities	■ Social Venture Network Standards of Corporate Responsibility
	■ Management philosophy	■ Nike Code of Conduct
	■ High road (aspirational)/ low road (rules of behaviour)	■ Global Sullivan Principles/ Glaxosmithkline Code of Conduct
Code function (e.g. Kolk *et al.* 1999; ILO, n.d.c.; Diller, 1999)	■ Guide or restrict corporate behaviour	■ Virtually all codes
	■ Influence other actors/ carry out self-regulation	■ Ethical Trade Initiative Base Code
	■ Operational or subscription	■ Social Venture Network Standards of Corporate Responsibility
	■ Model (acts as an example)	■ International Code of Ethics for Canadian Business
Progress over time/ historical progression (e.g. Mendes and Clark 1996)	■ First generation	■ Bell Canada Enterprises
	■ Second generation	■ WPP Code of Business Conduct
	■ Third generation	■ Royal Bank of Canada Code of Conduct
	■ Fourth generation	■ Responsible Care
	■ Fifth generation	■ CAUX Round Table Principles for Business

to the structure of the code document and the fact that guidance or clarification on code commitments are usually found within a separate document (Bondy 2003). They are typically written by a representative of the company or industry, with little or no input from outside groups, and are often a vision of where the managing group or board of directors would like the company to be in the future. Therefore they do not reflect the way in which the corporation currently operates, nor do they typically meet the needs of other stakeholders affected by the corporation. Furthermore, company codes are also subject to the whims of senior management (Sodeman 1995).

The Clean Clothes Campaign (1998) lists four major drawbacks of company codes:

1 Vaguely defined – corporate codes do not specify precisely the limits of their responsibility.
2 Incomplete – many company codes exclude the right to organize, refer only to child labour or in other ways are not complete.
3 Not implemented – an important flaw in company codes of conduct is the lack of information on how these codes are being implemented or monitored.
4 Not independently monitored – controlled or internal monitoring assumes a willingness to take the company at its word only.

The two major benefits associated with company codes are the assumption that by virtue of creating the code, the corporation recognizes the importance of mitigating CSR issues at least superficially, and that the code and resulting changes are driven from within and thus likely to be more successful where there is an intention to implement (WBCSD 2000).

Multi-stakeholder codes on the other hand are generally not aspirational, but determine the bare minimum of acceptable commitments to a wide variety of interested stakeholders. This results from a process of bargaining, negotiating and compromise between diverse groups coming from government, business coalitions, NGOs and academia, for example, where the aim is to meet as many of the needs as possible through generating consensus. According to Dickerson and Hagen (1998), these codes are actually superior as they produce a minimum normative consensus that can be applied universally. Both Dickerson and Hagen (1998) and Kolk *et al.* (1999) would agree that multi-stakeholder codes are better at articulating, guiding and assessing corporations on the business–society interface than are individually created or company codes. Resulting from the consensus process, Jeffcott and Yanz (2000) suggest that multi-stakeholder codes are seen to be more effective in dealing with issues related to the developing world and to supply chain management.

The resulting multi-stakeholder code can provide consistency and standardization of wider stakeholder expectations for companies participating in the codes and the stakeholders affected by the corporations. Also, it is argued that multi-stakeholder codes provide SMEs (small and medium-sized enterprises) with an opportunity to participate in the use of codes without having to undertake development costs, particularly those associated with stakeholder engagement (Blowfield 2000).

Multi-stakeholder codes also require more transparency and accountability from member corporations, as audit reports from company codes are usually provided only to management (Blowfield 2000) where assessments on implementation of multi-stakeholder codes are generally required by the organization that created the code and are therefore available publicly. Also, when corporations commit to these externally created codes, they create a more visible accountability relationship with key internal and external stakeholders.

What makes this argument so interesting is that although the literature suggests corporations should be using multi-stakeholder codes, the vast majority used by corporations are those created internally (OECD 1999; Bondy *et al.* 2004). This issue will be discussed in more detail below.

Principles- vs rules-based codes

Principles-based codes are typically a short list of statements that can cover a wider variety of issues because the commitments are not targeted at specific behaviours or actions and are meant to guide behaviour in a variety of contexts. Thus, they are more flexible and relevant over longer periods of time. By the nature of their structure, they require individuals to think before acting to ensure their behaviour is in line with the code. However, this flexible structure invites a variety of possible interpretations for each statement, and makes them notoriously difficult to measure and thus report.

Rules-based codes can be a large list of more specific behavioural commitments, although this is not always the case. The rules tell individuals what they can and cannot do based on commitments made in the code. This provides a clear indication of expected behaviour surrounding particular issues, and provides external parties with a clear indication of the commitments and actions to be taken by the organization. Rules-based codes can also be much easier to measure. The major problem with rules-based codes is that they cannot cover every situation that arises and thus will not be an effective guide in areas not covered by the code, and must be constantly updated to address omissions and the changing situations faced by corporations.

The most effective CSR code of conduct is one that combines both principles and rules. The code would include an introductory section describing the author's perspective on CSR, codes of conduct, the appropriate role for corporations in society, and instructions on how to use the code. The introduction would indicate priorities and anticipated timelines for implementation of different phases (if a company code), etc. and confirm that the code is not intended to act as a list of do's and don'ts, but that it provides specific commitments to attitudes and behaviour which may be more or less appropriate depending on the specific organizational context. The remaining text of the code would comprise each individual principle, with definitions of key terms (particularly those with vague or multiple meanings), how the term has been operationalized for action (or the rules for implementation), and the indicators to measure and report on progress.

The different types of codes and classification systems found in the literature help to highlight four important elements in understanding codes of conduct. The use of these four elements: code author, content, function within the corporation and 'genre', to classify codes show the importance of these characteristics in analysing and understanding them.

CODE CHARACTERISTICS

After having identified the nature and key types of codes we will now discuss in more detail the various characteristics of CoCs. Wotruba (1997) provides a succinct summary of the literature on the major dimensions upon which codes can be characterized. He lists five separate continuums under which all codes can be characterized to varying degrees.

1 Specific vs general – this dimension describes to what degree the commitments found in codes are focused on specific behaviours or general statements. Operational codes fall on the specific side as they indicate expectations for specific kinds of behaviour. By contrast, model codes are on the general side as they typically suggest more sweeping comments on preferred philosophies and appropriate corporate intentions towards particular issues or groups.
2 Comprehensive vs selective – this dimension focuses on the breadth of topics covered by the code. Individual corporate codes are usually more selective as they include only issues appropriate to the unique operating conditions of the corporation. Multi-stakeholder codes usually attempt to be more comprehensive and cover a wider range of issues to be applicable to more organizations or industries.
3 Positive vs negative – this dimension describes the tone of the code. Some codes are written as aspirational statements about intentions for behaviour in the future and therefore are more positive in nature (such as many internally written codes and/or principles-based codes) (Lad 1991; Aaronson and Reeves 2002). Other codes are written as a set of rules that indicate unacceptable behaviours (rules-based codes), indicating what members 'shall not do' and thus are negative in nature.
4 Voluntary vs mandatory – this dimension indicates the degree to which corporations undertake codes voluntarily. Although defined as a voluntary tool based on market issues, some codes are effectively mandatory for certain corporations in particular contexts. For instance, in the UK corporations must comply with the Combined Code if they want to be listed on the London Stock Exchange. Chemical industry associations require their members to comply with Responsible Care as part of their membership with the association, ensuring social and environmental impacts of the industry are prevented or mitigated. In these contexts, corporations are essentially forced to comply with the codes, making them mandatory.
5 Equilegal vs supralegal – this dimension describes the degree to which commitments listed in the codes are mere reflections of already existing legislation and standards (equilegal) or have moved beyond the minimum requirements of the legal environment (supralegal).

Each of the four code typologies differentiates between codes on content and structure, although in some cases this is done implicitly such as with the author typology.

Therefore, these typologies would appear differently on Wotruba's (1997) five continuums of code characteristics. For instance, the code type 'model' from within the author typology would tend towards the general, selective and positive sides of the first three continuums. By definition, these codes would certainly be voluntary (fourth continuum) and might fit anywhere on the fifth continuum depending on the focus of the individual code. A regulatory code from the content typology however is likely to be on the specific, selective, negative ends of the first three spectrums, varied where it sits on the fourth continuum and likely to be on the equi-legal side of the fifth continuum. Thus, code type indicates likelihood towards the appearance of certain content and structure.

The location of the respective codes on these five continuums can also indicate the likelihood of code effectiveness if implemented efficiently, and the credibility of the code according to external parties. As credibility depends on effective monitoring, enforcement and transparency (ILO n.d.a), codes written in such a way as to lend simplicity to these processes will be viewed as more effective. They will therefore generate more credibility for the corporation and its CSR initiatives and create a stronger accountability relationship with key stakeholders.

EVALUATING CODES OF CONDUCT AS A TOOL FOR SUSTAINABLE CORPORATE GOVERNANCE

There is ongoing debate about whether codes of conduct are effective corporate governance tools which move organizations towards increased sustainability and conformity to societal expectations. Discussions of code effectiveness inevitably evaluate their structural and functional benefits and limitations particularly to determine if codes are in fact capable of helping facilitate changes in the impacts of corporations on society. A variety of perspectives influence this debate. Industries, businesses, NGOs and governments each have their own reasons for supporting or being concerned with codes, and may push for changes to make codes more effective for their own needs. The following discussion is summarized in Table 8.2 below and a more complete list of benefits and limitations can be found in Appendix 8.A.

Benefits of codes

Primarily, codes are flexible documents that can be tailored to individual corporations, industries, countries, international contexts, issues or groups (Aaronson and Reeves 2002). Therefore, corporations can identify those commitments applicable to their operational considerations, stakeholder base and governmental requirements (as is the case in the US) (Ruhnka and Boerstler 1998). This flexibility allows for creative and innovative solutions to complex social and environmental problems, and also allows for rapid changes to commitments required to keep pace with the changing needs of

Table 8.2 *Summary of code benefits and limitations*

Benefits	*Limitations*
■ Flexible, can be uniquely tailored ■ Relatively inexpensive ■ Provide space for innovation and creative problem solving of targeted issues ■ Create potential for competitive advantage ■ Mitigate need for governmental regulation or intervention ■ Level playing field of competitors within same industry ■ Create order and structure in transboundary environment ■ Enhance trust, customer loyalty and reputation ■ Allow stakeholder influence in governance decisions ■ Create pressure to follow through on commitments through formalization and publication of commitments ■ Create benchmark for measurement and identification of progress	■ Lack accountability mechanisms (monitoring, sanctions) ■ Cannot enforce proper implementation ■ Often written as broad philosophical statements, therefore hard to measure ■ Adopters already leaders in industry and with CSR issues ■ Over-represented in industries with high visibility, customer products, focus on brand image or reputation and large environmental or social impacts, and under-represented in industries with low visibility, primarily business-to-business sales or where production costs are a large part of final sale price ■ Lack expectations for suppliers ■ Unknown to majority of employees ■ Do not include complaints process or whistleblower protection

the marketplace, corporation and/or stakeholders (Australian Government 1997; WBCSD 2000).

Codes are less costly to create, implement, administer, monitor and enforce than legislation or legal regulation. The reduced costs of regulation achieved through codes are in essence transferred from governments to corporations, as all costs of internal codes are borne by the corporation. The same is true of corporations that implement multi-stakeholder codes. However, as the corporation only commits to activities applicable to its operations, the costs are less for them in the long term as they only deal with appropriate issues and not those mandated for all corporations by legislation. Not only do codes reduce the cost of regulation with regard to development and implementation, they also reduce costs to the legal system as stakeholders use avenues other than the courts to seek remedies from the corporation. Code disputes must be addressed through non-legal or market routes such as trade associations or consumer groups (Wotruba 1997; Gibson 2000; Carroll and McGregor-Lowndes 2001) as they are not enforceable in law except as part of a contract.

If codes based on certain issues are used by a large enough percentage of corporations, the codes can mitigate the need for additional government legislation. This is particularly true when the codes proactively cover issues of potential concern to stakeholders, which in turn can help corporations avoid external pressure such as negative media attention and consumer boycotts that in some cases can be the impetus for government legislation (Wotruba 1997; Gibson 2000).

Industry or multi-stakeholder codes can ensure a level playing field where all corporations within a set of criteria undertake the same costs of implementation and administration of the code, thereby, maintaining fair competition between the corporations. These external codes can also create a transparent benchmark from which to build trust with stakeholders and create confidence in the industry (Gibson 2000; Martin 2003).

Codes are also very important in regulating corporations across borders. Governments and corporations recognize the importance of codes in being able to create some consistency in cross-border operations and transactions resulting from the lack of effective international institutions in creating structure in the international context (Carroll and McGregor-Lowndes 2001; Martin 2003).

Codes can actually provide economic benefits to corporations through increased customer loyalty and reputation, and can enhance trust in corporations that make steps to effectively implement the code (Wotruba 1997; Sethi 2002). Creating and effectively implementing a code can create a competitive advantage for the corporation and/or help to create a niche market with stakeholders who judge corporations by not only what they produce but also how they produce it. The competitive advantage created by codes can also restrict new entrants to the market because of the costs associated with competing on CSR issues as well as product and price issues (Wotruba 1997; Gibson 2000).

Development and implementation of effective and credible codes requires the creation of partnerships with other organizations, or disclosure to other organizations not solely focused on profit motives. Thus, codes allow other organizations to influence the philosophies or decisions corporations make regarding their social and environmental impacts and/or leverage their behaviour (Jenkins 2002; Sethi 2002; Martin 2003; World Resources Institute 2003).

By virtue of making public commitments to social and environmental issues, corporations make themselves more visible and vulnerable to external pressure and negative attention should they fail to achieve their social and environmental objectives (Gibson 2000; Jenkins 2002). This visibility that results from code adoption also helps to create an accountability relationship with key stakeholders because it identifies responsibilities and commitments and suggests intended actions. This in turn gives stakeholders some power to ask questions surrounding implementation and performance, and to demand rectification of identified problems. In essence, committing to a code provides a subtle power shift away from corporations to interested stakeholders by allowing them a voice and the opportunity to directly affect corporate decision-making.

Codes can also create a benchmark from which corporations can be measured, audited and held publicly accountable and can encourage corporations to place the same expectations on their suppliers, thereby inducing more corporations to be socially and environmentally responsible (Jenkins 2002; World Resources Institute 2003). Thus codes, whether multi-stakeholder or company code, can act as a set of criteria in enabling the measurement of corporations and other organizations in relation to their non-economic issues and commitments.

Limitations of codes

The two most common critiques of codes are the lack of accountability mechanisms such as monitoring provisions and sanctions, and the inability or unwillingness of corporations to effectively implement code commitments. Many areas for concern with codes deal with the way in which they are written. Many codes are written as vague and/or broad philosophical concepts with little to no information on specific actions to be taken or plans for implementation, and the meaning of commitments can vary depending on the perspective and intent of the reader. The impact of codes with more general commitments is difficult to measure and it can therefore be hard to determine if the corporation is in fact living up to them. Often codes deal with specific issues that result from negative media attention, such as Nike and child labour, or are specific to a certain group of issues such as labour or the environment, without the inclusion of other pertinent issues from different areas. For instance, many organizations such as the ILO, Ethical Trading Initiative, etc. have developed codes dealing only or primarily with labour issues. These codes lack the same attention to other issues such as human rights, the environment, community issues, etc. and thus only deal with one area of corporate impact.

Codes with vague or broad commitments also create problems because they are open to a wide variety of interpretations which in turn create unforeseen expectations from stakeholders who understand the commitment differently from the corporation. This problem is enhanced because corporations have limited resources and must choose appropriate initiatives which are within their means to implement. This means that not all issues mentioned by stakeholders can be dealt with by corporations regardless of their sincerity to act.

Since codes are intended to fill regulatory voids, the concern over implementation and enforcement is a serious one. If corporations effectively implement codes and work on continual improvement of their social and environmental objectives, codes become increasingly difficult to implement. The easiest and most obvious areas for improvement are usually the first to be accomplished. Although these early successes help to encourage buy-in from corporations and their employees, once the easiest tasks are completed it becomes increasingly difficult to continue the same level of progress in achieving new social and environmental objectives. This is the problem of 'low-hanging fruit' – once it is gone, the amount of resources required to continue 'picking fruit' may outweigh the benefits to the corporation and its stakeholders.

Another critique is that individual corporations that adopt codes are usually already leaders in the industry or innovative with regard to CSR issues and it is usually the same corporations who are members of multiple voluntary initiatives. Multi-stakeholder codes suffer from low membership and are typically used as model codes, not adopted as written.

Codes are also found to be over-represented in industries with highly visible consumer products, brands or corporate images (such as apparel or other consumer goods industries) or large environmental or social impacts (such as extractive or pharmaceutical industries) and under-represented in industries with low consumer visibility, business-to-business sales or where the cost of production is high in proportion to the price of the product. In practice, codes are often found to have few provisions requiring social and environmental responsibility of suppliers, and focus primarily on issues that are either of large importance in the media, or have the ability to heavily impact the corporation in some way.

There is also a concern that corporations do not make their employees or other stakeholders aware of codes they have committed to, nor are they translated into languages that employees in other countries can understand. In other cases, the codes are critiqued for not having complaints procedures or secure channels for employees to indicate non-compliance within the corporation without fear of retaliation (Wotruba 1997; Diller 1999; Gibson 2000; Carroll and McGregor-Lowndes 2001; Jenkins 2002; Sethi 2002; Martin 2003; World Resources Institute 2003).

Often, this debate includes the use of different code types to illustrate benefits and limitations identified by the author. For instance, business coalitions tend to favour model or corporate codes because of the flexibility (structural) and transboundary (functional) nature of these code types. Many NGOs on the other hand favour intergovernmental or operational codes as they often prescribe right and wrong action (functional) and create minimum thresholds based on stakeholder consensus (structural).

In essence, the literature suggests that codes have the potential to be a powerful tool for self-regulation of corporations but only where the intent to implement co-exists with adoption. Codes can fill a global regulatory and governance gap that can be unique to specific corporate contexts or stakeholder viewpoints, where corporate intentions are formalized, creating greater transparency and accountability with respect to the business–society interface. However, the code must be developed with at least minimal consideration of affected stakeholders, methods for measuring corporate performance with it, and how it will be implemented for it to be an effective and credible tool amongst stakeholders.

ENCOURAGING SUSTAINABILITY BY COCs?

Clearly, the literature indicates that codes are quite varied in type, content, structure and use. But how does this translate into MNC practices? This penultimate section will discuss motivations for corporations using codes, the relationship between codes and broader sustainability goals and finally look at whether codes are an effective tool for encouraging sustainability within corporations.

It turns out that MNCs, regardless of their home culture, may in fact articulate a small set of similar motivations for code adoption. Although the motivations articulated are generally in keeping with the four main groups assumed in the literature (stakeholder regulation, stakeholder communication, competitive advantage and mitigation of risks and/or threats), these motivations appear to be similar in different cultures. Figure 8.1 is based on our study of the top 50 MNCs in Canada, the UK and Germany and illustrates the most common motivations presented by corporations across these cultures (Bondy *et al.* 2004).

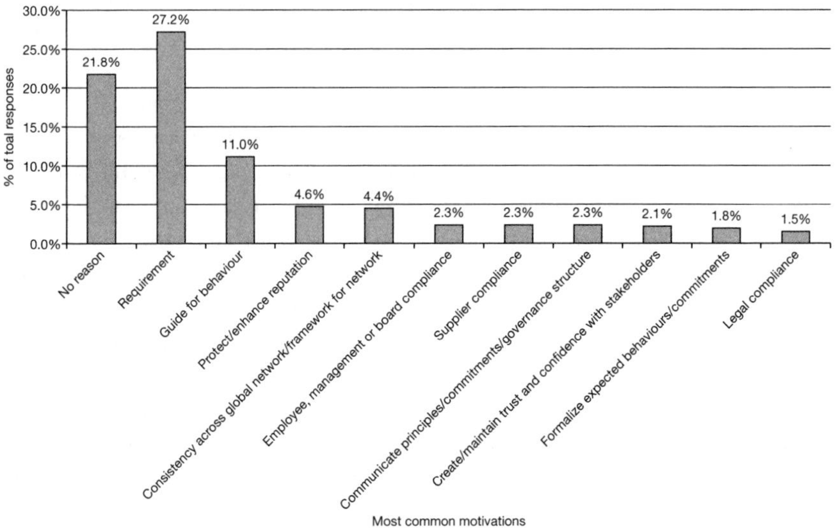

Figure 8.1 *Most common motivations articulated for adopting codes*

Based on this research, when MNCs provide a motivation for adopting a code that is not mandatory,[1] they list guides for behaviour, protection and/or enhancement of corporate reputation, consistency across a global framework, compliance of key stakeholders, communication of commitments, creating and/or maintaining trust, formalization of commitments and legal compliance most commonly. Thus, motivations for MNCs using codes to engage in CSR seem to be converging on a global scale around areas related to strategic business interests, communication and compliance.

Interestingly, there does not appear to be a relationship between the type of code used by the corporation and their reason for adopting it. In some cases there was a synergy between the type of code and the motivation (such an industry code and adopting it to gain membership with the industry and to protect its reputation), while in other cases the type of code and the motivation for adopting it were disconnected (such as a company code and adopting it to create or maintain trust of key stakeholders). The code type, and the benefits and limitations associated with these did not appear to have any kind of systematic impact on the motivations presented for adopting codes, regardless of the type adopted.

Evidence from this study suggests that in fact codes are not primarily a tool of sustainability-related goals. To foster those, companies tend to resort more to other tools such as reports, policies, dedicated websites, etc. Going back to the definition of sustainability provided at the start, this study suggests that codes on aggregate do not in fact significantly further social and environmental imperatives for business success or deal in any meaningful way with the social and environmental externalities of business activities. However, some of the codes in our sample are excellent examples of both furthering sustainability imperatives and including some externalities of business functions, but this is not true in the aggregate. Thus, codes are more often tools for governing organizational imperatives rather than governing the corporation towards increased sustainability.

CONCLUSION: CAN CODES ENCOURAGE CORPORATIONS TO ACT SUSTAINABLY?

Arguably, codes are not a panacea for solving problems in the business–society interface and corporations, governments and the public need to understand better the nature, potential, restrictions and appropriate contexts of codes. They are certainly not, and cannot be, a catch-all solution to regulating corporations and the business–society interface. Codes provide one way of helping corporations understand the complexities of sustainability, and act as a guide for awareness and implementation of these issues. Inside a corporation, codes need to be a part of a much larger system of cultural commitments, values, accountability, actions and continual improvement, etc. They need to be embedded within the corporation's attitudes and actions, while enhancing its strategic direction.

Codes though may have a particular potential in the areas of risk identification and management. Codes written by external parties can help the corporation to identify additional areas of potential risk on non-economic issues. They may help to identify potential threats to brand image or reputation, physical environmental liabilities, or processes, facilities, products or services with potential for environmental and social liabilities. Due to the flexibility of codes, as new risks are identified based on changes within the global marketplace, they can easily be modified and enhanced to respond with commitments to reducing negative and enhancing positive impacts, thus becoming part of a risk management strategy. In this way, codes can also be a powerful tool for risk management and an impetus for corporate scanning of potential future issues.

Codes themselves cannot change a corporation's behaviour. The success or failure of a code is dependent on the corporation's desire, ability and available resources to implement code commitments. Therefore, a good code, with clear language, strong commitments and a base philosophy similar to the one of the adopting corporation is much more likely to produce effective initiatives, but cannot determine how successfully a corporation will engage in CSR. In the literature on CoCs, there are few unequivocal recommendations with regard to implementation. Exceptions include Newton (1995), who stressed the importance of maximizing the *participation* of organization members in the development stage in order to encourage commitment and 'buy-in' to the principles and rules of the code. Webley (2001) further contends that in order for codes to have credibility, companies must be willing to *discipline* employees found in breach of them. Similarly, Treviño *et al.*'s (1999) survey revealed that *follow-through* (such as detection of violations, follow-up on notification of violations, and consistency between the policy and action) tended to be much more influential on employee behaviour than the mere presence of a code, regardless of how familiar employees might be with it. These are sensible suggestions and findings. However, clear research findings relating to the effect of codes and their implementation on employee decision-making and behaviour are still relatively limited (Cassell *et al.* 1997).

These considerations about the key role of code implementation are linked to a more fundamental debate about the relation between bureaucratic control – of which CoCs are an important mechanism – and the ethical behaviour of individuals (Crane and Matten 2004: 132–7). This issue is critical in determining the potential of CoCs to foster sustainable corporate behaviour. Bureaucracy has been argued to have a number of effects on ethical decision-making (Weber 1947; Jackall 1988; Bauman 1989, 1993; ten Bos 1997; Kornberger *et al.* 2004). In particular, sceptics argue that individual morality tends to be subjugated to the functionally specific rules and roles of the bureaucratic organization. Thus, effective bureaucracy essentially 'frees' the individual from moral reflection and decision-making since s/he needs only to follow the prescribed rules and procedures laid down to achieve organizational goals. This can cause employees to act as 'moral robots', simply following the rules rather than thinking about why they are there, or questioning their purpose. This particular criticism has been reiterated in some recent studies on CoCs (Schwartz 2000; Kornberger *et al.* 2004). Clearly, CoCs will only function if the broader culture of the organization is oriented towards sustainability and a code thus is just one supporting tool to foster this goal (Sims and Brinkmann 2003).

Most importantly, codes, if developed appropriately, can provide a set of criteria for use by corporations and their auditors to measure performance on social, environmental and economic related initiatives and actions. Codes can thus become a powerful tool useful to all key stakeholders in strengthening the business–society relationship and rebalancing power between groups within society. This process will take time, as corporations and key stakeholders determine what the critical terminology means and how codes are to be operationalized, implemented, administered and measured.

NOTE

1 Mandatory codes refer to those codes corporations must comply with to become members of certain bodies or groups. For instance, to be listed on the London Stock Exchange, companies are expected to comply with the Combined Code which deals specifically with corporate governance issues. Other examples of codes deemed mandatory in this study include the German Code of Corporate Governance and Responsible Care.

REFERENCES

Aaronson, S. and Reeves, J. (2002) *The European Response to Public Demands for Global Corporate Responsibility*, National Policy Association. Available at: http://www.bitc.org.uk/docs/NPA_Global_CSR_survey.pdf (accessed 3 November 2003).

Aguilera, R.V. and Cuervo-Cazurra, A. (2004) 'Codes of good governance worldwide: what is the trigger?', *Organization Studies*, 25(3): 415–43.

Alexander, J. (1997) 'On the right side', *World Business*, 3(1) Jan/Feb: 38–41.

Australian Government (1997) 'Grey-letter law: report of the Commonwealth Interdepartmental Committee on Quasi-regulation', Commonwealth Interdepartmental Committee on Quasi-regulation. Online. Available at: http://www.pc.gov.au/orr/greyletterlaw/chapter3.pdf (accessed 23 April 2002).

Ayres, I. and Braithwaite, J. (1992) *Responsive Regulation: Transcending the Deregulation Debate*, New York: Oxford University Press.

Bauman, Z. (1989) *Modernity and the Holocaust*, Cambridge: Polity Press.

Bauman, Z. (1993) *Postmodern Ethics*, London: Blackwell.

Beck, U. (1994) 'The reinvention of politics: towards a theory of reflexive modernization' in U. Beck, A. Giddens and S. Lash (eds) *Reflexive Modernization*, Stanford: Stanford University Press, pp. 1–55.

Beck, U. (1996) 'Risk society and the provident state.' in S. Lash, B. Szerszynski and B. Wynne (eds) *Risk, Environment and Modernity*, London: Sage, pp. 27–43.

Beck, U. (1997a) *The Reinvention of Politics*, Cambridge: Polity Press.

Beck, U. (1997b) 'Subpolitics, ecology and the disintegration of institutional power', *Organization and Environment*, 10(1): 52–65.

Blowfield, M. (2000) 'Ethical sourcing: a contribution to sustainability or a diversion?', Natural Resources Institute. Online. Available at: http://www.eti.org.uk/pub/resources/othpub/pdfs/nret-susdev.pdf (accessed 2 June 2002).

Bondy, K. (2003) 'A new method for evaluating the quality of corporate social responsibility codes of conduct', MEDes Degree, University of Calgary, Calgary.

Bondy, K., Matten, D. and Moon, J. (2004) 'The adoption of voluntary codes of conduct in MNCs: a three-country comparative study', *Business and Society Review*, 109(4): 449–77.

Carroll, P. and McGregor-Lowndes, M. (2001) 'A standard for regulatory compliance? Industry self-regulation, the courts and AS3806-1998', *Australian Journal of Public Administration*, 60(4): 80–91.

Cassell, C., Johnson, P. and Smith, K. (1997) 'Opening the black box: corporate codes of ethics in their organizational context', *Journal of Business Ethics*, 16: 1077–93.

Clean Clothes Campaign (1998) 'Codes of conduct for transnational corporations: an overview', Clean Clothes Campaign. Online. Available at: http://www.cleanclothes.org/codes/overview.htm (accessed 12 August 2002).

Crane, A. and Matten, D. (2004) *Business Ethics – A European Perspective. Managing Corporate Citizenship and Sustainability in the Age of Globalization*, Oxford: Oxford University Press.

Deakin, N. and Walsh, K. (1996) 'The enabling state: the role of markets and contracts', *Public Administration*, 74 (Spring): 33–48.

Dickerson, C. and Hagen, K. (1998) *Corporate Codes of Conduct*, American Society of International Law, Proceedings of the Annual Meeting, Washington: 265–77.

Diller, J. (1999) 'A social conscience in the global marketplace? Labour dimensions of codes of conduct, social labelling and investor initiatives', *International Labour Review*, 138(2): 99–129.

Emmelhainz, M.A. and Adams, R.J. (1999) 'The apparel industry response to "sweatshop" concerns: a review and analysis of codes of conduct', *Journal of Supply Chain Management*, Summer: 51–7.

Forcese C. (1997) *Commerce with Conscience: Human Rights and Corporate Codes of Conduct*, Canada: International Centre for Human Rights and Democratic Development.

Gibson, R. (ed.) (1999) *Voluntary Initiatives and the New Politics of Corporate Greening*, Peterborough, Ontario: Broadview Press.

Gibson, R. (2000) *Encouraging Voluntary Initiatives for Corporate Greening: Some Considerations for More Systematic Design of Supporting Frameworks at the National and Global Levels*, Voluntary Initiatives Workshop, United Nations Environment Programme. Online. Available at: http://www.uneptie.org/outreach/vi/reports/encouraging_voluntary_initiatives.pdf (accessed 7 November 2003).

Giddens, A. (1990) *The Consequences of Modernity*, Stanford: Stanford University Press.

Gilbert, N. and Gilbert, B. (1989) *The Enabling State. Modern Welfare Capitalism in America*, Oxford: Oxford University Press.

Gordon, K. and Miyake, M. (2001) 'Business approaches to combating bribery: a study of codes of conduct', *Journal of Business Ethics*, 34: 161–73.

International Council on Human Rights Policy (2002) 'Beyond voluntarism: human rights and the developing international legal obligations of companies', International Council on Human Rights. Online. Available at: http://www.cleanclothes/ftp/beyond_voluntarism.pdf (accessed 17 November 2003).

International Labour Organization (ILO) (n.d.a) 'Corporate codes of conduct', ILO Bureau for Workers' Activities. Online. Available at: http://www.itcilo.it/english/actrav/telearn/global/ilo/code/main.htm (accessed 17 March 2004).

International Labour Organization (ILO) (n.d.b) 'Codes of conduct for multinationals', ILO Bureau for Workers' Activities. Online. Available at: http://www.itcilo.it/english/actrav/telearn/global/ilo/code/main.htm (accessed 17 March 2004).

International Labour Organization (ILO) (n.d.c) 'Private initiatives and labour standards: a global look', ILO. Online. Available at: http://www.unglobalcompact.org/un/gc/unweb.nsf/content/ilostudy.html (accessed 18 October 2001), no longer available.

Jackall, R. (1988) *Moral Mazes*, Oxford: Oxford University Press.

Jeffcott, B. and Yanz, L. (2000) 'Codes of conduct, government regulation and worker organizing', Maquila Solidarity Network. Online. Available at: http://www.maquilasolidarity.org/resources/codes/bluebooklet.htm (accessed 20 February 2002).

Jenkins, R. (2002) 'Corporate codes of conduct: self-regulation in a global economy' in *Voluntary Approaches to Corporate Responsibility: Readings and a Resources Guide*,

United Nations Non-Governmental Liaison Service. Online. Available at: http://www.unsystem.org/ngls/documents/publications.en/development.dossier (accessed 6 November 2003).

Kaptein, M. (2004) 'Business codes of multinational firms: what do they say?', *Journal of Business Ethics*, 50: 13–31.

Kaptein, M. and Wempe, J. (2002) *The Balanced Company: A Theory of Corporate Integrity*, Oxford: Oxford University Press.

Kolk, A. (2005) 'Corporate social responsibility in the coffee sector: the dynamics of MNC responses and code development', *European Management Journal*, 23(2): 228–36.

Kolk, A. and van Tulder, R. (2004) 'Ethics in international business: multinational approaches to child labor', *Journal of World Business*, 39: 49–60.

Kolk, A., van Tulder, R. and Welters, C. (1999) 'International codes of conduct and corporate social responsibility: can transnational corporations regulate themselves?', *Transnational Corporations*, 8(1): 143–80.

Kornberger, M., Clegg, S.R., and Rhodes, C. (2004) '"Everyday I write the book" – on the relationship between ethics, practice and rules in organizations', Working Paper, University of Technology Sydney.

Lad, L. (1991) 'Industry self-regulation as interfirm and multisector collaboration: the case of the direct selling industry', *Research in Corporate Social Performance and Policy*, 12: 155–78.

Langlois, C. and Schlegelmilch, B. (1990) 'Do corporate codes of ethics reflect national character? Evidence from Europe and the United States' *Journal of International Business Studies*, 21(4): 519–39.

Leipziger, D. (2003) *The Corporate Social Responsibility Code Book*, Sheffield: Greenleaf Publishing.

Lenox, M. and Nash, J. (2003) 'Industry self-regulation and adverse selection: a comparison across four trade association programs', *Business Strategy and the Environment*, 12: 343–56.

Martin, J. (2003) 'industry self-regulation and small business: voluntary codes – industry self-regulation vs. co-regulation vs. government regulation', Australian Competition and Consumer Commission, Speech presented to National Alternative Dispute Resolution Advisory Council, 4 September, 2003. Online. Available at HTTP: http://www.accc. gov.au/speeches/2003/Martin_Voluntary_4903.pdf (accessed 7 November 2003).

Mendes, E. and Clark, J. (1996) 'The five generations of corporate codes of conduct and their impact on corporate social responsibility', Human Rights Research and Education Centre, University of Ottawa. Online. Available at: http://www.cdp-hrc.uottawa.ca/publicat/five.html (accessed 17 March 2004).

Moon, J. (2002) 'The social responsibility of business and new governance', *Government and Opposition*, 37(3): 385–408.

Organization for Economic Cooperation and Development (OECD) (1999) 'Corporate codes of conduct: an inventory', OECD. Online. Available at: http://www.oecd.org/ech/docs/codes.htm (accessed 12 February 2002).

Organization for Economic Cooperation and Development (OECD) (2001) 'Private initiatives for corporate responsibility: an analysis', OECD Directorate for Financial, Fiscal and Enterprise Affairs. Online. Available at: http://www.oecd.org/pdf/M0000 13000/M00013735.pdf (accessed 22 January 2002).

Orts, E.W. (1995a) 'Reflexive environmental law', *Northwestern University Law Review*, 89(4): 1227–340.

Orts, E.W. (1995b) 'A reflexive model of environmental regulation', *Business Ethics Quarterly*, 5(4): 779–94.

Pearson, R. and Seyfang, G. (2001) 'New hope or false dawn? Voluntary codes of conduct, labour regulation and social policy in a globalizing world', *Global Social Policy*, 1(1): 49–78.

Rezaee, Z., Elmore, R. and Szendi, J. (2001) 'Ethical behaviour in higher education institutions: the role of the code of conduct', *Journal of Business Ethics*, 30(2): 171–83.

Ruhnka, J. and Boerstler, H. (1998) 'Governmental incentives for corporate self-regulation', *Journal of Business Ethics*, 17(3): 309–26.

Scholte, J.A. (2003) *Globalization. A Critical Introduction*, 2nd edn, Basingstoke: Palgrave.

Schwartz, M. (2000) 'Why ethical codes constitute an unconscionable regression', *Journal of Business Ethics*, 23: 173–84.

Sethi, P. (2002) 'Standards for corporate conduct in the international arena: challenges and opportunities for multinational corporations', *Business and Society Review*, 107(1): 20–40.

Sethi, S. (2003) *Setting Global Standards: Guidelines for Creating Codes of Conduct in Multinational Corporations*, Hoboken, NJ: J. Wiley.

Sims, R.R. and Brinkmann, J. (2003) 'Enron ethics (or: culture matters more than codes)', *Journal of Business Ethics*, 45: 243–56.

Sodeman, W. (1995) 'Advantages and disadvantages of using the Brown and Perry database', *Business and Society*, 43(2): 216.

ten Bos, R. (1997) 'Business ethics and Bauman ethics', *Organization Studies*, 18(6): 997–1014.

ten Brink, P. (ed.) (2002) *Voluntary Environmental Agreements*, Sheffield: Greenleaf Publishing.

Treviño, L.K., Weaver, G.R., Gibson, D.G. and Toffler, B.L. (1999) 'Managing ethics and legal compliance: what works and what hurts', *California Management Review*, 41(2): 131–51.

Turner, B.S. (2000) 'Review essay: citizenship and political globalization', *Citizenship Studies*, 4(1): 81–6.

United States Council for International Business (2000) *Corporate Codes of Conduct: Overview and Summary of Initiatives*, United States Council for International Business. Online. Available at: http://www.uscib.org/index.asp?documentID=1434 (accessed 17 March 2004).

Weber, M. (1947) *The Theory of Social and Economic Organization*, trans. A.M. Henderson and T. Parsons, Oxford: Oxford University Press.

Webley, S. (2001) 'Values-based codes', in C. Moon, and C. Bonny (eds) *Business Ethics: Facing up to the Issues*, London: The Economist Books, pp. 159–60.

White, S. (2003) *The Civic Minimum*, Oxford: Oxford University Press.

Wood, G., Svensson, G., Singh, J., Carasco, E. and Callaghan, M. (2004) 'Implementing the ethos of corporate codes of ethics: Australia, Canada, and Sweden', *Business Ethics: A European Review*, 13(4): 389–403.

World Business Council for Sustainable Development (WBCSD) (2000) *Corporate Social Responsibility: Making Good Business Sense*, World Business Council for Sustainable Development. Online. Available at: http://www.wbcsd.ch/printpdf/CSR2000-Making%20Good%20Business%20Sense.pdf (accessed 18 February 2001).

World Resources Institute (2003) *World Resources 2002–2004: Decisions for the Earth: Balance, Voice, and Power*, United Nations Development Programme, World Bank, World Resources Institute. Online. Available at: http://pubs.wri.org/pubs_content_print.cfm?ContentID=1835 (accessed 14 October 2003).
Wotruba, T. (1997) 'Industry self-regulation: a review and extension to a global setting', *Journal of Public Policy and Marketing*, 16(1): 38–54.

APPENDIX 8.A

Advantages and limitations of voluntary initiatives and codes of conduct

Structural

Advantages

- code is applicable across boundaries and government jurisdictions;
- better suited to rapidly changing or complex contexts than regulations;
- allow for flexibility and creativity in designing solutions, help to create best practice;
- emphasis on prevention.

Limitations

- limited implementation or process information;
- limited scope of content;
- content not appropriate in certain industries or contexts;
- lack of monitoring, auditing or verification commitments;
- lack of information disclosure, reporting or feedback mechanisms;
- vague, ill-defined responsibilities towards suppliers, business partners, contractors and subcontractors;
- content focused on issues highly damaging to reputation;
- drafted with little or no help from variety of stakeholders;
- commitments weak or vague;
- cannot set or enforce limits specific to individual facilities;
- cannot deal with negligent or poor performers (free-riders).

Individual corporations

Advantages

- influence corporate behaviour;
- acceptance by firms of responsibility for activities;
- acceptance by firms of responsibility for supplier/business partner, contractor and subcontractor activities;

- protect or enhance reputation;
- not required to sign other agreements;
- establish management commitment;
- competitive advantage/race to the top;
- long-term cultural changes in business management;
- implemented wisely, can achieve change without forcing early retirement of capital stock and resultant loss in economy and jobs;
- encourage awareness of new or more efficient technologies.

Limitations

- may have negative, unintended effects;
- costs of development, implementation, auditing and/or certification;
- cannot be applied where no business self-interest;
- finite resources.

Societal

Advantages

- corporations accountable externally for code provisions;
- emphasize business not separate from remainder of society;
- create stakeholder confidence in corporation;
- improved dialogue and trust between industry and other two sectors;
- promote partnerships and shared ownership;
- can provide useful product information to consumers, reducing information asymmetries;
- help reduce compliance and enforcement costs.

Limitations

- limited adoption to date;
- adopted only by industry leaders;
- adopted due to external pressures, not for ethical or business reasons;
- concentrated in consumer goods sector;
- concentrated in firms that export or have overseas operations;
- codes seen as panacea;
- too many codes in existence;
- confusion over which codes are credible;
- suppliers faced with variety of different codes from different corporations;
- codes may undermine the position of trade unions;
- fear codes may replace regulations and government control over corporations;
- risk of creating trade barriers.

Chapter 9

The case of governance for sustainability at IAG

Suzanne Benn, Louise Wilson and Soochen Low

INTRODUCTION

This case study describes the strategies, structures and processes implemented at Insurance Australia Group (IAG) in 2003–2005 to facilitate the attainment of sustainability as an agreed purpose and a shared goal across the organization and to monitor its progress towards that goal. We see these initiatives as establishing a corporate governance framework for sustainability at IAG. In other words, they are mechanisms of governance whose role is to balance social, economic, environmental, individual and communal goals (Clarke 2004).

We draw from the work of Waddock *et al.* (2002) to argue that in order to implement this balanced approach the organization must adopt a values-based system of governance whose creation is dependent on the principles of inspiration, integration and innovation. In the case of governance for sustainability, inspiration can be interpreted as the development of a coherent culture around a vision of sustainability. According to Waddock *et al.* (2002), implementing this vision requires establishing codes of conduct and is dependent upon top-down support. The vision must be clarified and repeatedly articulated. Leadership must be open and responsive to high complexity. The second key principle of the governance system is integration, using reward, reporting, measurement and information systems as the basic systems for integration. Third, the systems of governance must be flexible and open enough to allow for innovation. This entails learning from past mistakes, reflective and reflexive learning systems, risk-taking and innovation.

Methodology

The researchers conducted semi-structured interviews with a cross-section of IAG employees, including: Mike Hawker (CEO, IAG), Rick Jackson (CEO, Personal Insurance), Sam Mostyn (Group Executive, Culture and Reputation), members of the Community and Environment team, HR and business managers. Other case material was obtained from secondary documents such as newspaper articles, company reports, annual staff engagement surveys, materials available on the IAG website and by discussions with Louise Wilson (Organisational Effectiveness, IAG).

Overview of IAG

IAG is currently Australasia's largest general insurance group – in 2004 it insured more than $800 billion worth of property. In 2004–2005 the net profit attributable to shareholders was $760 million, up $95 million from the previous year. The group owns the following insurance brands: NRMA Insurance, SGIO, SGIC, CGU and Swann Insurance in Australia, State Insurance and NZI in New Zealand, and CAA and RSA in Asia.

The organization has been through significant change and growth since 2000. Mike Hawker became CEO of NRMA Insurance Group Ltd (NIGL) in September 2001. In November 2001, shareholders of NIGL approved a change in name (to Insurance Australia Group Limited) to better reflect its size, diversity, geographical distribution and its aspirations. In January 2003 IAG acquired CGU and NZI. IAG has grown from 6,500 staff in 2002 to 12,000 in 2005 and over this period the share price has risen from $2.80 to $5.12.[1]

Sustainability at IAG is defined as being about ensuring the organization is around in the future for its customers, employees, community and shareholders. That involves:

- economic sustainability (building value for shareholders);
- human sustainability (safety, work–life balance, diversity);
- environmental sustainability (advocating climate change, reducing impact on the environment);
- social sustainability (reducing risk in the community such as crime, fires, car accidents etc).

The IAG Sustainability Report (2005) states that the company has made significant achievements towards becoming a sustainable organization. These achievements include:

- significant advancement in the firm's risk reduction community initiatives, in the areas of road and home safety, crime prevention, workplace safety and climate change;
- dramatically improving the firm's occupational health and safety (OH&S) performance;
- employees feeling positive about working at IAG, with 73 per cent of respondents to the annual survey saying they value IAG's focus on balancing social, environmental and financial responsibilities.

However, IAG faces challenges in the following areas:

- although IAG has implemented strong initiatives to improve its own environmental performance, it did not meet all of its environmental targets for the 2005 financial year;
- uncertainty and debate with some smash repairer groups about reform in the smash repair industry in New South Wales.

According to CEO Mike Hawker, true sustainability and enduring shareholder value comes from an understanding of the organization's purpose and achieving a balance between complex stakeholder priorities. In the next section we examine the strategy, structures and processes established at IAG to ensure the implementation of a coherent business model around the central theme of sustainability.

STRATEGIES

Establishing change leaders

The sustainability change programme at IAG is led by Mike Hawker, and it started when he became CEO in September 2001. According to Hawker, his crusade on behalf of sustainability was prompted by the massive storms in Sydney in 1999, Australia's largest insurance disaster. He is convinced that global warming relates to human activity and that it is the cause of the massive increase in insurance claims in recent years (Carruthers and Cornell 2005). Hawker identifies himself strongly with sustainability at IAG; he promotes corporate social responsibility as a core value and prioritizes risk and risk reduction as key issues. For example, Hawker himself takes the role of Chief Safety Officer. He is a strong advocate of Australia adopting policies to reduce the effects of climate change. He argues that sustainability values and governance are interrelated:

> The bigger the organization the more important it is to have a set of control structures to ensure that you are consistent in what you do and the two control structures that work are firstly values (a set of corporate values that don't change, they stand the test of time and the values describe the nature of people in the organization and describe how people will act). And the second one is a clear understanding throughout the organization of what it is you offer as a value proposition (purpose) to your customer. We think that the only way you get the consistent delivery is through a control mechanism which is value based and purpose based.

The only way to develop this clarity of understanding is through ongoing articulation of the sustainability vision and strategy. Hawker is not concerned at losing competitive advantage by broadcasting the change and governance programme employed at IAG to shift the organization to a stronger focus on sustainability. In his view, all organizations should be doing the same.

According to Hawker:

> The value set creates clarity of what we're doing and creates action and creates a framework of thinking, it creates a way of thinking in a consistent fashion so management starts to act consistently.

Setting the purpose

The governance system at IAG is underpinned by the concept that its customers are the community. IAG has developed a unifying purpose to address the expectations of its community role. IAG's stated organizational purpose is:

- paying claims;
- understanding and pricing risk;
- managing costs;
- reducing risk (through reducing effects of climate change, improving safety at home and work, and reducing crime).

The organizational purpose integrates with the values of honesty, transparency, teamwork, meritocracy and social responsibility, and is reinforced by the Executive team and through decisions, behaviours, processes and rewards. However, Hawker's view is that this does not make IAG a 'charity'. Instead: anything you do which does not increase shareholder value in an economic democratic capitalist society will not be sustainable in its own right. Hawker argues that governance mechanisms should be geared to the company's prime responsibility to ensure it is around in the long term. To do this the company must make a profit, and there will be times when it will be necessary to stringently cut costs. In Hawker's view, governance decisions should be made today with the intent of ensuring the organization is in good shape in 20–50 years.

The decision to prioritize sustainability and social responsibility objectives as a shared purpose was made because the organization recognized the need to consider all aspects of its impact on society and to respond to the loss of community trust currently experienced by the banking and insurance industry. Furthermore, reducing crime in the community and reducing the impacts of climate change result in fewer claims, and have a positive impact on IAG's financial position. Hence there is a strong business case for why sustainability and social responsibility is important for IAG. The overall strategy is to build social capital and maintain a social licence to operate through reducing theft, crime and safety risks for customers.

Rick Jackson, Chief Executive Officer, Personal Insurance, argues on behalf of a governance system that balances shareholder value creation with stakeholder value creation. For example, he describes IAG's decision to cap its return on equity to 15 per cent and to target return on equity of between 13 and 15 per cent as a survival strategy. In his view, insurers can learn a lot from the failure of the banking sector to balance the interests of shareholders and customers:

> that's the challenge for the insurance industry – How do you keep that balance and not have yourself legislated into control because you're seen to be overly greedy, or not caring enough for your customers, or not giving enough return to your shareholders?

Leadership frameworks

Leadership through a series of levels relating to different degrees of complexity is a key management strategy at IAG. The principle adopted under Hawker's leadership is that individuals in an organization have highly variable capacities to deal with complexity. According to Sam Mostyn, companies may fail because they have people in the very senior leadership positions who are very good on day-to-day tasks or management, but cannot cope with the degree of complexity you need to span and embed long-term sustainability in an organization. In a large organization the executive team must be planning/preparing for 5–10 years ahead and must be able to influence and balance political, economic, environmental and societal factors. Not everyone can comfortably deal with that level of complexity and the amount of greyness that comes with making decisions over that type of time horizon. In Mostyn's words:

> So one of the reasons we've been trying to embed a form of 'levels of work' is to have a rigour behind our choice of people at different levels in the organisation and trying to match the level of complexity of the job with the level of complexity that the person can actually feel comfortable with and to put fewer people in positions where they end up being so stressed and so unable to do their job.

In her view, companies that will be able to think sustainably and embed practices of good management to be around for the long term will require leaders who have the ability to deal with significant complexity and ambiguity. Mostyn conceives of 'levels of work' according to Elliot Jaques' concept of Stratified Systems Theory (1986), whereby individual employees are matched to their work environment depending upon capacity to deal with levels of complexity.

According to Mike Hawker, also working from this framework, IAG is now assessing the capability of individual managers in a much more rigorous way using a procedure called the Talent Matrix:

> what we're looking at is we're trying to assess those individuals' capability and outcomes in a very measurable and quite a robust way, . . . financial performance, people management performance, community interest, customer outcomes, values . . . and start to move people in a way that through that measurement those people who are performing well will get the first job offers.

Change mechanisms within the organization

From the top, strategy, direction and leadership around sustainability goals is clearly defined at IAG. As well, a culture change agenda is required to mobilize the workforce of over 12,000 people to be committed and united around this direction. Parallel to the top-down approach, the sustainability change committee is using bottom-up strategies to introduce sustainability into the respective divisions. The committee meets monthly, and includes one representative from each division of IAG. Change tactics include presentations by guest speakers to the committee on such topics as innovative ways of decreasing the organization's environmental impact.

IAG's response in 2004 to new legislation designed to improve consumer protection is illustrative of the organization's preparedness to address good governance issues in terms of its responsibilities to the community and social sustainability. Specialized change agents developed a change framework and change strategies to overcome staff resistance to new legislation designed to provide a consistent framework of consumer protection through full disclosure of product information. The change programme included creating stakeholder groups to champion the changes at the frontline and strong emphasis placed on communication and ongoing monitoring of performance outcomes (Hackman 2005).

Changing the supply chain

The sustainability of the smash repair industry is essential to IAG's business. This industry is currently at a crossroads with more than twice as many repair shops per vehicle in Australia than in the United Kingdom. IAG has taken steps to help the industry by investing $10 million over four years in apprenticeships, traineeships, business management training and succession planning courses. In 2005 IAG introduced a new Care and Repair service in NSW, a system that successfully operates in Queensland, Western Australia and South Australia. This service allows customers to take their damaged vehicle to one of IAG's assessment centres. However, there has been uncertainty and debate in NSW with the repairer groups about this system.

As part of the broader industry reform agenda, IAG established a network of Preferred Smash Repairers (PSRs) and although it encountered some criticism, the PSR strategy does enable management and control of environmental sustainability performance along the supply chain. The PSRs are selected based on factors such as operational performance and IAG's business needs, and are assisted by IAG to improve their operating efficiency, including their environmental and safety performance. The PSRs are also being assisted to develop a waste strategy which will reduce both operating costs and environmental damage.

Another tool designed to align IAG's environmental and economic goals through supply chain management is the Risk Radar tool. This online training tool aimed at building safe, environmentally sound workplaces is the first sustainability product for the IAG Group. Members of the PSRs network can obtain a discount on commercial insurance if the training plan is implemented and safety and environmental standards are met. The key idea is to offer financial incentives for behavioural changes which will reduce insurance risk. The tool is targeted at smash repairers, but it is currently being modified for use by farms and other businesses and has recently won the United Nations Association of Australia Triple Bottom Line Award.

Reducing risk in the community – community programmes

A shared understanding of the central importance of safety is crucial to achieving IAG's aim of adding stakeholder value through enabling a safer community, roads and workplace. To further this aim IAG has developed partnerships with community groups at a local, state and national level. One such partnership is with St John Ambulance. This is the first time St John Ambulance, initially reluctant to partner with a corporate, has taken part in such an initiative. The partnership involves St John becoming the primary supplier of first aid training to IAG with free four-hour first aid training sessions being made available to all IAG staff. The long-term aim is to offer free first aid training to all policyholders in order to reduce personal and community risk. The two organizations often put out co-branded communications and have commenced work on a number of other awareness-raising and mentoring programmes.

IAG also funds community grants with the aim of increasing staff involvement with the community. Over $10 million per year is spent on community programmes. In one example, a community grant supported a young crime offenders' programme in Newcastle, where indigenous community leaders and elders work with the police running cultural camps. The local managers of NRMA Insurance and the IAG employee who nominated the grant went to the camp. The feedback from this programme has generated staff engagement and an awareness in the organization of community-based problems. Links have now been developed with the Newcastle Police, who have recently approached the organization to offer 'drink drive' and other education programmes.

Another programme has entailed the purchase of a crime prevention van for the NSW Police Service, staffed by an IAG employee and a police education officer. The van is fitted out with demonstrated ways of reducing risk in the home and is being piloted in three regional areas. The value added to the community is being assessed through the reported number of burglaries. Moving forward, the NRMA Insurance databank will be used to identify priority areas for this vehicle.

Raising community awareness

The IAG Sustainability Report 2004 describes a number of strategies that IAG is working towards, helping its customers develop a better understanding of their risk profile. For instance, risks around the home are highlighted by the online help-house, and car theft is being targeted through the CrimeSafe programme which produces information on comparative vehicle crime safety features. Data such as research on tougher roofing products and the effects of climate change are to be made available on the IAG website.

IAG has processes in place to pursue a simultaneous top-down and bottom-up approach to develop and implement a community education strategy (IAG Stakeholder Relations 2004). Fostering sustainable communities is the aspect of sustainability which is most actively pursued by the education strategy at IAG. This interpretation requires a focus on safety, financial and social issues. Environmental issues are addressed by other parts of the organization.

According to Sam Mostyn, IAG's data on crime and risks can be extremely influential in raising community awareness:

> We looked at our data and saw that we had twice as many claims in three parts of NSW and they were Shellharbour, South Sydney and Dubbo. So we went into those areas and went to the police and local councils and said 'Is it worth us having a conversation with you to show you our data, our data is saying something that really disturbs us, you know your communities we don't, is it worth us sitting down with you to work out whether there is something in your community that's driving this crime?' We've called these our social capital investment programmes and in each case we have continued to work with those communities.

Reducing risk in the community involves awareness raising and education on crime reduction, fire safety and road safety, and partnering with organizations such as Rural Fire Brigade, ASIC (Australian Securities and Investment Commission) and teachers associations. Crime reduction initiatives include sponsoring a major researcher to visit from the UK to present to various groups.

STRUCTURE

Integrating sustainability into the organization

Considerable effort has gone into designing an effective structure at IAG for governance of the sustainability effort.

Sustainability is seen as being implemented at four levels:

Table 9.1 *Levels of sustainability at IAG*

Level	*Function/action*
Board	Nomination, remuneration and sustainability sub-committee
Executive	Specific divisional action plans; corporate strategy and culture
Corporate	Corporation-wide initiatives designed to implement the core values and organizational purpose across the organization; driving the sustainability strategy;
Operational	Sustainability champions lead initiatives designed to embed sustainability in the everyday aspects of the organization, involving a number of practical and specific roles at various levels

Each of the nine executives at IAG embeds sustainability into their planning. However, four members of the Executive Team have played a particularly strong leadership role in sustainability and are prominent in public forums concerned with sustainability in Australia.

They are:

CEO – Mike Hawker (by advocating his sustainability responsibilities as a leader of one of Australia's largest companies, and embedding the vision, values and purpose in the organization to enable it to become a sustainable organization).

Chief Risk Officer and Group Actuary – Tony Coleman (by highlighting climate change trends and using IAG data on natural disasters for climate change advocacy).

Group Executive, Culture and Reputation – Sam Mostyn (by establishing partnerships across the community to reduce risk, building a culture that is united around the purpose and values, and influencing organizations and leaders in the Australian community about sustainability).

CEO, Personal Insurance – Rick Jackson (by championing sustainability within his business and by sponsoring supply chain sustainability initiatives, particularly across the motor industry).

The role of the culture and reputation team

Sam Mostyn's key role is to manage a number of teams with sustainability functions, in relation to both internal (culture) and external (reputation) stakeholders. Responsibility areas of culture and reputation include human resources, organizational effectiveness, community and environment, government relations, and community affairs.

Senior management recognizes the ethos of sustainability cannot be prescribed from the top. As Sam Mostyn describes the progress to sustainability at IAG:

> I'd say we're well on the way to actually being sustainable but I would put it more at a sort of five to seven year opportunity for us rather than having achieved that in the first three years. There is an external perception by some that Sustainability is fully embedded in IAG, and that would be the wrong conclusion to draw right now. I think the first three years have been about raising consciousness and actually entering into a debate, a conversation with quite a large number of people in the company. I think what we've done really well is not try to prescribe what this means but to open that conversation and we've not been frightened of feedback from around the company.

But Mostyn also recognizes the need for all employees to internalize the vision – to move from a 'what Mike says' or 'they say this is what we should do' to a 'we believe, this is what we believe in, this is how we manage people, this is how we operate as a company, these are our belief systems, here's how we run this business'. For this reason, the change leaders at IAG acknowledge the value of internal schisms and debates. As Mostyn says:

> I think it's particularly interesting for us because we're about to go into a more difficult economic cycle as a sector and there are a lot of people in the company who would say, 'if this is real it will be embedded so deeply that we'll keep focusing on this and it will get us through tough times', another group saying 'it will be one of the first programmes to go because it must be costing us money to do this'. So I think that internal debate has been very healthy, there's no shutting it down, there's no telling people 'no this is the way it's going to be and if you don't like it you should just leave'.

Within Culture and Reputation, the task of designing sustainability strategy and measuring outcomes rests with Lynette Thorstensen (Head of Community and Environment). Lynette's role is to liaise with relevant internal and external stakeholders. She is charged with raising interest in sustainability across the organization and providing expert help when the interest is triggered. Her team also has the role of 'keeping the sustainability initiative honest' through pulling together the measurement indices. For instance, her team members coordinate the input required for the Dow Jones Sustainability Index and group-wide performance reporting in an annual sustainability report, in accordance with the Global Reporting Initiative.

Tying down the concept of sustainability can involve very different roles and procedures across the organization. The corporate service function of the Chief Financial Office (which comprises 120 employees) includes developing procurement guidelines and establishing monitoring guidelines, as well as developing eco-efficiency tools and measurement devices.

In Group Risk, under Tony Coleman, the team researches risk patterns and modelling, building social and environmental risk into risk management. Ambiguity is an emblematic challenge at IAG. As one interviewee put it: 'if you work here you have to deal with ambiguity'. In the Asset Management area, IAG is screening on corporate governance issues and is in early days of thinking about the best approaches to long-term sustainable investment opportunities.

The role of the flexibility and diversity team

The role of the flexibility and diversity team is to raise the sustainability profile, seen through the lens of work–life balance and diversity. The team is charged with lifting the awareness levels of management about diversity. One result has been a doubling in the number of indigenous employees. A key step in raising awareness is consideration and support of the initiatives at the local level.

Rather than the corporate view on sustainability, this IAG team has the responsibility to interpret sustainability through frameworks that establish a flexible working environment for the individual employee. The goal is to create a flexible workplace to enable work–life balance and a diverse workforce to facilitate equality. Primary drivers are higher rates of attraction and retention.

While the IAG Enterprise Agreement has a suite of flexibility options such as career breaks, work from home, flexi-time, childcare, emergency personal leave, and childcare leave on top of parental leave, the issue for the team has been implementing these goals in a smaller department. A current initiative aims to develop a more flexible work-pool focus in the highly structured work environment of Customer Service.

There is strong commitment across the organization to improve the representation of women in senior management. In 2005 women occupied 15 per cent of executive and 30 per cent of senior management positions. A mentoring programme has been established involving four senior women in a Chief Executive Senior Women Mentoring Program. The focus is on raising awareness rather than structural change.

At an operational level, all managers are required to attend Equal Employment Opportunity (EEO) training (with a focus on legislative and practical implications). The underpinning message is that workplace equality is essential.

PROCESSES

Establishing reporting systems

Governance is also about establishing policies and monitoring and reporting processes to ensure sustainability. Sustainability is not a single person issue at IAG but a matter of embedding it throughout the organization. Reflecting its success in reaching this goal, IAG won Special Award for Corporate Governance in the 2005 Australian Sustainability Awards, presented by Ethical Investor. Nominations of eligible Australian Stock Exchange listed companies were received from nine sustainability research groups. The nominations were reviewed by an expert judging panel. Special mention was made about the introduction of the Conflict of Interest Policy and ActionLine, the reporting mechanism to capture the most severe incidents of inappropriate activity within the organization and/or where an issue has been reported but no action taken.

In 2005 IAG was also granted AA ratings for Social Responsibility by RepuTex. RepuTex's annual survey of corporate social responsibility covers issues including corporate governance, environmental impact, workplace practices and the company's social impact. Only one firm received the higher AAA rating, while eleven others shared IAG's AA rating.

Measurement is critical to the process of embedding sustainability and ties into the fact that insurance is about collecting meaningful data with the expectation of long-term results. Under the rubric of governance for sustainability, IAG is moving from the disclosure of financials as required by regulation to include voluntary disclosure of other data such as human capital and environmental performance.

A key tool designed to achieve this outcome was the establishment of corporate targets for safety and for the reduction of emissions and other aspects of the environmental footprint. Working with the executives and the strategy team, members of the sustainability change management team have set targets for electricity usage, office paper, print paper, trade car fleet usage and air travel.

The IAG Sustainability Reports (2004, 2005) examined these targets. Setting targets for environmental and safety outcomes enables sustainability to be incorporated into the performance measurement system and annual planning and strategy discussions. The 2005 Sustainability Report stated that although strong initiatives have been implemented, IAG has not met all of its environmental targets for the year 2005. This is due to a number of factors including the challenge of balancing the need to reduce environmental impact while growing the business. For example, the firm knows that decisions taken to benefit customers through improved technology require additional computer servers, leading to an increase in CO_2 emissions.

In 2005–6, IAG took steps to address environmental performance by:

- improving measuring and reporting processes;
- setting more tailored divisional targets;
- rolling out action plans to address high environmental impact areas; and
- engaging IAG people around improving performance.

IAG is also targeting its single greatest contributor to CO_2 emissions – electricity – by developing and implementing an energy management plan for major sites. In 2004 a process to further the organizational strategy concerning the development of a social licence to operate and with the aim of ascertaining what the community thinks are the attributes of excellence for an insurance company, IAG surveyed approximately 2,000 community leaders. The findings are developed in a Stakeholder Report (IAG Pty Ltd 2004). Almost 80 per cent of survey respondents said working to secure safer roads, homes and workplaces for Australians is the most important challenge facing their community. Seventy-one per cent highlighted reducing crime as a high priority for their community and just under one-third of respondents stated IAG should take the lead in working to reduce greenhouse gas emissions.

Monitoring engagement

A survey-based instrument is used to assess the level of engagement with the sustainability goals. The 2005 employee engagement scores were average for a financial institution (54 per cent engagement with a response rate of 86 per cent, up from 45 per cent engagement in 2003).

In the 2005 Your Voice Survey,

- Seventy-three per cent of respondents surveyed said 'The organization's position on safety, environment and community is important and meaningful for me'.
- Seventy-four per cent of respondents surveyed said 'I am proud of IAG's role in helping to reduce and share financial risks across the community'.

The sustainability change team is looking at where sustainability can add value by making insurance more exciting and more positive, focusing for instance on how insurance enables people to have better and more secure lives. This is what Sam Mostyn says to sceptics in the organization who see corporate social responsibility as a temporary fad:

> If this world is changing the external environment in which we're operating, the ability to attract talented people is changing. . . . And they're different people, they're not going to be the people we've traditionally been able to recruit and we're not actually, even today, addressing one hundred per cent of the addressable market by ignoring part-time women, and older work force members, so we're killing our own ability to do that if we don't address one hundred per cent of the market and think collaboratively and be flexible about what we're going to do.

Management at IAG is aware of the relationship between corporate reputation and corporate performance, including employee attraction and retention. Attempts are being made to improve the current employee retention rate of 19.50 per cent (IAG Sustainability Report 2005). Preliminary indications from recent trials are that a more flexible management and governance system can alleviate problems with low retention rate in call centres (call centres being the business units with the highest turnover).

In our interviews, Mike Hawker made the point that the purpose and values enshrined through a focus on sustainability can build staff satisfaction and commitment, benefit the financial bottom line and contribute to the long-term survival of the firm.

Monitoring occupational health and safety (OHS)

The first internal annual OHS report (2002) showed IAG's OHS performance was considerably poorer than the average insurance company. It stated:

- The number of claims per 1,000 employees is around five times the industry average.
- The average claim cost is 44 per cent of the industry average.
- Total claims cost per employee is around 2.2 times the industry average.

(Workplace Health and Safety IAG 2002)

This indicates that IAG experienced a greater number of smaller claims than similar organizations with the total cost per employee being slightly above double the industry average.

The report also stated that IAG systems may encourage a greater rate of reporting than other organizations (although still under-reporting of actual occurrence) and may reflect more pro-active management of claims. This revelation shocked the organization into instigating governance measures designed to monitor and measure safety. The OHS Management system was structured to align with AS/NZS 4801 capturing the elements of policy, planning, implementation, measurement and evaluation, management review and continued improvement, with a focus on a number of underpinning key priority areas:

- leadership
- communication
- use of technology
- decentralizing management of risk.

In implementing the safety management programme, IAG made the link between cultural change and safety, as well as using results and data to continue to drive motivation forward.

The safety programme at IAG is led by an organization-wide Steering Committee composed of the CEO and ten executive/senior managers from across the organization. To support the Steering Committee is a specialist OHS team. This team includes psychologists, nurses and business risk managers, provided with data analysis support. Under a consultation framework developed with the Finance Sector Union, agreement has been reached to have at least one representative, trained in OHS consultation, at each site as point of contact and as a technical resource. This has resulted in a network of more than 300 OHS representatives and 20 building OHS committees consulting on local and corporate OHS issues.

As a large workers' compensation insurer, IAG recognizes that it must practise what it preaches to maintain credibility of its sustainability profile. The *besafe* programme was instigated to work right throughout the organization to reduce workplace harm and foster a safety culture. The *besafe* initiative was complemented by a range of other OHS process-based initiatives including the development of online OHS training for all employees (currently completed by 84 per cent of all employees), compulsory manager training, the introduction of an electronic accident and incident reporting process, and risk radar (an online OHS self-assessment process for all worksites). These technical improvements assisted in generating awareness, promoting leadership and decentralizing risk.

The initiatives resulted in a 20 per cent reduction of workplace accidents in the 2003–2004 period, with a further 22 per cent reduction in LTIFR (Lost Time Injury Frequency Rate) in 2004–2005. IAG has also realized a 57 per cent reduction in workers' compensation claims costs in the 2004–2005 year. Outstanding improvements in the annual culture survey confirmed the clear link back to employee engagement.

Further internal processes such as a timely reporting rate, timely follow up, OHS training rates, quality of managers' comments as well as types and costs of incidents are collated and reported internally on a monthly basis. This information helps to maintain and drive the commitment to cultural change, as well as highlighting potential issues that may arise. The main injuries are slips, trips and falls which involve smaller cost claims. However, the big causes of concern are the increase in stress and overuse injuries.

The safety programme is currently targeting ergonomics, stress and driver safety, where the potential for injury is very high. Local health and well-being initiatives are also helping to address the main causes of concern. Safety and community work are linked through the IAG relationship with St John Ambulance, a relationship which is unique to the insurance sector, with corporate leadership now being demonstrated through success in a number of awards (including the NSW WorkCover 2005 Safe Work Award for Best OHS management system).

Monitoring for change

According to the Manager of OHS: just doing the measurement has increased the reporting rate. Recent safety programme initiatives include the creation of a role specifically designed to monitor data which is expected to result in a much more robust system. Having now implemented industry benchmarking and with two years of internal data, IAG can compare different parts of the organization and look at trends from year to year. Safety purists in the organization still count the number of fire extinguishers and whilst the Safety Manager states this is critical, a key challenge is reinforcing the broad perspective and 'pushing back the accountabilities'. The numbers need to be very visible for us to analyse accountabilities and responsibilities. IAG has decreased its Lost Time Injury Frequency Rate to 5.3 per million hours worked compared to 6.7 per cent in the 2004 financial year, and 80 per cent of managers have completed OHS training (up from 26 per cent in 2003).

Measuring community leadership

IAG's crime prevention strategy is another way of reducing risk of claims and is very dependent on measurement. Not only are cars rated according to their level of security but Car Park Security Ratings are also available. Areas of crime are targeted which are hot spots, characterized by a low number of police and high burglary rate. The results show a decreased level of burglary with a 27 per cent overall crime reduction. By using the data that it collates from paying claims, IAG can play a strong community leadership role by working with organizations and using this data to address community issues (whether it be crime, road safety or climate change). In this way, an insurance company is in a powerful position to change behaviour and drive societal change.

Sustainable procurement

Sustainable procurement processes are another example of governance fostering sustainability. IAG has a procurement policy that it uses to measure and evaluate suppliers or potential suppliers. These criteria include sustainable environmental practices and socially responsible behaviour. An example of this is that IAG has now purchased over 120 Toyota Prius hybrid vehicles for its fleet. These cars use approximately 50 per cent less petrol than comparative cars and emit 90 per cent less greenhouse gases. Toyota reported that the initial purchase of 26 vehicles was the largest business order of the Prius since the first model was launched in Australia in 2001.

DISCUSSION: GOVERNANCE CHALLENGES

Broadening the sustainability vision

The strong leadership around sustainability at IAG has led to a perception both internally and externally that it is already embedded into the business model. But Mike Hawker acknowledges much headway is still to be made. However, he is confident that the company has a strong culture and a well-established set of values upon which the sustainability platform can be built:

> Culture is about the sustainability of a set of principles over a long period of time, and management is just a passing parade within the middle of it. So culture should be hard to change, should be hard to build, but should be very powerful if it's built well.

In his view, there are synergies between insurance, with its strong focus on measurement, and a governance system which permits employee flexibility and initiative: 'We want a culture where managers will take a chance. We are there to help them when they make mistakes'.

A number of senior managers recognize that the governance framework should include strategies, structures and processes that can move the organizational understanding of sustainability to a less restrictive focus. According to one manager we interviewed, many employees still think of sustainability as recycling or environmental gases, not thinking of the social, safety or financial literacy aspects. And according to the Manager, OHS: 'Safety is not seen as sustainability. Some people here see sustainability as the environment. We need to get them to recognize that it is about the organization being around in the future'.

Achieving consistency

Implementing this broad, integrated vision of sustainability presents many challenges, highlighted by these comments from IAG sustainability change agents, set out in Table 9.2

These comments reflect the fact that the governance system does not attempt to enforce commitment to sustainability in the management ranks. Rather, as we have discussed, the organization is attempting to build the right culture though implementing strategic, structural and process-based change through bottom-up as well as top-down

Table 9.2 *Perceptions of sustainability challenges at IAG*

Comments by IAG change agents
'The change programme in place now at IAG does not reflect the history of the organization. A culture of stability does not necessarily facilitate change'.
'The business model can tend to be Sydney-centric. Identity and fragmentation are issues – SGIO and SGIC are retail brands and were acquired as different companies. The organization has gone from 3,000 to 12,000 employees in five years. Five acquisitions in five years. Different parts of IAG have different cultural backgrounds.'
'Although some of the leading executives are very positive about sustainability, not all of the managers have embraced the concept and support the change programme. Some act as leaders but others are indifferent'.
'The tightening insurance market will test IAG's level of commitment to sustainability'.
'IAG has not yet released an environmental product to the marketplace (such as pay-as-you-drive insurance or discounts for hybrid cars)'.

procedures. Therefore the situation is now that some managers fully embrace it (and the complexity and the challenges that it brings), while others maintain their short-term traditional view of their accountabilities as a manager.

Corporate challenges

According to Lynette Thorstensen (Head of Community and Environment) future challenges for the governance of sustainability in IAG, relevant to the sector in general, are concerned with:

- Assets and investments: it's now important that the sector makes sure it has its own house in order in relation to its ecological footprint, its suppliers and its investments.
- Achieving environmental targets: IAG did not meet all of its environmental targets for the 2005 year. The firm needs to ensure that it takes into account the impact of growing its business internationally in the targets it sets, and to ensure that all business units actively work to meet set targets.
- Professional development: there are opportunities for more exciting and challenging opportunities for professional development (especially for employees in line roles). These could include global study tours of other organizations (to view how they are embedding sustainability) and/or to immerse people in real social issues.
- Integrated campaigns/social marketing: IAG needs to find new and innovative ways to link sustainability to genuine market differentiation for our customers.

This should mean innovative best practice forms of social marketing and integrated campaigns (where the firm simultaneously reinforces in marketing with customers and media the work it is doing with community partnerships).

- Management commitment: through workshops and face-to-face sessions, IAG can do more work with small groups and with every manager across the business, to generate debate and discussion. The responsible change agents search constantly to find better and more persuasive ways of articulating the business case for these people. The firm also needs to introduce more stringent attention to integrating sustainability into performance objectives.

Finally, IAG is in a race against time. The values, the culture and the sustainability commitment needs to be so well embedded that should there be a substantial leadership shift, the commitment to the community and sustainability will remain strong.

If we return to Waddock *et al.* (2002) and their key values-based governance principles of inspiration, integration and innovation, we can see that IAG has attempted to address each of these areas of organizational concern. The study has affirmed the role that leadership plays in inspiring and revisioning an organization around the motif of sustainability. We have also seen how IAG has worked to integrate sustainability in a very pragmatic approach, based on both top-down and bottom-up systems of governance. While the model of governance is influenced by the structured and hierarchical levels of work concept espoused by Jaques (1986), IAG initiatives such as emphasis on cross-level and function sustainability champions reflect more circular forms of decision-making advocated by organization theorists such as Romme (1999). A key issue for the success of this model will be how these systems of governance can draw together the elements of sustainability into an integrated purpose for IAG, yet allow for the flexibility required of the interconnected and innovative organization of the future.

CONCLUSION

As one of Australia's leading businesses, very much in the public eye, the risks of IAG taking an advocacy role in sustainability are high. The governance strategies, processes and structures IAG has selected to manage this risk have been described in this study. But as Mike Hawker himself points out (Carruthers and Cornell 2005), IAG functions within the wider governance framework of government policy-making. At this level, more complex measures are needed to measure the economic and environmental costs of doing nothing, versus the costs of working to foster sustainability.

NOTE

1 As at 10am, Wednesday 7 December 2005.

REFERENCES

Carruthers, F. and Cornell, A. (2005) 'End of the dry argument', *Australian Financial Review*, 9 December.

Clarke, T. (2004) 'Introduction: theories of governance – reconceptualising corporate governance theory after the Enron experience' in T. Clarke (ed.) *Theories of Corporate Governance*, London: Routledge, pp. 1–31.

Hackman, K. (2005) 'Providing customers with the "right help": implementing financial services reform in Insurance Australia Group', *Journal of Change Management*, 5: 345–55.

IAG Pty Ltd, (2004) 'We're listening . . . , summary of results – community issues and priorities survey 2004', IAG. Online. Available at: http://www.iag.com.au/pub/iag/sustainability/publications/media/05-08-08%20IAG%20Stakeholder%20Report%202005.pdf (accessed 10 August 2005).

IAG Stakeholder Relations (2004) 'Improving the community's understanding of insurance', IAG Community Education Strategy Discussion Paper.

IAG Sustainability Report (2004) 'The fewer the risks the better for everyone', IAG. Online. Available at: http://www.iag.com.au/pub/iag/sustainability/publications/report/2004/index.shtml (accessed 15 September 2005).

IAG Sustainability Report (2005) 'It's just good business', IAG. Online. Available at: http://www.iag.com.au/pub/iag/sustainability/publications/report/2005/index.shtml (accessed 4 December 2005).

Jaques, E. (1986) *The Requisite Organization*, Arlington: Cason Hall and Co.

Romme, A. Georges L., (1999) 'Domination, self-determination and circular organizing', *Organization Studies*, 20(5): 801–31.

Waddock, S., Bodwell, C. and Graves, S. (2002) 'Responsibility: the new business imperative', *Academy of Management Executive*, 16(2): 132–49.

Workplace Health and Safety IAG (2002) '2001–2002 workplace incidents and occupational compensation claims report', unpublished report, IAG.

apter 10

ı he civil regulation of corporations

Towards stakeholder democracy

Jem Bendell and Aarti Sharma

INTRODUCTION

> How can we call our society democratic when many of its most powerful institutions are closed to governance from outside and are run as oligarchies from within?
>
> Henry Mintzberg (1989, p. 328)

Today, corporations are everywhere. The number of 'transnational corporations' (TNCs) has risen nearly ten-fold since 1970, and their turnovers dwarf that of many national economies. One-third of world trade occurs between factories and offices of TNCs (ILO 2000). On the one hand, their involvement in processes meeting basic needs, such as food, shelter, medicines and infrastructure, makes them directly relevant to billions of people worldwide. On the other, their ability to escape state-based regulation, and even dictate that regulation, has given rise to growing concerns about their accountability. Corporate organizations have emerged as a superpower in our global economy (Bendell, 2004). As the historical balance between governments and business has been upset through globalization, we are challenged to think creatively about how international corporations can be governed by society.

In this chapter, we discuss the concept of 'civil regulation' (Murphy and Bendell 1997; Bendell 2000) and question whether it offers a novel channel for participatory democratic governance of the global economy. Using a typology of civil regulation, supported with international cases, we demonstrate how voluntary associations of people can influence changes in corporate policies and practices on sustainable development issues. The concept of civil society is used to theorize these voluntary associations, and to then explore the extent to which novel business–civil society relations may provide a means of democratizing global economic activity in a context of the weakening independence of governments from corporate interests. Concepts of democracy are, of course, contested, with historical debates between advocates of representative democracy and participatory democracy. Modern twists to this debate involve cosmopolitan, deliberative and associative conceptions of democracy, among others. Engaging with concepts and techniques of democracy poses a significant challenge. One popular conception of democracy is that in a democratically governed society a community of people should have meaningful participation in decisions and processes that affect them and they should not be systematically adversely affected by another group of people without being able to rectify the situation (Dahl 1961). This means that any organization can be assessed in terms of democracy: organizations should be accountable to those they affect – particularly those who are negatively affected.

Some have argued that voluntary corporate responses to sustainable development challenges, often in partnership with non-governmental organizations, can pose a threat to democracy if it leads to the view that they are sufficient and that state regulation and court action are not needed (Klein, 2000). By reviewing existing empirical work, conducted by these authors and others, we conclude that in some instances civil regulation is providing a means of democratic participation in society, in the sense that it allows some of those who are affected by corporations to influence their activities. However, we also describe how many of these processes are weak or not driven by the interests of affected parties. Consequently, we need to 're-place' our understanding of democracy as something that can be pursued at the 'sub-political' realm of non-state actor interaction. By doing this, our analysis and subsequent advice may help people to govern corporations. This chapter is therefore an introduction to civil regulation, and an invitation for further work on the issues of power and democracy that arise.

CIVIL REGULATION

The concept of 'civil regulation' was introduced to policy debates on sustainable development in 1999, in a publication by the UN Research Institute of Social Development (UNRISD) on novel partnerships between businesses and non-governmental organizations (Murphy and Bendell 1999). It theorized those partnerships in the context of a wide variety of NGO campaigns on corporations, ranging from confrontational to collaborative, and suggesting that these were having a cumulative effect that could be understood as the quasi-regulation of business by 'civil society'. Before progressing in exploring the nature of these relations, it is important to clarify what is meant by 'civil' and by 'regulation'.

Civil is a direct reference to 'civil society'. At various times in the history of Western political thought, the term 'civil society' has been used to describe the realm of networks and associations that result from people coming together, voluntarily, to work towards progressive change in their local and extra-local communities. The term is contested, with some suggesting it usefully describes all forms of association, whatever their purpose, and others being more explicit about the role of shared values in making it a category of social importance (Edwards 2003). Some prefer to delineate a type of value or effect that is 'civil', suggesting that the usefulness of the term 'civil society' will be in how it allows us to understand matters of the common good (Knight and Hartnell 2000). Others are uncomfortable with deciding what is or is not a 'civil' value or action (Keane 1998).

In the initial proposition of civil regulation, civil society was used to describe the sphere of associational life formed by people coming together for a primary purpose other than commerce or attaining governmental power (Murphy and Bendell 1999; Bendell 2000). The term 'civil groups' therefore refers to formal or informal organizations and networks that are both not-for-profit and non-governmental, and 'civil actors' as individuals who participate themselves in those forms of associational life.[1] Despite not explicitly positing a shared value set amongst these diverse actors, there was a suggestion that civil society's engagements with corporations might be a process that democratized economic activity (Bendell 2000). In this chapter we adopt the same broad conception of civil society as all forms of not-for-profit, non-governmental associational activity, but question whether this 'civil' activity can lead to the democratization of economic activity.

Regulation is popularly understood as something done by governments. However, work on lead company regulation of their industries (Teubner 1996) suggests that regulation can be useful if understood in a broader context. From a re-working of Kant's (1964) ideas, a regulatory framework can be defined as a norm-creating and norm-enforcing system, which must exhibit the following five components:

- an *agent*, or agents, which can make choices between alternative norms of behaviour;
- alternative *norms* of behaviour between which to choose;
- a *subject*, be it something or someone, upon which a chosen norm is imposed;
- a *resolution* regarding which of the alternative norms should apply to the subject;
- a *mechanism* for ensuring that the chosen norm is adhered to by the subject(s).

In terms of a national government and the legislature, the *resolution* regarding which *norm* to choose is called 'legislation' and the preferred *norm* is called a 'law'. However, it is incorrect to assume a government to be the *only* agent that can consider different *norms* of behaviour and make *resolutions* about which should apply to different *subjects*, and then use a *mechanism* to ensure compliance.

Civil regulation recognizes civil society as the *agent* where different *norms* of behaviour for corporations are debated. Civil groups then make *resolutions* about the standards that should be upheld by the *subjects* of the regulation, in this case the corporations. These 'resolutions' are diverse, taking the form of campaign goals, or the standards set out in codes of conduct and certification systems. The regulatory framework is completed by *mechanisms* for ensuring compliance. In civil regulation these mechanisms range from the specific to the diverse. A system of auditing and certification, for example, is a specific mechanism for enforcement. These mechanisms are ultimately enforced through a range of processes, which together constitute the commercial rationale for companies to respond to civil society. These include the benefits of a positive reputation for relations with communities, regulators, the media, customers, investors and potential critics, and impacts on staff motivation and retention, and opportunities for innovation (Bendell 2000).

Different civil groups/actors may be inclined to different types of activity that directly influence the corporate policy and practice on sustainable development issues. A typology of civil regulation is helpful in understanding various types of civil actions and how those influence corporates, in terms of their social responsibility (Bendell 2000). This typology is based on the following two variables:

- 'place' of the civil action in relation to the market – whether or not the civil group/actor is dependent on raising revenue in the market economy;
- 'style' of the civil action in relation to the corporate activity being influenced – whether the civil group/actor conflicts or collaborates with the mainstream companies concerned.

The typology recognizes the following four types of corporate-influencing civil actions (illustrated in Figure 10.1): forcing change, promoting change, facilitating change and producing change.

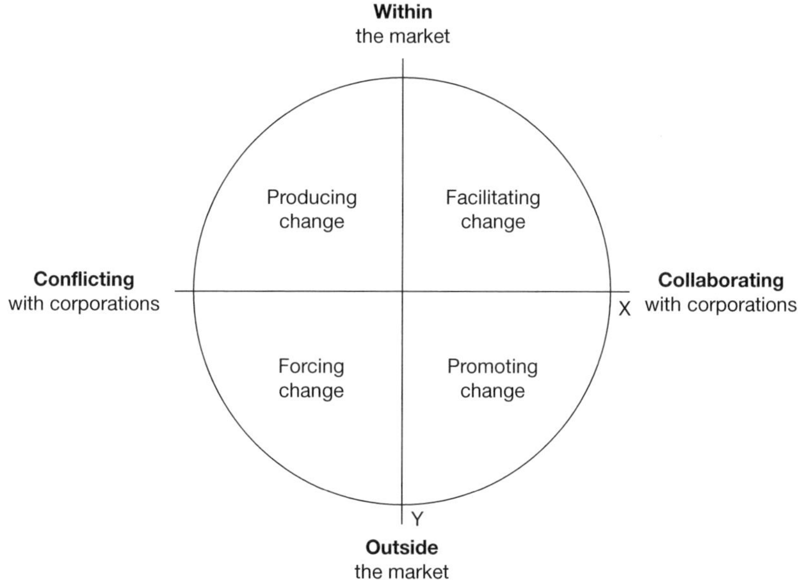

Figure 10.1 *Typology of civil group engagement with, to change, corporations*

The approach taken is the result of a number of factors, such as the ideology of the civil group/actor, the skills they possess, the success or failure of previous campaigns, and the responsiveness of the businesses in question. In the following sections we explain these forms of action with examples, before discussing their cumulative effect as the civil regulation of corporations.

Forcing change

Civil groups may use force to bring about changes in corporate policy and practice. Various 'pester pressure' tactics may be employed at various levels to provoke change in corporate actions. At the activist level, civil groups may organize consumer boycotts, media-friendly stunts awkwardly exposing executives to questions fired by journalists, demonstrations at corporate offices, retail outlets, or annual general meetings (AGMs). A tactic of general advocacy may be employed to create outcry amongst people in government, the UN system, the media and the wider business community.

Civil regulating Monsanto: in pursuit of a GM-free world

> Monsanto's field trials . . . will be reduced to ashes in a few days. These actions will start a movement of direct action by farmers against biotechnology, which will not stop until all the corporate killers like Monsanto, Novartis, Pioneer etc. leave the country . . . [T]hese actions can also pose a major challenge to the survival of these corporations in the stock markets. Who wants to invest in a mountain of ashes, in offices that are constantly being squatted (and if necessary even destroyed) by activists?
>
> Professor Nanjundaswamy, (1998, quoted in Bendell 2000: 14)

In 1998, Indian farmers in the Karnataka region, chanting 'Cremate Monsanto' and 'Stop Genetic Engineering', uprooted and burnt genetically engineered cotton fields in front of the mass media. Civil groups including the Karnataka State Farmers Association, were calling on the biotechnology company Monsanto to 'get out of India', and for the government to ban field tests and imports of genetically modified (GM) seeds and crops. This was just one episode in a global campaign against Monsanto – orchestrated by diverse, autonomous, yet Internet-working, civil groups covering issues such as farmer security, environmental risk, consumer health and corporate power. Most governments had been supportive of the commercialization of genetic modification (GM) technology, so activists had decided to target the companies directly. This civil campaign meant that the market for GM products dried up as retailers said they would not sell food with GM ingredients. Monsanto was forced into a number of policy U-turns, including the shelving of its 'terminator technology' (infertile seeds) and the provision of royalty-free licences for its technologies that might help the development of vitamin-A enriched rice. These moves were not enough to save the company from evaporating investor confidence, and its share price fell to the extent that is was taken over (Bendell 2001). The public demise of Monsanto made people realize that the previous high-profile row in the mid-1990s between Shell and environmental groups over the Brent Spar oil platform and with human rights groups over its operations in Nigeria were not unique. Governmental approval for the conduct of large corporations was not enough to save Shell from severe criticism that compelled these companies to change their policies and practices.

Civil regulating GlaxoSmithKlein: in pursuit of a humane mission

One of the most high-profile forcing change campaigns did not involve a boycott but general advocacy to create outcry amongst people in government, the UN system, the media and the wider business community. The issue was how pharmaceutical companies were hindering the treatment of millions of people living with Human Immunodeficiency Virus and Acquired Immune Deficiency Syndrome (HIV/AIDS) in the global south by their pricing and patenting of anti-retroviral drugs. Civil groups like Médecins Sans Frontières (MSF – doctors without borders) had been campaigning on this issue for a while and were joined by others including the British aid agency Oxfam. They published a report on the largest pharmaceutical company in the world, GlaxoSmithKlein (GSK), in which they called on the company to either slash the costs of its drugs for treating diseases in poor countries or give up its patents on those drugs. UN Secretary General Kofi Annan joined the calls for action, especially when 39 pharmaceutical companies went to the Pretoria High Court to challenge a South African law aimed at easing access to AIDS drugs. The companies claimed that the law unfairly invalidated patent protections by giving the health minister broad powers to produce – and import more cheaply – generic versions of drugs still under patent. The fact that more than 4.5 million South Africans were infected with HIV, while five of the corporations suing the government had global sales more than three times South Africa's national budget, highlighted the imbalance. 'It is indefensible for billion-dollar drug companies to take South Africa to court to stop it buying cheap essential medicines' said Oxfam Policy Director Justin Forsyth. 'This court case demonstrates how powerful drug companies are bullying poor countries just so they can protect their patent rights on life-saving medicines' (quoted in Bendell 2001: 8).

Within weeks the pharmaceutical industry dramatically dropped its case against the government, and began cutting the costs of their drugs. *The Financial Times* suggested the companies were fighting a price war as they sought to outbid each other and generic manufacturers to supply cheap AIDS drugs to Africa. This 'price war' reached a significant point when Pfizer Inc. announced it would offer an antifungal medicine at *no charge* to HIV/AIDS patients in the 50 least-developed countries where the disease was most prevalent (Bendell 2001).

These tactics of *forcing change* are often successful in raising an issue and gaining a general commitment from a corporation, and hence may no longer seem so confrontational when corporations start responding positively. However, the significance of these campaigns for enabling greater regulation of corporate practice by those they affect depends on the subsequent processes of implementation, which we return to below.

Promoting change

Civil groups may attempt to influence corporations by operating from outside the market on a voluntary basis and donating their time, resources and money in order to *promote change* in corporate behaviour. This may involve dialogue between civil groups, companies and consultants, advising companies on best practice, negotiating agreements, endorsing or promoting best practice (thereby supporting ethical consumerism and investment), conducting and publishing helpful research, or jointly developing new products or techniques.

Civil regulating industrial relations: in pursuit of a global dialogue

Some trade unions have begun responding to the global reach of large corporations by coordinating amongst themselves and seeking to engage companies at the global level. National trade unions have been working together to increase affiliation to global federations such as the International Union of Food, Agricultural, Hotel, Restaurant, Catering, Tobacco and Allied Workers' Associations (IUF), the International Federation of Building and Wood Workers (IFBWW), and the International Confederation of Free Trade Unions (ICFTU). Together these federations help give a global voice to the 200 million members of trade unions worldwide (Graham 1998: personal communication). Many such federations have signed framework agreements with large international corporations. These agreements allow unions to deal with corporations at a global level on the basis of common principles, including the fundamental rights of workers that are incorporated in core conventions of the International Labour Organization (ILO), while also upholding the principle that disputes should be resolved by local union representatives. In 2001 the International Federation of Chemical, Energy, Mine and General Worker's Unions (ICEM) signed one of these agreements with the oil company Statoil. ICEM's Ian Graham (1998) believes these agreements offer 'one of the best chances yet of improving global companies' communications with their stakeholders – in the interests of the community as a whole.' Statoil's Vice-President, Geir Westgaard, says his company's agreement with ICEM 'made good business sense' because civil groups 'are globe-spanning knowledge-based organizations. They give us early warning of problems we should be aware of, and allow us to take early action to mitigate risks' (Bendell 2001: 9).

Facilitating change

Instead of collaborating voluntarily with corporations to help them change their behaviour, civil groups may operate from 'inside' the market by selling their services to *facilitate change* in corporate practice. Such actions may include providing consultancy services to help companies with strategy, policy and organizational change, or setting up reputed networks or institutions that provide endorsements, accreditation or certification for corporates and thereby enhance the company's reputation in the business community and consumer market. Therefore, the success of such civil actions depends on their ability to sell their services.

Civil regulating timber industry: in pursuit of responsible forestry

Civil groups like the Soil Association certify food products on the basis of organic criteria, and wood products on the basis of responsible forestry standards. Their forestry certification work is overseen and accredited by another civil group, called the Forest Stewardship Council (FSC), which aims to provide a credible guarantee to consumers that wood products come from well-managed forests. FSC is a membership body, bringing together stakeholders from different sectors and with different and sometimes opposing views, to agree to standards for responsible forestry and how forest inspections should be carried out by accredited certifiers, as well as how products should be traced from certified forests and then labelled and advertised in stores. Within ten years of its founding, hundreds of logging operations, accounting for millions of hectares of forest, had been certified within the FSC system. FSC illustrates the way new institutions are being established to oversee social and environmental standards for corporate practice. Other examples include the Marine Stewardship Council, Social Accountability International and the Global Reporting Initiative.

Producing change

Civil action may also attempt to *produce change* in the market, by providing alternative production and trading systems based on a different value system from mainstream business practice. Many civil groups have helped to establish trading companies that operate to standards such as fairtrade or organic agriculture. These approaches can be considered combative to mainstream corporations as, initially, they seek to compete with them in the marketplace.

Civil regulating through fair trade: in pursuit of helping disadvantaged producers

In the 1950s and 1960s some companies began purchasing goods from disadvantaged producers with a view to promoting their development as part of 'goodwill selling' and later 'solidarity trade' (Tallontire *et al.* 2001). Examples included Traidcraft in the UK and Fair Trade Organisatie (formerly SOS Wereldhandel) in the Netherlands. Subsequently fairtrade labelling organizations emerged, the first and probably best known being Max Havelaar. In 1997 they joined up with similar organizations in other countries, to form 'FLO' – Fairtrade Labelling Organizations International. By 2001 this group had 17 member organizations. They issue fairtrade labels to manufacturers or importers whose production or supply of a particular product meets specified standards, including the payment of a guaranteed price that includes a 'social premium' to fund development activities. Today you can buy fairtrade coffee, tea, bananas, sugar, orange juice and cocoa. The market for fairtrade products grew steadily throughout the 1990s, averaging $400 million in retail sales each year in Europe and the USA, equivalent to 0.01 per cent of global trade (Littrell and Dickson, 1999). The fairtrade product that first grabbed a sizeable market share was the banana in Switzerland, which reached a 15 per cent market share by the end of the 1990s. Tallontire and colleagues have noted, however, that there remains a large gap between the number of people who claim to prefer goods with ethical characteristics and the actual sales figures for fairtrade consumption (Tallontire *et al.* 2001). Nevertheless, as demand for fairtrade products has grown, large companies such as Starbucks and Nestlé have begun to offer fairtrade products, illustrating how companies can change their approach, therefore challenging the assumption that particularly civil actions are confrontational rather than collaborative.

Power and democracy in civil regulation

In the last decade collaborative relations between businesses and civil groups have moved from being unusual arrangements to centrepieces of international policy-making on sustainable development. This was highlighted when the 2002 World Summit on Sustainable Development (WSSD) secretariat announced over 200 partnerships involving different civil groups, companies and/or governments, as official 'Type II' outcomes of intergovernmental process. Therefore the contemporary upturn in civil group engagement with corporations has now existed for long enough for us to gain insight into the initial civil regulation hypothesis that it would promote the democratic governance of corporations in a global economy.

On the one hand, there is evidence in support of the democratization hypothesis. The very existence of 'forcing change' and 'producing change' tactics from civil groups is an indicator of the existence and use of civil and political rights, that is essential to democracy, as much as it is an indicator of initial grievances. In addition, they have helped fuel positive responses to promoting and facilitating change tactics from civil groups that have helped to drive tangible changes on a variety of issues. Millions of forest hectares certified as well-managed, and thousands of factories privately inspected for labour standards violations, are tangible results that provide benefit to the communities and workers concerned.

Conversely, there is growing evidence that these civil group tactics are having a very limited impact on democratizing corporate activity. The ability of 'forcing change' tactics to deliver tangible results in accordance with the interests of those most affected by corporate practice is dependent on the 'promoting change' and 'facilitating change' activities – namely the various partnerships, codes and certification systems that have been adopted. Examination of the accountability of these initiatives to those who are (presumably) intended to benefit, as well as the appropriateness of the discourse they help to create about the issues being addressed, poses a challenge to the democratizing hypothesis. In some cases civil groups in the global North have been found to marginalize the interests and role of local groups in the global South. For example, environmental groups like Conservation International have been criticized for arranging deals between itself, governments and multinational companies that exclude local groups, particularly on issues such as bio-prospecting (Choudry 2003). Research on the social auditing overseen by Social Accountability International (SAI) also identifies problems with its accountability (Bendell 2005). SAI is a New York based civil group that in 1997 developed a standard called SA8000, against which the conditions in workplaces worldwide could be assessed, and certified as compliant. Although SAI presents the processes of standard implementation, monitoring, certification and accreditation as largely technical, not political exercises, research has demonstrated that they have marginalized some of the approaches and interests of Southern civil groups (Bendell 2005).

This situation is due in part to the fact that a key impetus for voluntary corporate responses to civil action arises from a corporation's need to manage the risks of its reputation being damaged due to the influence of Northern civil groups on the media, consumers, investors, staff and regulators. Therefore it is the concerns of Northern civil groups that are key to processes of civil regulation. The relationship between these civil groups and other opinion-formers in the North, and intended beneficiaries of their work in the global South, is therefore key. One implication of this for civil groups is how they manage their own downwards accountability to the constituents they are meant to serve. Few civil groups 'active in ethical trade are accountable to the people they claim to represent, and where they have adequate international networks they do not manage these to systematically understand and present the views of their so-called constituencies' argues Blowfield (2004: 87). This echoes existing debates about the accountability of civil groups in public policy advocacy and service provision (Edwards and Hulme 1996).

There are reasons why corporate executives could also be concerned about the limited accountability of Northern civil groups to their Southern counterparts and the intended beneficiaries of their actions. In terms of reputation management, unless the intended beneficiaries are engaged, it is not certain that the challenges they face will be addressed, and thus problems will not be resolved, providing material for future reputation-damaging campaigns. In addition, some sustainable development issues pose challenges beyond reputational concerns; HIV/AIDS, climate change, poverty and conflict all present risks to the future expansion of business in the global South, and thus the long-term strategies of international companies. Institutional investors like pension funds should also be interested in this, as they invest across whole sectors, and need to see the threats to long-term portfolio arising from problems like AIDS, poverty and climate change effectively tackled, rather than ensuring preservation of the reputation of individual companies. Tackling these problems effectively would be helped by good information exchange with intended beneficiaries, and for activities to have credibility with, and a mandate from, those beneficiaries. In essence, far-sighted fiduciaries and business leaders may have an interest in civil regulation processes actually providing a democratizing effect.

CONCLUSION

Corporations today face a range of civil groups that employ a variety of tactics to try and influence their behaviour. Many corporations are having to respond to these civil groups in ways that add weight to the concept of civil regulation: the quasi-regulation of business by civil society. What this means for the democratization of corporate activity is currently unclear. On the one hand there are concerns with an anti-democratic corporatism developing (Ottaway 2001), while on the other hand there is evidence of limited, but nevertheless promising, avenues for people who are affected by corporations to influence them through civil action.

Given this mixed picture, the current enthusiasm for stakeholder participation and partnership needs to evolve towards a closer consideration of accountability and democracy. The concept of 'stakeholder democracy' could be used as a conceptual frame for business–civil society interactions. Stakeholder democracy is a new term describing an ideal system of governance of a society where all stakeholders in an organization or activity have the same opportunity to govern that organization or activity. Stakeholder groups are key to this process, as well as being the subjects of democratic governance themselves (Bendell 2005).

Future research on civil regulation should consider the dynamics of power in stakeholder relations. Key will be consideration of the power of discourse production, and how it is shaped by particular interests (Bendell, forthcoming). Also important will be analysis of the relationship between deliberation and action, or compulsion. Deliberation cannot be divorced from issues of compulsion – if a nation state had a parliament that was ignored by the monarch, then it would not be considered a democracy, and neither should a stakeholder process that has limited powers of implementation.

As globalization fractures traditional mechanisms for exercising democratic control over economic actors, so we need a triple democratization of state, market and civil society. This will require all of us to become aware of the democratic dimensions and implications of the work we do.

NOTE

1 This is a null-definition, defining what the primary purpose is not, rather than what it is. A positive definition for civil society is offered in Bendell (forthcoming), but is beyond the scope of this chapter.

REFERENCES

Bendell, J. (ed.) (2000) *Terms for Endearment: Business, NGOs and Sustainable Development*, Sheffield, UK: Greenleaf Publishing.

Bendell, J. (2001) 'World review', *Journal of Corporate Citizenship*, 3: 8–23.

Bendell, J. (2004) 'Barricades and boardrooms: a contemporary history of the corporate accountability movement', Programme Paper 13, UNRISD. Online. Available at: http://www.unrisd.org/80256B3C005BCCF9/(httpPublicationsHome)/$First?OpenDocument (accessed 9 December 2005).

Bendell, J. (2005) 'In whose name? The accountability of corporate social responsibility', *Development in Practice*, 5(3 and 4): 362–74.

Bendell, J. (forthcoming) *Our Power: The Civilisation of Globalisation*, Sheffield, UK: Greenleaf Publishing.

Blowfield, M. (2004) 'Implementation deficits of ethical trade systems: lessons from the Indonesian cocoa and timber industries', *Journal of Corporate Citizenship*, 13: 77–90.

Choudry, A. (2003) 'Privatizing nature, plundering biodiversity', *Seedling*, October: 17–22.

Dahl, R.A. (1961) *Who Governs? Democracy and Power in an American City*, New Haven, CT: Yale University Press.

Edwards, M. (2003) *Civil Society*, London: Polity Press.

Edwards, M. and Hulme, D. (eds) (1996) *Beyond the Magic Bullet: NGO Performance and Accountability in the Post-Cold War World*, West Hartford, CT: Kumarian Press.

Graham, I. (1998) 'Unions from Venus, CEOs from Mars? Crossing the void in stakeholder communications', paper presented at the First Annual ETI Conference in London, December 1998.

International Labour Organization (2000) *Sustainable Agriculture in a Globalised Economy*, International Labour Organization, Geneva Switzerland. Online. Available at: http://www.ilo.org/public/english/dialogue/sector/techmeet/tmad00/tmadr.htm (accessed 9 December 2005).

Kant, I. (1964) *Groundwork of the Metaphysic of Morals*, New York: Harper and Row.

Keane, J. (1988) *Democracy and Civil Society*, London: Verso.

Klein, N. (2000) *No Logo*, London: Flamingo.

Knight, B. and Hartnell, C. (2000) 'Civil society: is it anything more than a metaphor of hope for a better world?', *Alliance*, 5(3): 16–18.

Littrell, M.A. and Dickson, M.A. (1999) *Social Responsibility in the Global Market: Fair Trade of Cultural Products*, Thousand Oaks, CA: Sage.

Mintzberg, H. (1989) *Mintzberg on Management: Inside our Strange World of Organisations*, New York: Free Press.

Murphy, D.F. and Bendell, J. (1997) *In the Company of Partners: Business, Environmental Groups and Sustainable Development Post-Rio*, Bristol: The Policy Press.

Murphy, D.F. and Bendell, J. (1999) 'Partners in time? business, NGOs and sustainable development', paper 109, United Nations Research Institute for Social Development. Online. Available at: http://www.eldis.org/static/DOC7703.htm (accessed 9 December 2005).

Ottaway, M. (2001) Corporatism goes global: international organizations, NGO networks and trans-national business', *Global Governance*, vol. 7, no. 3, September. Online. Available at: http://www. ceip.org/files/publications/Global Corporatism.asp (accessed in March 2004).

Tallontire, A.M., Greenhalgh, P., Faustine, B. and Kyamanywa, J. (2001) *Diagnostic Study of FLO Registered Coffee Producers in Tanzania and Uganda*, Chatham, UK: Natural Resources Institute.

Teubner, G. (ed.) (1996) *Global Law without a State*, Aldershot: Artmouth.

Chapter 11

The materiality of sustainability

Corporate social and environmental responsibility as instruments of strategic change?

Thomas Clarke

INTRODUCTION

A substantial increase in the range, significance and impact of corporate social and environmental initiatives in recent years suggests the growing materiality of sustainability. Once regarded as a concern of a few philanthropic individuals and companies, corporate social and environmental responsibility appears to be becoming established in many corporations as a critical element of strategic direction, and one of the main drivers of business development, as well as an essential component of risk management. Corporate social and environmental responsibility (CSR) seems to be rapidly moving from the margins to the mainstream of corporate activity, with greater recognition of a direct and inescapable relationship between corporate governance, corporate responsibility, and sustainable development.

The burgeoning importance of this newly revived movement is demonstrated by the current frequency and scale of activity at every level (Calder and Culverwell 2005: 43). Among international organizations, the United Nations is coordinating a public-private partnership between UNEP and 170 banks, insurers and asset managers worldwide including Deutsche Bank, Dresdner Kleinwort Wasserstein, Goldman Sachs, HSBC and UBS to explore the financial materiality of environmental, social and governance (ESG) issues to securities valuation (UNEP 2004c). Early in 2005 the UN convened a group of 20 of the world's largest institutional investors to negotiate a set of principles for responsible investment, which will be published in a *Working Capital Report* in early 2006 as a guide for the investment community on how to incorporate environmental, social and governance issues into their investment decision-making and ownership processes. This builds on the work of the UN Global Compact with more than 1,500 corporate signatories, which is working with the world's leading stock exchanges and the World

Federation of Exchanges to advance the principles of corporate responsibility in capital markets and with public corporations (UN 2000).

In 2005, institutional investors representing 21 trillion dollars in assets came together for the third Carbon Disclosure Project meeting, collectively requesting the world's largest corporations to disclose information on greenhouse gas emissions and their approach to the management of carbon risks (UNEP FI 2005a). Finally, 36 of the world's largest banks, representing more than 80 per cent of the global project finance market, have adopted the Equator Principles, a set of voluntary principles outlining environmental, social and human rights disciplines associated with project finance above $50 million (Freshfields Bruckhaus Deringer 2005a). The principles originally were developed by the International Finance Corporation (IFC), the private sector investment arm of the World Bank. The OECD also is active in the promotion of corporate social responsibility in its guidelines for the operations of multinational corporations; and the European Union is actively encouraging corporate social responsibility as the business contribution to sustainable development (OECD 2000; European Commission 2003a, 2004). At the national level, a growing number of governments in Europe and across the globe have identified strongly with the call for corporate social and environmental responsibility, even with the evident difficulties in applying the Kyoto Protocol and creating an effective international climate policy regime.

At the corporate level the World Business Council for Sustainable Development and the World Economic Forum Global Corporate Citizenship Initiative have projected corporate responsibility into the minds of the international business elite (WBCSD 2002, 2004; WEF 2005). Other business organizations active in promoting CSR include the Business Leaders Initiative on Human Rights, the Conference Board, Business in the Community, and Business for Social Responsibility. A large number of leading corporations have signed up for the Global Reporting Initiative and more than 2,000 international corporations now publish reports on their CSR performance (many accessible on www.csrwire.com) (GRI 2002). Reinforcing the new found willingness on the part of corporate executives to disclose their commitments to CSR are the new indices including the Dow Jones Sustainability Index and FTSE4Good. Finally there are a proliferating number of consultancies, NGOs and campaign groups offering guidance and actively monitoring CSR activities along the entire length of the global value chain (World Bank 2003).

Questions are often addressed to the sincerity of corporate social and environmental initiatives; the legality of company directors engaging in these concerns; equally, the legality of the trustees of investment institutions attending to these interests; and the verifiability of CSR activities and outcomes. The aim of this chapter is to clarify the continuing and emerging legal and commercial basis for corporations to pursue corporate social and environmental responsibility; to outline the ongoing legal and material support for institutional trustees to prioritize socially and environmentally responsible investments; to examine developments in verification on corporate reporting of CSR performance; and to consider some illustrations of current best practice.

The integrity of CSR

Despite the recent burst of enthusiasm for corporate social and environmental responsibility in some quarters of the business community, the concept and practice still provokes a degree of understandable scepticism, partly due to CSR's record of lapsing into amoral apologetics for unacceptable corporate behaviour (Najam 2000; Christian Aid 2004; Corporate Responsibility Coalition 2005; OECD Watch 2005). David Vogal in a review conducted for the Brookings Institute, *The Market for Virtue: The Potential and Limits of CSR* (2005), contends there are many reasons why companies may choose to behave more responsibly in the absence of legal requirements to do so, including strategic, defensive, altruistic or public spirited motivations. However, despite pressure from consumers for responsibly made products, the influence of socially responsible investors, and the insistent call for companies to be accountable to a broader community of stakeholders, there are important limits to the market for virtue:

> CSR is best understood as a niche rather than a generic strategy: it makes sense for some firms in some areas under some circumstances. Many of the proponents of corporate social responsibility mistakenly assume that because some companies are behaving more responsibly in some areas, some firms can be expected to behave more responsibly in more areas. This assumption is misinformed. There *is* a place in the market economy for responsible firms. But there is also a large place for their less responsible competitors. . . . Precisely because CSR is voluntary and market-driven, companies will engage in CSR only to the extent that it makes business sense for them to do. Civil regulation has proven capable of forcing *some* companies to internalize *some* of the negative externalities associated with *some* of their economic activities. But CSR can reduce only some market failures.
>
> (Vogal 2005: 3–4)

Vogal concludes that CSR has a multidimensional nature, and that companies, like individuals, do not always exhibit consistent moral or social behaviour, and may behave better in some countries than others depending on the social and environmental policies existing there. Since the origins of capitalism, there have always been more or less responsible firms and though it may be heartening that executives in many highly visible firms may become more responsive (if only as a result of external stakeholder pressures), the reality is that the amounts wasted on the losses due to financial fraud, and the very substantial – and some would argue unwarranted – increases in executive compensation in corporations in the recent period far exceed any resources companies have devoted to CSR.

In a similar vein, Deborah Doane, who is Chair of the Corporate Responsibility Coalition in the UK, is sceptical regarding optimism about the power of market mechanisms to deliver social and environmental change, referring to the key myths informing the CSR movement as:

- The market can deliver both short-term financial returns and long-term social benefits.
- The ethical consumer will drive change.
- There will be a competitive 'race to the top' over ethics amongst businesses.
- In the global economy countries will compete to have the best ethical practices.

In support of her argument these are largely mythological trends she highlights: the insistence of stock markets upon short-term results, and the failure of companies to invest in long-term benefits; the considerable gap between green consciousness expressed by consumers and their consumer behaviour; the inconsistency between companies' alignment to CSR schemes and their successful efforts to bring about the sustained fall in corporate taxation in the US and other jurisdictions in recent decades; and finally the evidence emerging in developing countries of governments competing to *reduce* their insistence on the observance of social and environmental standards to attract international investment (Doane 2005).

It may well be the case that further legislative and regulatory intervention will be required to ensure all corporations fully respond to the growing public demand that they recognize their wider social and environmental responsibilities. However, it is useful to examine how far CSR objectives can be achieved within existing law and regulation. If there is substantial evidence of leading corporations demonstrating that it is possible to voluntarily commit to social and environmental performance and to achieve commercial success – perhaps because of, rather than in spite of, ethical commitments – then it will be more straightforward to press for the legislative changes necessary to deal with corporations that refuse to acknowledge their wider responsibilities, as well as finding appropriate legislative support for companies that wish to develop further their CSR commitments.

In the meantime the practical fact is that corporations and governments currently are struggling with an 'almost bewildering array of international CSR initiatives' (Calder and Culverwell 2005:7; McKague and Cragg 2005). Reviewing the efforts to develop CSR following the World Summit on Sustainable Development, a survey by the Royal Institute for International Affairs of stakeholders from governments, businesses and civil society groups identified a range of significant weaknesses in current approaches to promoting CSR which governments should seek to address:

- an over-proliferation of CSR initiatives at the international level and lack of clarity about how these initiatives relate to each other in a coherent way;
- an excessive focus on getting businesses to make commitments to CSR and not enough focus on enabling them to implement them effectively;
- an absence of credible monitoring and verification processes of CSR initiatives;
- a lack of effective mechanisms of redress for communities affected by companies that flout national or international norms on sustainable development or human rights;

- a lack of engagement with developing country governments and their sustainable development priorities (e.g. economic development and poverty reduction);
- a failure to bridge the governance gap created by weak public sector governance of the private sector in many developing countries;
- the limited impact on national and international sustainable development goals;
- a lack of government involvement and/or investment in international CSR initiatives, which is contributing significantly to their underperformance.

(Calder and Culverwell 2005: 7)

Defining social and environmental sustainability

The rapidly developing interest in sustainability and corporate social and environmental responsibility has resulted in a plethora of definitions and interpretations of the two concepts from international agencies, consultancies and practitioners (Calder and Culverwell 2005; McKague and Cragg 2005). A first difficulty is that the most commonly employed acronym CSR refers to corporate social responsibility, though in most interpretations it is meant to include environmental responsibility also. The use of the simpler term corporate responsibility and acronym CR is not widespread, though it would more readily embrace all corporate responsibilities. The UN's recent adoption of the environmental, social and governance (ESG) acronym may become influential, since it explicitly links governance to social and environmental responsibility.

More confusingly still, in some definitions CSR is subsumed under sustainability, while in others sustainability is included within CSR. One source of this confusion is that often different levels of analysis are being addressed. At the highest level the sustainability of the planet is at issue and at lower levels, the sustainability of economies and societies, industries and organizations. Corporate sustainability is a critical issue because of the economic scale and significance of these entities and their growing impact on the economy, society and the environment. 'Corporations have magnified capacities relative to individuals, in their financial resources, scale of operations, organizational capacity and capacity for social and individual harm' (Redmond 2005: 1). Once the primary (in some cases sole) concern was to produce goods and services that might generate the profits to achieve the financial sustainability of the corporation (everything else was written off as externalities). Increasingly today, the social and environmental impact of the corporation will be assessed in deciding whether it is viable or not, by governments, regulators, or other stakeholders, even if the corporations' management are reluctant to make this assessment. The *licence to operate* can no longer be readily assumed for any corporation, and in an increasing number of contexts needs to be earned with verifiable evidence of the social and environmental responsibility of the corporation.

Definitions of CSR and sustainability range from the basic to the most demanding, from a specific reference to a number of necessary activities to demonstrate responsibility, to a general call for a comprehensive, integrated and committed pursuit of social and environmental sustainability. The following representative range of definitions of CSR is in ascending order from the least to the most demanding:

- The integration of stakeholders' social, environmental and other concerns into a company's business operations (EIU 2005: 2).
- The commitment of businesses to contribute to sustainable economic development by working with their employees, their families, the local community and society at large to improve their lives in ways which are good for business and for development (WBCSD 2002).
- Corporate social responsibility is at heart a process of managing the costs and benefits of business activity to both internal (for example, workers, shareholders, investors) and external (institutions of public governance, community members, civil society groups, other enterprises) stakeholders. Setting the boundaries for how those costs and benefits are managed is partly a question of business policy and strategy and partly a question of public governance (World Bank 2002: 1).
- A concept whereby companies integrate social and environmental concerns in their business operations and in their interaction with their stakeholders on a voluntary basis (EU 2001).
- A company's commitment to operating in an economically, socially, and environmentally sustainable manner, while recognizing the interests of its stakeholders, including investors, customers, employees, business partners, local communities, the environment, and society at large (Certified General Accountants Association of Canada 2005: 20).
- CSR is essentially about how the company makes its profits, not only what it does with them afterwards. CSR is about how the company manages first, its core business operations – in the boardroom, in the workplace, in the marketplace, and along the supply chain; second, its community investment and philanthropic activities; and third, its engagement in public policy dialogue and institution building (Kennedy School of Government Corporate Responsibility Initiative: 2004: 33).
- A business approach embodying open and transparent business practices, ethical behaviour, respect for stakeholders and a commitment to add economic, social and environmental value (SustainAbility 2005).
- Sustainability performance refers to an organization's total performance, which might include its policies, decisions, and actions that create social, environmental and/or economic (including financial) outcomes (AccountAbility 2005: 10).

Sustainability as a whole (planet, environment, and species) is an altogether more ambitious project with more expansive definitions than CSR. Corporations have a vital role to play in this also, beginning with a modest recognition of their necessary subordination to the interests of maintaining a balanced ecosystem. Sustainability is defined as:

- Meeting the needs of the present generation without compromising the ability of future generations to meet their needs (Bruntland Commission 1987).
- Sustainable development, sustainable growth, and sustainable use have been used interchangeably, as if their meanings were the same. They are not. Sustainable growth is a contradiction in terms: nothing physical can grow indefinitely. Sustainable use is only applicable to renewable resources. Sustainable development is used in this strategy to mean: improving the quality of human life whilst living within the carrying capacity of the ecosystems (IUCN, UNEP, WWF 1991).

Putting the entire field into perspective, according to the Global Reporting Initiative (GRI) (2002) *Sustainability Reporting Guidelines*:

- Environmental impact means an organization's impact on living and non-living natural systems, including eco-systems, land, air and water. Examples include energy use and greenhouse gas emissions.
- Social impact means an organization's impact on the social system within which it operates. This includes labour practices, human rights and other social issues.
- Economic impact means an organization's impact both direct and indirect on the economic resources of its stakeholders and on economic systems at the local, national and global levels.

From the margins to the mainstream

However challenging the prospects, there are growing indications of large corporations taking their social and environmental responsibilities more seriously, and of these issues becoming more critical in the business agenda. KPMG since 1993 have conducted an international survey of corporate responsibility every three years which has revealed the developing prevalence of this commitment (Table 11.1). Surveying the largest 100 companies in a sample of advanced industrial OECD countries (with the addition of the Global 250 companies from 1999), KPMG (2005a) find a steadily rising trend in companies issuing separate corporate responsibility annual reports. From 13 per cent of the national 100 companies reporting on corporate responsibility matters in 1993, by 2005 this had risen to 33 per cent (up to 41 per cent if including information in annual reports). A more substantial increase in the Global 250 reporting occurred with 35 per cent reporting in 1999 and 52 per cent in 2005 (64 per cent including information in annual reports). Publication of corporate responsibility reports as part of the annual financial reports of companies often implies the issue is regarded as of greater salience, and companies often progress from separate to integrated CSR and financial reports.

More importantly, the substance of company reports is changing, from purely environmental reporting up until 1999, to sustainability reporting (social, environmental and economic), which has become the mainstream approach of the G250 companies, and is becoming so among the national 100 companies. The two leading countries in terms

Table 11.1 *KPMG CSR surveys 1993–2005 (KPMG)*

Survey year	*1993*	*1996*	*1999*	*2002*	*2005*
Research set (s)	Top 100 in 10 countries	Top 100 in 13 countries	Top 100 in 11 countries and Global 250	Top 100 in 19 countries and Global 250	Top 100 in 16[1] countries and Global 250
Total number of companies included	810	1,300	1,100+	1,900+	1,600+
Response rate	85%	69%	98%	96%	98%
N100: Percentage of companies with CR reports	13%	17%	24%	23% (28% for 11 countries in 1999)	33% (41% including CR information in annual reports)
G250: Percentage of companies with CR reports	–	–	35%	45%	52% (64% including CR information in annual reports)

Source: KPMG (2005a) International Survey of Corporate Responsibility Reporting, *KPMG International.*

Note: 1 Refers to 15 of OECD countries (Australia, Belgium, Canada, Denmark, Finland, France, Germany, Italy, Japan, the Netherlands, Norway, South Africa, Spain, Sweden, UK, US) and South Africa.

of separate corporate responsibility reporting are Japan (80 per cent of top 100 companies) and the UK (71 per cent of top 100 companies) in 2005. The industrial sectors with the highest environmental impact tend to lead in reporting (in one sense self-evidently important, in another sense deeply curious). At the Global 250 level, over 80 per cent of companies report in electronics and computers; utilities; automotive; and oil and gas sectors. The most remarkable increase in the Global 250 was in the finance sector, with a doubling of the rate of CSR reporting from 24 per cent in 2002 to 57 per cent in 2005. At the national level over 50 per cent of top 100 companies are reporting in utilities; mining; chemicals and synthetics; oil and gas; and forestry and paper sectors.

Finally the KPMG survey reveals a balanced range of business drivers for CSR reporting (Table 11.2), beginning with economic considerations (74 per cent of companies); ethical considerations (54 per cent); innovation and learning (53 per cent); employee motivation (47 per cent); risk management (47 per cent) and access to capital (39 per cent). The survey suggests there were solid business reasons for acting and reporting on CSR:

> The economic reasons were either directly linked to increased shareholder value or market share or indirectly linked through increased business opportunities, innovation, reputation, and reduced risk. Thirty-nine per cent of the companies reported improved shareholder value, and one in five (21 per cent) reported increased market share as an important reason for sustainability.
>
> (KPMG 2005a: 18)

Table 11.2 *Drivers for corporate social responsibility (KPMG)*

Driver	%
Economic considerations	74
Ethical considerations	53
Innovation and learning	53
Employee motivation	47
Risk management or risk reduction	47
Access to capital or increased shareholder value	39
Reputation or brand	27
Market position (market share improvement)	21
Strengthened supplier relations	13
Cost saving	9
Improved relationships with governmental authorities	9
Other	11

Source: KPMG (2005a) International Survey of Corporate Responsibility Reporting, *KPMG international.*

In a further recent international survey of 136 corporate executives and 65 executives of institutional investors on the importance of corporate responsibility (CR) the Economist Intelligence Unit (EIU) discovered a similar growth in interest:

> A total of 88 per cent of executives said that CR is a 'central' or 'important' consideration in decision-making. This compares with 54 per cent of executives who said it was a 'central' or 'important' consideration five years ago. The biggest percentage change between now and five years ago was among European executives. A total of 46 per cent said CR was 'central' or 'important' five years ago compared with 84 per cent at the present time. In Asia, the proportion rose from 49 per cent to 82 per cent and in North America from 66 per cent to 88 per cent. The survey of professional investors reveals a sharper trend. Eighty-one per cent of those surveyed said CR was currently a 'central' or 'important' consideration in their investment decisions, compared with 34 per cent who said it was 'central' or 'important' five years ago. In fact, 14 per cent of them said CR was not a consideration at all five years ago. Now, not a single investor said it was not a consideration.
>
> (EIU 2005: 5)

As with the gap noticed earlier between consumer consciousness and behaviour, it is likely there will be a mighty gap between the expressed concerns of executives for corporate responsibility and their actual behaviour in different circumstances in the exigencies of difficult situations. However, simply expressing concerns is an advance over stony faced refusals to even acknowledge responsibilities that may have occurred in the past. 'Corporate responsibility is really about ensuring that the company can grow on a sustainable basis, while ensuring fairness to all stakeholders', says N.R. Murthy, the chairman of an Indian IT firm, Infosys' (EIU 2005: 2). Though some of the expressed concern may be part of the discourse of political correctness, there do appear to be grounds for a significant shifting of opinion among executives, as the EIU comments:

> Until recently, board members often regarded corporate responsibility as a piece of rhetoric intended to placate environmentalists and human rights campaigners. But now, companies are beginning to regard corporate responsibility as a normal facet of business and are thinking about ways to develop internal structures and processes that will emphasize it more heavily. In the not-too-distant future, companies that are not focusing on corporate responsibility may come to be seen as outliers. As companies focus on non-financial performance, an important yardstick of corporate responsibility, the measurement of intangibles, such as customer satisfaction and employee morale, are likely to become less vague and more credible.
>
> (EIU 2005: 3)

One of the surprising results of the EIU survey was that after more than a decade of the exhortation of the primacy in all circumstances of shareholder value, the executives surveyed still possessed a balanced appreciation of the relative importance of key stakeholders to the company, identifying customers, employees and shareholders in that order (Figure 11.1). The EIU compiled some of the contextual highlights for these changes in executive views in the emerging evidence that corporate social and environmental responsibility is moving substantially from the margins to the mainstream of economic activity:

- The New York-based GovernanceMetrics International (GMI), which covers corporate governance and CR, now produces in-depth rating reports on 2,000 companies around the world and has a growing client base including TIAA-CREF, State Street Bank and ABP, the largest pension fund in Europe.
- More than 10,000 individuals and 3,000 listed companies have helped to develop the standards of the Global Reporting Initiative (GRI), an organization based in Amsterdam, trying to create a single global measure for CR performance. Among its corporate clients implementing GRI standards are Bayer, Canon, Deutsche Bank, General Motors, Heineken and Shell.
- A group of five major European institutional investors, including the second-largest pension fund in the UK and the largest pension fund in the Netherlands, jointly stated in October 2004 that they would allocate 5 per cent of their budgets for the purchase of non-financial research analysis of such topics as corporate governance, labour management and environmental practices.

- One in every nine investment dollars under professional management in the US is now invested in socially responsible funds. This amounts to US$2 trillion out of a total of US$19 trillion in investible funds, according to the 2003 report on socially responsible investing (SRI) produced by the Social Investment Forum, the national trade body for the SRI industry.

(EIU 2005:4–5)

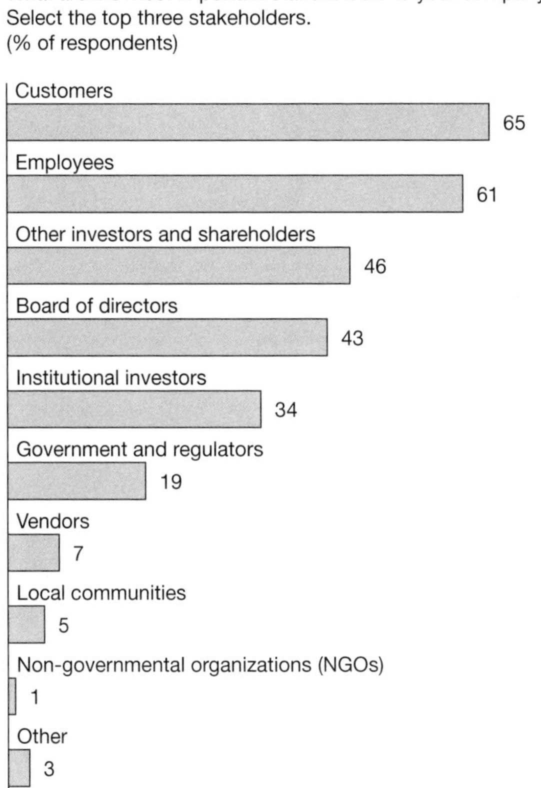

Figure 11.1 *Key stakeholders according to corporation executives (EIU)*

At the confluence of these multiple emerging initiatives and trends towards greater corporate social and environmental responsibility, there is emerging a dynamic stakeholder model for driving enlightened shareholder value (Figure 11.2). At many leading corporations the pieces of what admittedly is a very large and demanding puzzle are beginning to come together. The wider commitments to building engaged and inclusive relationships with employees, economic partners, the community and the environment becomes a means of achieving enlightened shareholder value through access to a lower cost of capital, enhanced reputation, minimized risks and new business opportunities.

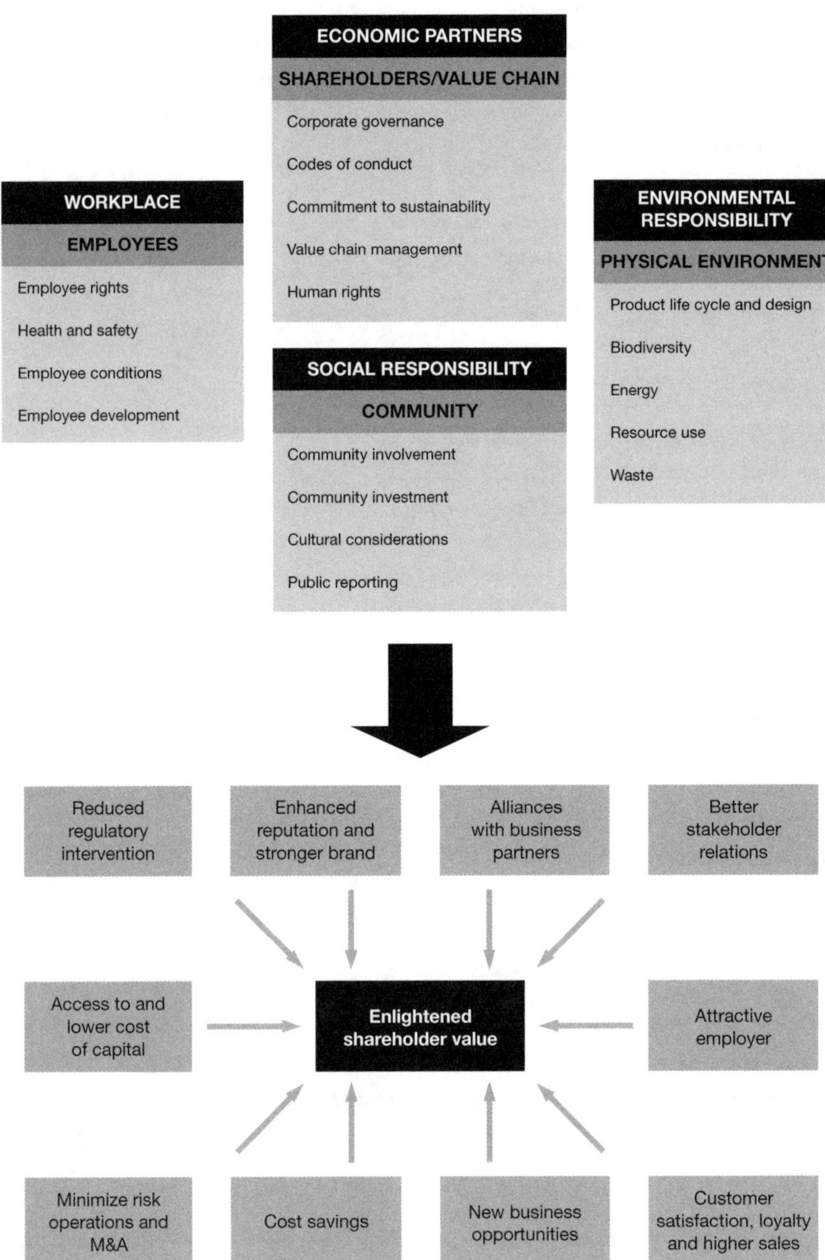

Figure 11.2 *CSR stakeholder model driving enlightened shareholder value*

Source: *Mays (2003: 11, 16)*

The legitimacy of CSR from a governance perspective

Corporations enlightened shareholder value? The duty to promote the success of the company

The impact of the adoption of corporate commitments to wider forms of social and environmental engagement and reporting will be determined essentially by initiatives of leading companies and, in turn, this will be influenced by the insistent pressures companies encounter from the market, investors and stakeholders, and the perceived commercial benefit of assuming a broader accountability. However, the role of the law and of accounting standards in establishing a framework of accountability and management discipline is a significant factor. Historical analysis of the perception of company directors' duties, including legal interpretations, reveals much greater sympathy for corporations adopting a wider view of their responsibilities than the recently imposed tenets of shareholder value would suggest.

This balance of pursuing market opportunities while maintaining accountability has proved a defining challenge for business enterprise since the arrival of the joint-stock company in the early years of industrialism. The accountability and responsibility of business enterprise was constantly subject to question, and historically failed this test often in the view of the public. Maurice Clark deplored how business 'inherited an economics of irresponsibility' from the laissez-faire beliefs and practices of early industrialism (1916). He argued business transactions do not occur in isolation, but have wider social and economic consequences that need to be considered, impacting directly on employment, health and the environment. He insisted legal regulation may be required to ensure protection from abuses, but that this could never replace a general sense of responsibility in business that goes beyond the letter of the law, preventing competitive forces leading to a race to the bottom. Hence the periodic outbreak of destructive competition needed to be restrained in Clark's view by 'an economics of responsibility, developed and embodied in our working business ethics' (1916).

The debate concerning the true extent of the accountability and responsibility of business enterprise has continued to the present day, punctuated by occasional public outrage at business transgressions, and calls for greater recognition of the social obligations of business. At the height of the economic depression in the United States in 1932, Dodd made a dramatic plea in the pages of the *Harvard Law Review*:

> There is in fact a growing feeling not only that business has responsibilities to the community but that our corporate managers who control business should voluntarily and without waiting for legal compulsion manage it in such a way as to fulfill these responsibilities.

This resonated with Berle and Means' insistence that large corporations 'serve not alone the owners or the control, but all society' (1933). Though Berle subsequently commenced a prolonged debate with Dodd on the subject of 'For whom are corporate managers trustees', Berle (1955) later conceded to Dodd's argument that management powers were held in trust for the entire community (Wedderburn 1985: 6).

Such forthright views did not remain at the level of academic speculation, but were often translated into legal, policy and business interpretations and practice. For example in Teck Corp Ltd v. Millar, the Supreme Court of British Columbia, while retaining the identification of company interests with those of shareholders, nonetheless was prepared to grant directors a license under their fiduciary duties to take into account wider stakeholder interests:

> The classical theory is that the directors' duty is to the company. The company's shareholders are the company . . . and therefore no interests outside those of the shareholders can legitimately be considered by the directors. But even accepting that, what comes within the definition of the interests of the shareholders? By what standards are the shareholders' interests to be measured? A classical theory that once was unchallengeable must yield to the facts of modern life. In fact, of course, it has. If today the directors of a company were to consider the interests of its employees no one would argue that in doing so they were not acting bona fide in the interests of the company itself. Similarly, if the directors were to consider the consequences to the community of any policy that the company intended to pursue, and were deflected in their commitment to that policy as a result, it could not be said that they had not considered bona fide the interests of the shareholders.
>
> (Teck Corp Ltd v. Millar 1973: 313–4)

Wedderburn (1985: 12) documents an equivalent deep-seated and practical commitment of corporate responsibility to a wide constituency in the post-war beliefs of leaders of the British business community. A lively debate continues worldwide concerning the scope of directors' duties. In Australia the Corporations Act Section 181 obliges directors and other corporate officers to exercise their powers and discharge their duties

- in good faith and in the best interests of the corporation;
- for a proper purpose.

Under common law, directors are obliged to act in the interests of 'the company as a whole'. Traditionally this phrase has been interpreted to mean the financial well-being of the shareholders as a general body (though directors are obliged to consider the financial interests of creditors when the firm is insolvent or near-insolvent). A recent generation of financial economists helped to translate this broad shareholder *primacy principle* into a narrow pursuit of shareholder value. There is a wider interpretation of shareholder value which suggests that only when all of the other constituent relationships of the corporation – with customers, employees, suppliers, distributors and the wider community – are fully recognized and developed can long-term shareholder value be released. However, the restrictive definition of shareholder value has often been associated with short-termism and a neglect of wider corporate responsibilities in the interests of immediate profit maximization. Concerns have arisen that directors who do wish to take account of other stakeholder interests may be exposed.

Traditionally, commercial law in many European countries has supported a sense of the wider social and environmental obligations of companies, which continues despite a recent enthusiasm for the principle of shareholder value, as some large European companies for the first time seek the support of international investors. The UK has stood apart from Europe as an influential exponent of the Anglo-American market-based approach to corporate governance. However, in an effort to jettison the company law rhetoric formed in the nineteenth century, and to make the law more accessible a Company Law Review (CLR) steering group was established. The ensuing consultative document *Modern Company Law for a Competitive Economy: Developing the Framework* (2000) proposed for the first time that there should be a statutory statement of directors' duties (presently the core components of those duties are found in case law), and made a significant step in the direction of endorsing fuller corporate social and environmental reporting:

> Current accounting and reporting fails to provide adequate transparency of qualitative and forward looking information which is of vital importance in assessing performance and potential for shareholders, investors, creditors and others. This is particularly so in the modern environment of technical change, and with the growing importance of 'soft', or intangible assets, brands, know-how and business relationships. The full annual report must be effective in covering these, both as a stewardship report and as a medium of communication to wider markets and the public . . . we believe the time has come to require larger companies to provide an operating and financial review, which will cover the qualitative, or 'soft', or intangible, and forward looking information which the modern market and modern business decision making requires, converting the practice of the best run companies into a requirement for all.'
>
> (CLR 2000: 180–1)

These issues were extensively considered in the UK for several years in the deliberations of the Modern Company Law Review. Two approaches were considered:

- a pluralist approach under which directors' duties would be reformulated to permit directors to further the interests of other stakeholders even if they were to the detriment of shareholders;
- an enlightened shareholder value approach allowing directors greater flexibility to take into account longer-term considerations and interests of various stakeholders in advancing shareholder value.

In considering these approaches, the essential questions of what is the corporation and what interests it should represent are exposed to light, as Davies eloquently argues:

> The crucial question is what the statutory statement says about the interests which the directors should promote when exercising their discretionary powers. The common law mantra that the duties of directors are owed to the company has long obscured the answer to this question. Although that is a statement of the utmost importance when it comes to the enforcement of duties and their associated remedies, it tells one nothing about the answer to our question, whose interests should the directors promote? This is because the company, as an artificial person, can have no interests separate from the interests of those who are associated with it, whether as shareholders, creditors, employers, suppliers, customers or in some other way. So, the crucial question is, when we refer to the company, to the interests of which of those sets of natural persons are we referring?
>
> (Davies 2005: 4)

As a member of the Corporate Law Review Steering Group, Davies goes on to defend the enlightened shareholder value view, suggesting the pluralist approach produces a formula which is unenforceable and paradoxically gives management more freedom of action than they previously enjoyed. An Australian legal expert, Redmond, endorses this critique of widening the scope of directors' duties too greatly:

> The pluralist or multifiduciary model rests on a social, not a property, view of the corporation. It identifies the corporate purpose with maximising total constituency utility. This is an indeterminate outcome measure which poses particular difficulties in translation into a legally enforceable duty. The indeterminacy of the criteria for decision and performance measurement also points to a probable loss of accountability for directors since it offers broad scope to justify most decisions. It is difficult to resist the conclusion of the UK review that either it confers a broad unpoliceable policy discretion on managers themselves or must give a broad jurisdiction to the courts. The model needs either practical rehabilitation or a superior performance metric. It is not clear where either might be found.
>
> (Redmond 2005: 27)

In the resulting UK Company Law Reform Bill (2005) the enlightened shareholder value view has prevailed in Clause 156, which defines the essential directoral duty as:

> Duty to promote the success of the company
>
> 1 A director of a company must act in the way he considers, in good faith, would be most likely to promote the success of the company for the benefit of its members as a whole.
>
> 2 Where or to the extent that the purposes of the company consist of or include purposes other than the benefit of its members, his duty is to act in the way he considers, in good faith, would be most likely to achieve those purposes.

3 In fulfilling the duty imposed by this section a director must (so far as reasonably practicable) have regard to:

(a) the likely consequences of any decision in the long term,
(b) the interests of the company's employees,
(c) the need to foster the company's business relationships with suppliers, customers and others,
(d) the impact of the company's operations on the community and the environment,
(e) the desirability of the company maintaining a reputation for high standards of business conduct, and
(f) the need to act fairly as between members of the company.

4 The duty imposed by this section has effect subject to any enactment or rule of law requiring directors, in certain circumstances, to consider or act in the interests of creditors of the company.

This clause replaces the *discretion* of directors to have regard for stakeholder interests with a *duty* for directors to do this:

> As far as directors' duties are concerned, this is the heart of the enlightened shareholder value approach. The aim is to make it clear that although shareholder interests are predominant (promotion of the success of the company for the benefit of its members), the promotion of shareholder interests does not require riding roughshod over the interests of other groups upon whose activities the business of the company is dependent for its success. In fact, the promotion of the interests of the shareholders will normally require the interests of other groups of people to be fostered. The interests of non-shareholder groups thus need to be considered by the directors, but, of course, in this shareholder-centred approach, only to the extent that the protection of those other interests promotes the interests of the shareholders. The statutory formulation can be said to express the insight that the shareholders are not likely to do well out of a company whose workforce is constantly on strike, whose customers don't like its products and whose suppliers would rather deal with its competitors.
>
> (Davies 2005: 5)

In this way the Company Law Reform Bill treads a fine legal line between a sense of 'enlightened shareholder value', which is becoming best practice in many leading companies, and more radical claims for company law to adopt a more 'pluralist' sense of the ultimate objectives of the enterprise and the interests to be served. The reform manages this balancing act by suggesting that the pluralist objectives of maximizing company performance to the benefit of all stakeholders can best be served by professional directors pursuing commercial opportunities within a framework of standards and accountability:

> The overall objective should be pluralist in the sense that companies should be run in a way which maximises overall competitiveness and wealth and welfare for all. But the means which company law deploys for achieving this objective must be to take account of the realities and dynamics which operate in practice in the running of commercial enterprise. It should not be done at the expense of turning company directors from business decision makers into moral, political or economic arbiters, but by harnessing focused, comprehensive, competitive decision making within robust, objective professional standards and flexible, but pertinent accountability.
>
> (CLR 2000: 14)

The reform supports the ultimate power of shareholders to appoint or dismiss directors for whatever reasons they choose, and to intervene in management to the extent the constitution permits, and confesses:

> There is clearly an inconsistency between leaving these powers of shareholders intact and enabling or requiring directors to have regard to wider interests . . . the effect will be to make smaller transactions within the powers of directors subject to the broad pluralist approach, but larger ones which are for shareholders subject only to the minimal constraints which apply to them.
>
> (CLR 2000: 26)

It is likely that the modern company law proposals, should they reach the statute book, will over time facilitate the wider and more conscious adoption by UK companies of social and environmental commitments, and the willingness to report fully on them. In time it is possible that such social and environmental commitments will become part of a widespread company and management best practice, in the way that the commitment to quality in the production of goods and services has become universal.

Moreover, just as the UK in the publication of the Cadbury Code of corporate governance ultimately influenced a considerable number of other countries to adopt a similar code, it is possible that other countries (particularly those that share a common law tradition to the UK) will begin to review their company law with similar objectives in mind. Twin inquiries taking place into corporate responsibility in Australia are now traversing this terrain. The Corporations and Markets Advisory Committee (CAMAC) commenced in March 2005 to consider whether directors' duties under the Corporations Act 2001 should include corporate responsibilities or obligations to take into account certain classes of stakeholders. The Committee has just published an excellent Discussion Paper on *Corporate Social Responsibility* (available free at http://www.camac.gov.au).

The second inquiry, the Parliamentary Joint Committee on Corporates and Financial Services (PJC) began in June 2005 with a call for submissions on corporate social responsibility, and has received over 120 extensive submissions from companies, consultancies, academics and other interested parties (available at http://www.aph.gov.au/Senate/committee/corporations_ctte/corporate_responsibility/index.htm).

Together these inquiries will raise awareness of the issues involved in corporate responsibility considerably in Australia and it is likely that some significant modification of directors' duties will result.

The possibility that this will be accompanied by an extension of the requirements for company reporting to include social and environmental matters may appear to have receded with the UK Chancellor's dramatic abandonment of the obligatory Operating and Financial Review for listed companies in November 2005. However, this was in the context of the European Union's Accounts Modernization Directive (2003/51/EC) which also requires companies include environmental and social reports with their annual accounts necessary for an understanding of the companies performance. There is here an irresistible new agenda for corporate responsibility.

One reason the agenda of corporate responsibility is increasingly irresistible is that while legal liability of corporations is deepening, what has been described as an emerging and hardening *moral liability* is exerting increasing influence (Figure 11.3). In this respect the legislative process lags behind what society thinks, values and respects. Moral liability occurs when corporations violate stakeholder expectations of ethical behaviour in ways that put business value at risk. There is an increasing convergence between these two forms of liability, as corporations come under scrutiny both by the law and – often more immediately and pointedly – by public opinion (SustainAbility 2005: 5). A graphic illustration of this was the James Hardie building company, which having moved its corporate headquarters from Australia to the Netherlands, believed it had escaped responsibility for the legal liabilities of its remaining Australian subsidiaries to the thousands of asbestos victims now dependent on a seriously underfunded and almost bankrupt medical foundation Hardie had left behind to meet their claims. Massive public disapproval in Australia and internationally, and a commission of inquiry combined with the threat of legislative intervention, dragged James Hardie back to face the consequences of its irresponsible actions over many decades in the Australian market (Jackson 2004).

The legitimacy of CSR from a governance perspective

Investment institutions' effective portfolio management: the duty to address ESG issues?

Similar forces that are impressing corporations towards taking a greater regard of CSR issues are guiding investment institutions towards addressing environmental, social and governance issues more directly in their investment policies and practices. In the UNEP Finance Initiative on *The Materiality of Social, Environmental and Corporate Governance Issues to Equity Pricing* (2004c) the interest of a growing number of institutional investors in approaches to asset management that explicitly include environmental, social and governance (ESG) criteria and metrics, either for ethical reasons or as relevant to investment performance, was considered. Critical intermediaries are the brokerage firms that often have paid less consideration to ESG issues, often because they are driven

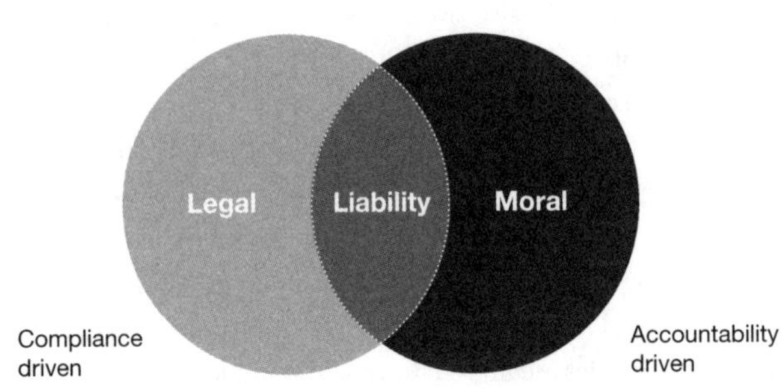

Existing (legal)		Emerging (moral)
Court of law	→	Court of public opinion
Time – limited	→	Time – unlimited
Compliance to letter	→	Compliance to spirit
Ownership	→	Association
Money	→	Goodwill/badwill

Figure 11.3 *Legal and moral liability are converging*

by short-term performance. A group of 11 international brokerage firms' analysts were commissioned to examine a range of industry sectors regarding the relevance of ESG to investment performance, and to submit detailed reports. Briefly their conclusions were:

- Environmental, social and governance criteria affect shareholder value both in the short and long term, and in some cases the effects could be profound. Research to determine the financial materiality of these criteria should use longer time spans than is currently employed for financial analysis.
- Governments could reduce barriers to environmental, social and corporate governance analysis by mandating and standardizing the inclusion of these criteria in national and international corporate disclosure frameworks.
- Innovative techniques are being developed to perform financial analyses of environmental, social and corporate governance criteria in response to growing investor demand, including ranking surveys, portfolio analysis of best and worst performers, and scenario analysis to evaluate potential impact of upcoming regulation on sectors.

The survey discovered that brokerage houses in Europe are increasingly willing and able to respond to demand for ESG research. In contrast, brokerage houses in the United States referred to perceived difficulty in analysis due to barriers associated with inadequate disclosure of these criteria.

A further fascinating research project of the UNEP Finance Initiative considered *A Legal Framework for the Integration of Environmental, Social and Governance Issues into Institutional Investment* (2005b). The current value of assets managed by the investment industry worldwide is estimated at US$42 trillion, pension fund assets in the US and UK alone amounting to US$7.4 trillion. However, the weighty responsibility of deciding where these assets are invested lies not with the owners, but with a small number of principals and agents.

> By influencing the way investments are made, the legal factors that inform the decisions made by this relatively small group have a profound effect on the behaviour of the entities in which these assets are invested and ultimately on the environments and societies with which these investment vehicles interact.
>
> (UNEP FI 2005b: 6)

Despite the increasing evidence that ESG issues do have a material impact on the financial performance of securities and increasing awareness of the importance of assessing ESG-related risks, the effort to achieve a greater regard for ESG issues in investment decision-making is often resisted on the basis that institutional principals and their agents are legally prevented from taking account of these issues. Just as it is assumed corporate directors can only be committed to shareholder value, it is often assumed that investment trustees can only be directed towards profit maximization. However, the survey conducted by the international law firm Freshfields Bruckhaus Deringer confirms categorically that in each of the jurisdictions examined (France, Germany, Italy, Japan, Spain, UK, US, Australia and Canada) investment decision-makers retained some degree of discretion as to how they might invest the funds they control.

In the common law jurisdictions (US, UK, Australia and Canada) the rules are articulated in statute and in court decisions. In the other jurisdictions as civil law applies, rules are articulated as codes or in statutes. Though in none of the jurisdictions do rules prescribe how principals should integrate ESG considerations into their decisions, in most cases it is left to principals to determine their investment approach within their legal obligations.

Fiduciary duties are the key discretionary limits of investment decision-makers in common law countries, the most important duties being the duty to act prudently and the duty to act in accordance with the purpose for which investment powers were granted (the duty of loyalty) (Figure 11.4).

In the US, the modern prudent investor rule, which incorporates both a duty of care and a duty of loyalty, emphasizes modern portfolio theory and provides that:

- Investments are assessed not in isolation but in the context of their contribution to a total investment portfolio.
- There is no duty to 'maximize' the return of individual investments, but instead a duty to implement an overall investment strategy that is rational and appropriate to the fund.
- The investment portfolio must be diversified, unless it is prudent not to do so; and
- the prudence of an investment should be assessed at the time the investment was made and not in hindsight.

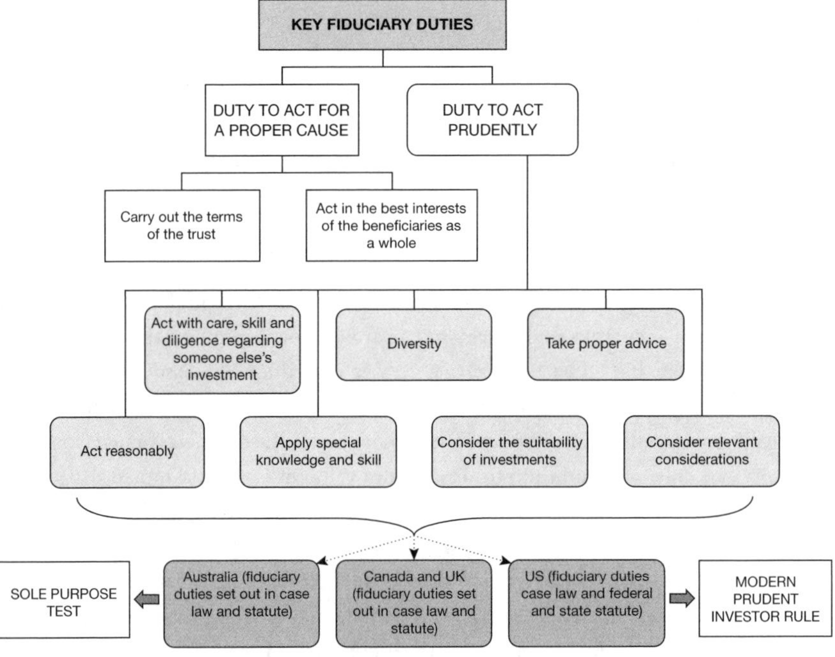

Figure 11.4 *Fund trustees' fiduciary details*

Source: Freshfields, Bruckhaus and Deringer. A legal framework for the integration of environmental, social and governance issues into institutional investment October 2005. *UNEP Finance Initiative Innovative Financing for Sustainability*

The effect of the modern prudent investor rule is that institutional decision-makers are given latitude to follow a wide range of diversified investment strategies. Provided their choice of investments is rational and economically defensible, they are free to construct a balanced portfolio (UNEP FI 2005b: 8). Other jurisdictions stipulate the duty to act conscientiously in the interests of beneficiaries, to seek profitability, recognize the portfolio approach to modern investment, and in some jurisdictions, limits on the types of assets which may be selected for particular funds.

Two things which are critical in all jurisdictions are following the correct process, and pursuing proper objectives in terms of acting only in the interests of the beneficiaries. As with other investment criteria, different considerations will be given different weight, according to how conditions are defined and analysed. In some circumstances it may be decided that ESG considerations have little material impact on financial performance relevant to a particular investment. However, this does not justify failure to identify such considerations and to assess the weight. It is becoming increasingly difficult to argue that ESG considerations are difficult to quantify, since good will and intangibles are now readily quantified. A majority of the jurisdictions surveyed have already legislated to require investment decision-makers, particularly of pension funds to disclose the extent to which they take ESG considerations into account.

There is increasingly credible evidence that ESG considerations have a vital role to play in the proper analysis of investment value, and cannot be ignored as they would result in investments being given inappropriate value, for example:

> Climate change is an obvious example of an environmental consideration that is recognised as affecting value. Following the recent release of a report by Mercer Investment Consulting noting the financial impact that climate change has already had on companies' costs, revenues, assets and liabilities, the UK Carbon Trust expressed the view that 'Pension fund trustees have a duty to address the financial risk posed by climate change when making investment decisions'.
>
> (UNEP FI 2004a: 11)

Investment institutions are not only becoming more alert regarding the ESG issues in their investment portfolio, they are also beginning to take a proactive stance in terms of engaging in the environmental, social and governance performance of the corporations they invest in (Figure 11.5). Both in the US and UK the traditional passivity of the investment institutions is being cast aside in favour of more active involvement. Certainly they continue to prefer quiet influence to open confrontation, but in an increasing number of instances, the institutional investors have demonstrated a willingness to use their power to insist on higher standards of governance, and there are some indications this may occur more frequently in future on wider ESG issues.

Corporate reporting of CSR

If the revival of interest in CSR is to continue to develop, and not descend into apologetics as previous efforts have done, and if the current wave of interest in ESG issues in the investment community is to bear fruit in more enduring returns, then what is absolutely critical is the accuracy and verifiability of corporate disclosure regarding CSR performance. In this regard the Global Reporting Initiative (GRI) Principles are an invaluable tool for working towards international confidence in the trustworthiness of corporate reporting. The overall aim of the GRI-based reporting is to:

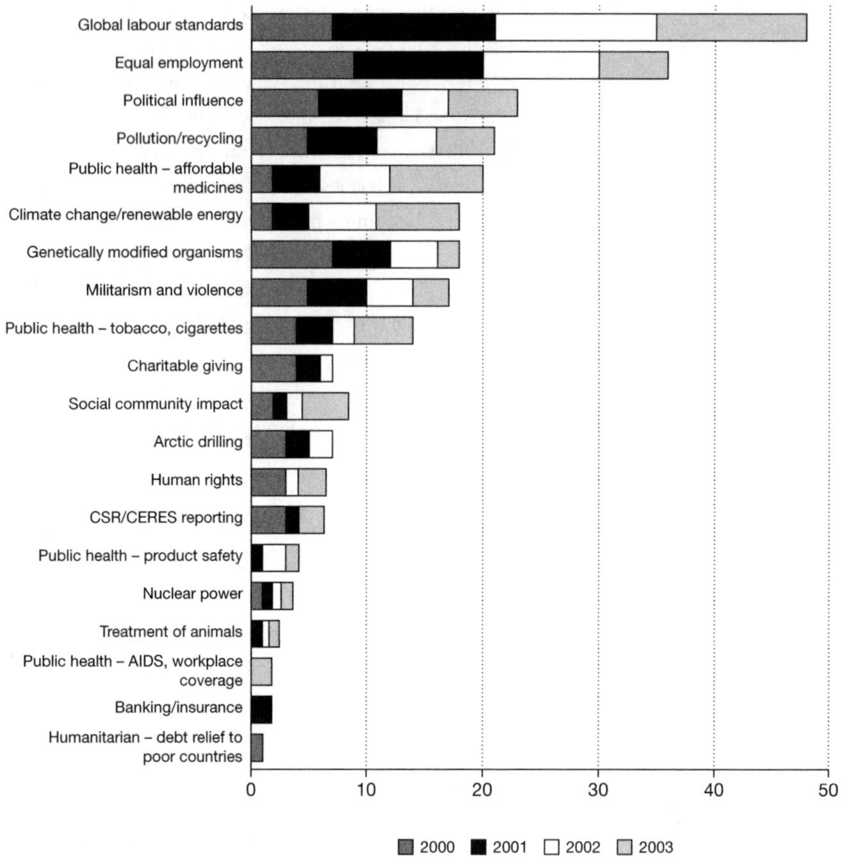

Figure 11.5 *Institutional investor voting 2000–3*

Source: Monks, Miller and Cook (2004).

- provide a balanced and reasonable representation of an organization's sustainability performance;
- facilitate comparability;
- address issues of concern to stakeholders.

The GRI reporting principles are the underpinnings of corporate report content, and as such are as important as the content itself. The reporting principles are:

- Transparency: full disclosure of the processes, procedures and assumptions in report preparation are essential to its credibility.
- Inclusiveness: the reporting organization should engage its stakeholders in preparing and enhancing the quality of reports.

- Auditability: reported information should be recorded, compiled, analysed and disclosed in a way that enables internal auditors or external assurance providers to attest to its reliability.
- Completeness: all material information should appear in the report.
- Relevance: reporting organizations should use the degree of importance that report users assign to particular information in determining report content.
- Sustainability context: reporting organizations should seek to place their performance in the broader context of ecological, social or other issues where such context adds significant meaning to the reported information.
- Accuracy: reports should achieve a degree of exactness and low margin of error to enable users to make decisions with a high degree of confidence.
- Neutrality: reports should avoid bias in selection and presentation of information and provide a balanced account of performance.
- Comparability: reports should be framed so as to facilitate comparison with earlier reports as well as with reports of comparable organizations.
- Clarity: information should be presented in a manner that is understandable by a maximum number of users while still maintaining a suitable level of detail.

(GRI 2002: 6)

The work of developing, implementing and verifying these reporting standards for corporate social and environmental responsibility will continue for many years to come, replicating the effort that is now being made in the quest to achieve better measurement and reporting of intangibles. However, the whole edifice of CSR and ESG analysis and valuation will rest on the adequacy and rigour of reporting standards.

Future developments: the redesign of the corporation

It could be argued that the whole corporate social and environmental responsibility project, however worthy, is probably too little and too late. A more sympathetic view is that in its revived form CSR represents a new beginning in corporate reform that may be built on to create more substantial and enduring results. Certainly further efforts will be required to further ensure the accountability of corporations, on a universal and not simply voluntary basis. In extending accountability, directors of corporations should be licensed to have regard for the interests of other stakeholders, and to accept the costs of enterprise operations beyond what they are legally required to assume (Redmond 2005: 28).

A group of business and community leaders in the US have projected a vision of Corporation 2020 based on the imperative to redesign the corporation. The principles they advocate are that the purpose of the corporation is to harness private interests to serve the public interest, that fair returns to shareholders should not be at the expense of the legitimate interests of other stakeholders, that corporations should operate sustainably, and that corporations distribute wealth produced equitably among those who contribute to the creation of that wealth. Robert Hinkley offers a 28-word amendment to directors' duties which states that they are to act in the interests of the company 'but not at the expense of the environment, human rights, public health and safety, dignity or employees, or the welfare of communities in which the corporation operates' (Luis 2005).

It is possible to envisage a business world not characterized by the bipolar disorder of the ongoing shareholder/stakeholder debate. The effective integration of corporate social and environmental responsibilities could potentially release greater value for both shareholders and wider stakeholders (Figure 11.6). That is, moving beyond compliance, to creating new value through new products and services that meet societal needs and collaborating to solve the complex and demanding social and environmental problems that threaten to grow beyond our control. Corporations capable of working on investors, stakeholders, and societies' interests in a collaborative, creative and productive way would require a fundamental redesign of the concept of the corporation and the

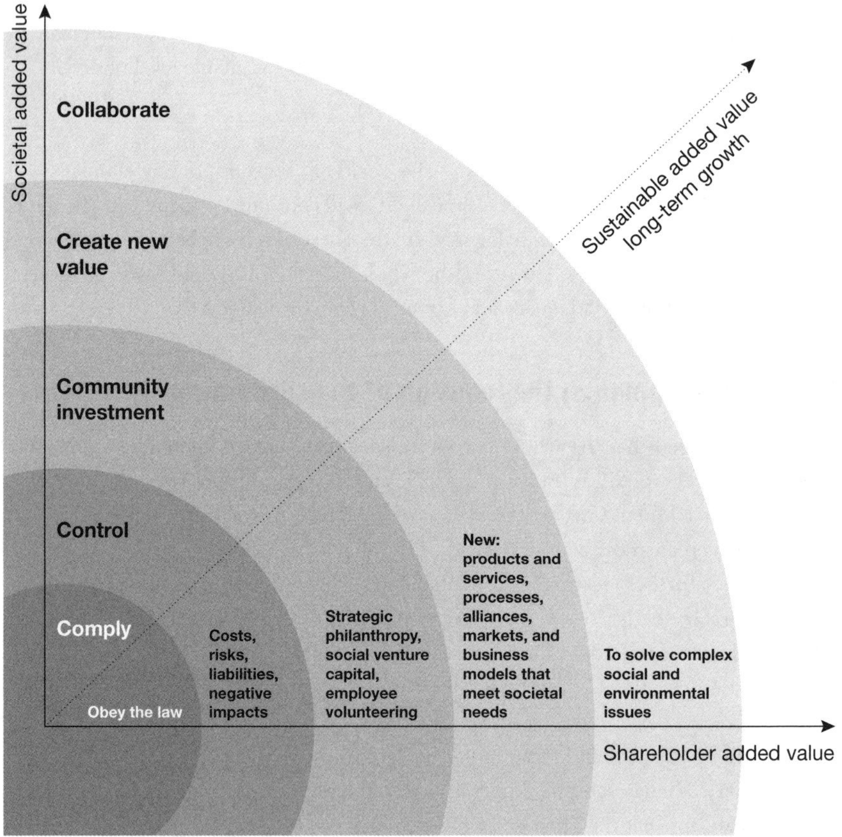

Figure 11.6 *Corporate strategies to deliver value to society*

Source: Kennedy School of Government Corporate Responsibility Initiative (2004).

institution of the market. At this stage both prospects appear remote. However, we live in an industrial world where the problem of material production has essentially been solved. The primary remaining global dilemmas are that overproduction and massive surpluses still coexist with desperate poverty and need, and that the resource base for industry is rapidly depleting and damaging, potentially irreparably, the eco-system. It is possible that confronting these dilemmas will force the rethinking of corporate objectives, structures, and activities that is necessary.

BIBLIOGRAPHY

AccountAbility (2005) *Stakeholder Engagement Standard,* London.

AccountAbility.American Law Institute (1994) *Principles of Corporate Governance: Analysis and Recommendations (Volume 1),* Philadelphia, PA: American Law Institute Publishers.

AMP Capital Investors (2005) *Financial Payback from Environmental and Social Factors,* Sydney: AMP.

AMP Henderson Global Investors (2003) *SRI Team Position Papers,* AMP Henderson Global Investors. Online. Available at: http://www.sustainablefuturefunds.com/research _ position.asp

Association of British Insurers (2004) Risk, Returns and Responsibility, London: Association of British Insurers. Online. Available at: http://www.abi.org.uk.

Australian Councils of Super Investors (2005) *Corporate Social Responsibility: Guidance for Investors,* Discussion Paper, September, Sydney: ACSI.

Australian Stock Exchange (2003) *Principles of Good Corporate Governance and Best Practice Recommendations,* Sydney: Australian Stock Exchange.

Baxt, R. (1976) 'The duties of directors of public companies – the realities of commercial life, the contradictions of the law, and the need for reform', *Australian Business Law Review,* 4: 289.

Bendell, J. (2004) *Barricades and Boardrooms: A Contemporary History of the Corporate Accountability Movement,* Geneva: United Nations Research Institute for Social Development. Online. Available at: http://www.unrisd

Berle, A.A. (1931) 'Corporate powers as powers in trust', *Harvard Law Review,* 44: 1049.

Berle, A.A. (1935) 'For whom corporate managers are trustees: a note', *Harvard Law Review,* 45: 1365.

Berle, A.A. (1955) *The 20th Century Capitalist Revolution,* New York: Harcourt Brace and Co.

Berle, A.A. and Means, G.C. (1933) *The Modern Corporation and Private Property,* Commerce Clearing House, New York: Harcourt Brace.

Bielefeld, S., Higginson, S., Jackson, J. and Ricketts, A. (2004) 'Directors' duties to the company and minority shareholder environmental activism', *Company and Securities Law Journal,* 28: 40.

Blair, M. and Stout, L. (1999) 'A team production theory of corporate law', *Vanderbilt Law Review,* 85: 247.

Blair, M. and Stout, L. (2001) 'Director accountability and the mediating role of the corporate board', *Washington University Law Quarterly,* 79: 403.

Brennan, G. (2002) 'Law values and charity', *Australian Law Journal*, 76: 492.
Bruntland Commission (1987) *Our Common Future*, Oxford: Oxford University Press.
Business Council of Australia (2001) *Towards Sustainable Development – How Leading Australian and Global Corporations are Contributing to Sustainable Development*, May, Sydney: BCA.
Calder, F. and Culverwell, M. (2005) *Following up the World Summit on Sustainable Development Commitments on Corporate Social Responsibility*, Royal Institute of International Affairs, London: Chatham House.
Carbon Trust (2005) 'A climate for change: a trustee's guide to understanding and addressing climate risk.' Online. Available at: http://www.thecarbontrust.co.uk
Certified General Accountants Association of Canada (2005) *Measuring Up: A Study on Corporate Sustainability Reporting in Canada*, Vancouver: CGA.
Christian Aid (2004) *Behind the Mask: The Real Face of Corporate Social Responsibility*, London: Christian Aid.
Clark, M. (1916) 'The changing basis of economic responsibility', *Journal of Political Economy*, 24(3): 13–19, in, T. Clarke (ed.), *Corporate Governance: Critical Perspectives on Business and Management*, London: Routledge, 2005, pp. 45–60.
Clarke, T. (2004) *Theories of Corporate Governance*, London: Routledge.
Company Law Review Steering Group (CLR) (2000) *Modern Company Law for a Competitive Economy: Developing the Framework*, London: Department of Trade and Industry.
Co-operative Insurance (2002) 'Sustainability Pays'. Online. Available at: http://www.forumforthefuture.org.uk/publications/default.asp?pubid=16
Corfield, A. (1998) 'The stakeholder theory and its future in Australian corporate governance: a preliminary analysis', *Bond Law Review*, 10: 213.
Corporate Responsibility Coalition (2005) *Corporate Social Responsibility in the Finance Sector in Europe*, London: Corporate Responsibility Coalition (CORE).
Corporations and Markets Advisory Committee (2005) *Corporate Social Responsibility: Discussion Paper*, Sydney: Australian Government.
Corporation of London, (2002) 'Financing the future — the London principles'. Online. Available at: http://www.cityoflondon.gov.uk/living_environment/sustainability/sustainable_finance.htm
CPA Australia (2005) *Sustainability Reporting: Practices, Performance and Potential*, Melbourne: CPA Australia.
CSR Wire 'The Corporate Social Responsibility Newswire Service'. Online. Available at: http://www.csrwire.com/csr/index.mpl?arg=all
Davies, P. (2005) 'Enlightened shareholder value and the new responsibilities', WE Hearn Lecture at the University of Melbourne Law School, 4 October.
Department of the Environment and Heritage (2003a) *The Materiality of Environmental Risk to Australia's Finance Sector*, Canberra: Commonwealth of Australia. Online. Available at: http://www.deh.gov.au/industry/finance/publications/index.html
Department of the Environment and Heritage (2003b) *The State of Public Environmental Reporting in Corporate Australia*, Canberra: Commonwealth of Australia. Online. Available at: http://www.deh.gov.au/industry/finance/publications/index.html
Department of the Environment and Heritage (2003c) *Triple Bottom Line Reporting in Australia – A Guide to Reporting Against Environmental Indicators*, Canberra: Commonwealth of Australia. Online. Available at: http://www.deh.gov.au/industry/finance/publications/index.html

Department of the Environment and Heritage (2004) 'Triple bottom line report: our environment, social and economic performance', September, Canberra, Australia.

Digby, Q. and Watterson, L. (2004) 'Pursuing profit, productivity and philanthropy: The legal obligations facing corporate Australia', *Keeping Good Companies*, June, Sydney: Chartered Secretaries Australia.

Doane, D. (2005) 'The myth of CSR', *Stanford Social Innovation Review*, Stanford University Graduate School of Business, Fall 2005, 23–9.

Dodd, E.M. (1932) 'For whom are corporate managers trustees?', *Harvard Law Review*, 45: 1145, in T. Clarke (ed.), *Corporate Governance Critical Perspectives on Business and Management*, London: Routledge, 2005, pp. 61–75.

EIU (2005) 'The importance of corporate responsibility', White Paper, London: The Economist Intelligence Unit Ltd.

Elkington, J. (1997) *Cannibals with Forks: The Triple Bottom Line of 21st Century Business*, Oxford: Capstone Publishing.

Entine, J. (2003) 'The myth of social investing: a critique of its practice and consequences for corporate social performance research', *Organization & Environment*, 16(3): 352–68.

The Equator Principles (2003) – A framework for banks to manage environmental and social issues in project financing. Available at: http://www.equator-principles.com

Ernst & Young (2002) *Corporate Social Responsibility of Global Companies*, New York: Ernst & Young.

European Commission (2002a) *Corporate Social Responsibility: A Business Contribution to Sustainable Development*, Brussels: European Union.

European Commission (2002b) *Communication Concerning Corporate Social Responsibility: A Business Contribution to Sustainable Development*, Brussels: European Union.

European Commission ((2003a) *Corporate Social Responsibility: A Business Contribution to Sustainable Development*, Brussels: European Union.

European Commission (2003b) *EU Multi-Stakeholder Forum on Corporate Social Responsibility*, Brussels: European Union.

European Commission (2004) *Corporate Social Responsibility: National Public Policies in the European Union*, Brussels: European Union.

European Union (2001) *Promoting a European Framework for Corporate Social Responsibility*, Brussels: European Union.

Freshfields Bruckhaus Deringer (2005a) *The World Bank is Not Enough, Equator Principles Survey 2005, Part 1 The Banks*, London: Freshfields Bruckhaus Deringer.

Freshfields Bruckhaus Deringer (2005b) *A Legal Framework for the Integration of Environmental, Social and Governance Issues into Institutional Investment*, October, London: Freshfields Bruckhaus Deringer.

Fujita, T., Kanai, T., Teranishi, K., Yamamoto, Y. and Nikko Citigroup (2004) 'The global environment and socially responsible investment: environmental technologies fuelling zones of growth', in, *The Materiality of Social, Environmental and Governance Issues to Equity Pricing*, Geneva: UNEP, pp. 33–7.

Garz, H., Kudszus, V., Volk, C. and West L.B. (2004) 'Insurance and sustainability: playing with fire' in *The Materiality of Social, Environmental and Governance Issues to Equity Pricing*, Geneva: UNEP, pp. 47–50.

Gauthier, C. (2005) 'Measuring corporate social and environmental performance: the extended life cycle assessment', *Journal of Business Ethics*, 59: 199–206.

Gilles, V., Wright, A., Amusategui L. and Cipelletti, M. and UBS (2004) 'European emissions trading scheme' in *The Materiality of Social, Environmental and Governance Issues to Equity Pricing*, Geneva: UNEP, pp. 41–6.

Global Reporting Initiative (GRI) (2002) *Sustainability Reporting Guidelines*, Amsterdam: GRI. Online. Available at: http://www.globalreporting.org

Grandmont, R., Grant, G., Silva, F. and Deutsche Bank (2004) 'Beyond the numbers – corporate governance: implication for investors', in *The Materiality of Social, Environmental and Governance Issues to Equity Pricing*, 17–18, Geneva: UNEP.

Group of 100 Incorporated (G100) (2003) 'Sustainability: a guide to triple bottom line reporting'. Online. Available at: http://www.group100.com.au

Hale, K. (2003) 'Corporate law and stakeholders: moving beyond stakeholder statutes', *Arizona Law Review*, 45: 823.

Hancock, E. (2005) 'Corporate risk of liability for global climate change and the SEC disclosure dilemma', *Georgetown International Environmental Law Review*, 233: 249.

Horrigan, B. (2002) 'Fault lines in the intersection between corporate governance and social responsibility', *University of New South Wales Law Journal*, 25: 515.

Husted, B.W. and Allen, D.B. (2000) 'Is it ethical to use ethics as strategy?', *Journal of Business Ethics*, 27: (1–2), 21–31.

Hutton, W. (2001) *Putting Back the P in Plc: Public Companies and a New Corporate Citizenship*, London: The Industrial Society.

Institute for Sustainable Futures (2005) 'Mainstreaming SRI: a role for government', Sydney: Institute for Sustainable Futures, University of Technology.

IUCN, UNEP and WWF (1991) *Caring for the Earth. A Strategy for Sustainable Living*, Gland, Switzerland.

Jackson, D.F. (2004) 'Report of the special commission of inquiry into the medical research and compensation foundation', Sydney: New South Wales Government.

Jones, T. M. (1995) 'Instrumental stakeholder theory: a synthesis of ethics and economics', *Academy of Management Review*, 20(2): 404–37.

Kennedy School of Government Corporate Responsibility Initiative (2004) 'Leadership, accountability and partnership: critical trends and issues in corporate social responsibility', Report of Launch Event, 4 March 2004, Harvard University.

Klein, E. and Du Plessis, J. (2005) 'Corporate donations, the best interest of the company and the proper purpose doctrine', *University of NSW Law Journal*, 28: 69.

KPMG (2005a) 'International survey of corporate responsibility reporting', June, KPMG. Online. Available at: http://www.kpmg.com

KPMG (2005b) *The State of Sustainability Reporting in Australia*, Sydney: KPMG, CAER and Deni Green Consulting Services.

Kurtz, L. (1997) 'No effect, or no net effects? Studies on socially responsible investing', *Journal of Investing*, Winter: 37–49.

Kytle, B. and Ruggie, J. (2005) *Corporate Social Responsibility as Risk Management: A Model for Multinationals*, Boston: Kennedy School of Government.

Luis, C. (2005) 'People v. profits: a false dichotomy?' *University of California Davis, Business Law Journal*, 6(533).

McConvill, J. and Joy, M. (2003) 'The interaction of directors' duties and sustainable development in Australia: setting off on the uncharted road', *Melbourne University Law Review*, 27: 116.

McKague, K. and Cragg, W. (2005) *Compendium of Ethics Codes and Instruments of*

Corporate Responsibility, September, Toronto: Schulich School of Business, York University.

Mays, S. (2003) 'Corporate sustainability – an investor perspective', Canberra: Department of Environment and Heritage, Commonwealth of Australia.

Minerals Council of Australia (2004) 'Enduring value: the Australian minerals industry framework for sustainable development', Melbourne: MCA.

Monks, R., Miller, A. and Cook, J. (2004) 'Shareholder activism on environmental issues: a study of proposals at large US corporations 2000–2003', *Natural Resources Forum*, 28: 317–30.

Najam, A. (2000) 'World Business Council for Sustainable Development: the greening of business or a greenwash?', *Yearbook of International Cooperation on Environment and Development 1999/2000*, London: Earthscan Publications, 65–75.

OECD (1976, 2000) *Guidelines for Multinational Enterprises*, Paris: OECD.

OECD (2004) *Principles of Corporate Governance*, Paris: OECD.

OECD Watch (2005) *Five Years On: A Review of the OECD Guidelines and National Contact Points*, Amsterdam: Centre for Research on Multinational Corporations.

Parkinson, J. (1994) *Corporate Power and Responsibility: Issues in the Theory of Company Law*, Oxford: Clarendon Press.

Pleon (2005) *Accounting for Good: The Global Stakeholder Report*, Dusseldorf: Pleon Kohtes Klewes GmbH.

Redmond, P. (2005) *Submission Parliamentary Joint Committee on Corporations and Financial Services Inquiry into Corporate Responsibility*, Canberra: Commonwealth of Australia.

Report of the Special Commission of Inquiry into the Medical Research and Compensation Foundation (Jackson Report) (2004), Sydney: New South Wales Government.

Schroder, M. (2003) *Socially Responsible Investments in Germany, Switzerland and the United States: An Analysis of Investment Funds and Indices*, Mannheim: Centre for European Economic Research.

Sethi, S.P. (2003) *Setting Global Standards, Guidelines for Creating Codes of Conduct in Multinational Corporations*, London: John Wiley & Sons.

Smith, N.C. (1990). *Morality and the Market: Consumer Pressure for Corporate Accountability*. London: Routledge.

Solomon, J. F., Solomon, A. and Norton, S. D. (2002) 'Socially responsible investing in the UK: drivers and current issues', *Journal of General Management*, 27(3): 1–13.

Sparkes, R. and Cowton, C.J. (2004) 'The maturing of socially responsible investment: a review of the developing link with corporate social responsibility', *Journal of Business Ethics*, 52(1): 45–57.

Statman, M. (2000) 'Socially responsible mutual funds', *Financial Analysts Journal*, May/June: 30–9.

SustainAbility Ltd/UNEP (2002) 'Trust us — the global reporters 2002 survey of corporate sustainability reporting', SustainAbility Ltd/UNEP. Online. Available at: http://www.sustainability.com

SustainAbility (2005) *The Changing Landscape of Liability: A Director's Guide to Trends in Corporate Environmental, Social and Economic Liability*, London: SustainAbility.

Teck Corp Ltd v Millar (1973) *Delaware Law Review* 33, (3d).

UK Department for Environment, Food and Rural Affairs (2005) *Environmental Key Performance Indicators: Reporting Guidelines for UK Business*, London: UK DEFRA.

UN (1992) *Rio Declaration on Environment and Development*, Geneva: UN.

UN (2000) *Global Compact*, Geneva: UN.

UNCTAD (2004) *Development and Globalisation: Facts and Figures*, Geneva: UN.

UNEP Finance Initiative (2002a) *Climate Change and the Financial Services Industry*, Geneva: UNEP.

UNEP Finance Initiative (2002b) *Financing for Sustainable Development*, Geneva: UNEP.

UNEP Finance Initiative (2002c) *Financing Sustainable Energy Directory: A Listing of Lenders and Investors*, Geneva: UNEP.

UNEP Finance Initiative (2002d) *Foreign Direct Investment: Financing Sustainability*, Geneva: UNEP.

UNEP Finance Initiative (2002e) *Industry as a Partner for Sustainable Development: Finance and Insurance*, Geneva: UNEP.

UNEP Finance Initiative (2002f) *Sustainable Venture Finance*, Geneva: UNEP.

UNEP Finance Initiative (2003a) *Environmental Disclosure in Financial Statements*, Geneva: UNEP.

UNEP Finance Initiative (2003b) *Mainstreaming Sustainable Investment*, Geneva: UNEP.

UNEP Finance Initiative (2003c) *Risk, the Environment, and the Role of the Insurance Industry*, Geneva: UNEP.

UNEP Finance Initiative (2004a) *Generation Lost: Young Financial Analysts and Environmental, Social and Governance Issues*, Geneva: UNEP.

UNEP Finance Initiative (2004b) *Implementing Responsible Investment*, Geneva: UNEP.

UNEP Finance Initiative (2004c) *The Materiality of Social, Environmental and Corporate Governance Issues to Equity Pricing*, Geneva: UNEP.

UNEP Finance Initiative (2004d) *Values to Value: A Global Dialogue on Sustainable Finance*, Geneva: UNEP.

UNEP Finance Initiative (2005a) *CEO Briefing on the Future of Climate Change Policy: The Financial Sector Perspective*, Geneva: UNEP.

UNEP Finance Initiative (2005b) *A Legal Framework for the Integration of Environmental, Social and Governance Issues into Institutional Investment*, October, Geneva: UNEP.

U.S. Environmental Protection Agency (US EPA) (2000) *Green Dividends? The Relationship between Firms' Environmental Performance and Financial Performance*, Washington: Office of Corporate Environmental Management. Online. Available at: http://www.epa.gov/ocempage

Vogel, D. (2005) *The Market for Virtue: The Potential and Limits of Corporate Social Responsibility*, Washington DC: Brookings Institute.

Waddock, S. (2003) 'Myths and realities of social investing', *Organization & Environment*, 16(3): 369–80.

Waddock, S. (2004) 'Creating corporate accountability: foundation principles to make corporate citizenship real', *Journal of Business Ethics*, 50: 1–15.

Waddock, S.A. and Graves, S.B. (1997) 'The corporate social performance–financial performance link', *Strategic Management Journal*, 18(4): 303–19.

Wedderburn of Charlton, Lord (1985) 'Southey Memorial Lecture 1984: The social responsibility of companies', *Melbourne University Law Review*, 15: 4.

Welford, R. (2002) 'Globalisation, corporate social responsibility and human rights', *Corporate Social Responsibility and Environmental Management*, 9(1): 1–7.

Wells, H. (2002) 'The cycles of corporate social responsibility: an historical retrospective for the twenty-first century', *Kansas Law Review* 51: 77.

Williams, C. (2002) 'Symposium: corporations theory and corporate governance law. Corporate social responsibility in an era of economic globalisation', *University of California Davis Law Review*, 35: 705.

World Bank Group (2002) *Public Sector Roles in Strengthening Corporate Social Responsibility: A Baseline Study*, Washington, DC: WBG.

World Bank Group (2003) *Strengthening Implementation of Corporate Social Responsibility in Global Supply Chains*, October, Washington, DC: WBG.

World Bank Group (2004) *Public Sector Roles in Strengthening Corporate Social Responsibility: Taking Stock*, Washington, DC: WBG.

World Business Council for Sustainable Development (WBCSD) (2002) *Corporate Social Responsibility: The WBCSD's Journey*, WBCSD, Vernier, Switzerland: Atar Roto Presse SA.

World Business Council for Sustainable Development (WBSCD) (2004) *Running the Risk*, Geneva: WBCSD, Altar Roto Presse, SA.

World Economic Forum (WEF) (2005) *Mainstreaming Responsible Investment*, Geneva: World Economic Forum.

Zadek, S. (2004) 'The path to corporate responsibility', *Harvard Business Review*, December, 82(12): 125–32.

Index

Page numbers in *Italics* represent Tables and page numbers in **Bold** represent Figures